Political Cycles and the
Macroeconomy

Political Cycles and the Macroeconomy

Alberto Alesina and
Nouriel Roubini with
Gerald D. Cohen

The MIT Press
Cambridge, Massachusetts
London, England

This book was set in Palatino on the Monotype "Prism Plus" PostScript Imagesetter by
Asco Trade Typesetting Ltd., Hong Kong.

Printed and bound in the United States of America.

Library of Congress Cataloging-in-Publication Data

Alesina, Alberto.
  Political cycles and the macroeconomy / Alberto Alesina and
  Nouriel Roubini with Gerald D. Cohen.
     p.   cm.
  Includes bibliographical references and index.
  ISBN 0-262-01161-1 (alk. paper)
  1. Political science—Economic aspects. 2. Business cycles—
Political aspects. 3. Economic policy—Political aspects.
I. Roubini, Nouriel. II. Cohen, Gerald, 1966–   . III. Title.
JA77.A43   1997
339.5—dc21   97-14051
                                                      CIP

To our parents

J

Contents

Acknowledgments   xi

1 **Overview**   1
   1.1 Organization of the Book   8
   1.2 How Does This Book Relate to Previous Research?   11
   1.3 Technical Level of This Book   13

2 **Opportunistic Models**   15
   2.1 Introduction   15
   2.2 The Traditional Opportunistic Model: The Political Business
       Cycle   17
   2.3 Rational Opportunistic Models   22
   2.4 Rational Retrospective Voting   33
   2.5 Conclusions   36
   Appendix   37

3 **Partisan Models**   45
   3.1 Introduction   45
   3.2 The Traditional Partisan Model   46
   3.3 The Rational Partisan Model   51
   3.4 Welfare Properties of Partisan Cycles   57
   3.5 A Rational Partisan Model with Retrospective
       Voting   59
   3.6 Discussion and Conclusions   61
   Appendix   64

4   Political Cycles in the United States   67
4.1   Introduction   67
4.2   Previous Empirical Results   70
4.3   Data and Basic Statistics   73
4.4   Specification of the Empirical Tests   82
4.5   Evidence on the Partisan Theories   83
4.6   Evidence on Political Business Cycles   93
4.7   Political Cycles in Monetary Policy   95
4.8   Political Cycles in Fiscal Policy   102
4.9   Discussion: Alternative Hypotheses   107
4.10 Conclusions   108
Appendix   109

5   Polls, Electoral Uncertainty, and the Economy   111
5.1   Introduction   111
5.2   The Electoral Option and Its Application to Models of
      Partisan Politics   112
5.3   Political Information and Financial Markets:
      An Overview   124
5.4   Conclusion   134
Appendix A   135
Appendix B   137
Appendix C   139

6   Political Cycles in Industrial Economies   141
6.1   Introduction   141
6.2   Previous Empirical Results   143
6.3   Data and Specification of Empirical Tests   145
6.4   Evidence on the Rational Partisan Theory   148
6.5   Traditional Partisan Theory   163
6.6   Level versus Growth Effects   166
6.7   Evidence on Political Business Cycles   167
6.8   Endogenous Elections and Opportunistic Policy-
      makers   170
6.9   Conclusions   173
Appendix   174

7   Political Cycles and Macroeconomic Policies: Evidence from Industrial Democracies   185

7.1   Introduction   185

7.2   Data and Specification of Empirical Tests for Monetary Policy   186

7.3   Evidence on Partisan Effects in Monetary Policy   188

7.4   Evidence on Political Business Cycle Effects in Monetary Policy   196

7.5   Electoral and Partisan Determinants of Fiscal Policy and Budget Deficits   201

7.6   Conclusions   207

Appendix   208

8   Political Cycles and Central Bank Independence   211

8.1   Introduction   211

8.2   Independent Central Banks   213

8.3   Political Cycles and Central Bank Independence   218

8.4   A Note on the "Contracting" Approach   223

8.5   Conclusions   224

Appendix   225

9   Political Parties, Institutions, and Budget Deficits   227

9.1   Introduction   230

9.2   Political Models of Budget Deficits   240

9.3   Opportunistic and Partisan Effects on Fiscal Policy Revisited   245

9.4   Normative Implications   247

9.5   Conclusions   248

Appendix   250

10 Conclusions   253

10.1 Summary of Results   253

10.2 Are Political Cycles Going to Disappear?   259

Notes   265

References   285

Index   297

Acknowledgments

The research effort that led to this book started about ten years ago. Since then we have received comments from many colleagues, students, and friends. We can mention only a few: James Alt, Robert Barro, Olivier Blanchard, Brock Blomberg, Giancarlo Corsetti, Jon Faust, Morris Fiorina, Roberta Gatti, Gregory Hess, Douglas Hibbs, Sylvia Maxfield, William Nordhaus, Roberto Perotti, Torsten Persson, Kenneth Rogoff, Howard Rosenthal, Jeffrey Sachs, Ron Schachar, Kenneth Shepsle, and Guido Tabellini. We are also very thankful to the four anonymous referees engaged by the MIT Press; they went well beyond the call of duty in providing detailed and very useful comments. Material covered in this book was presented in many seminars and used in courses. We are very grateful to all the seminar participants and students for their comments.

For financial support throughout these years, Alesina is grateful to the National Science Foundation, the Sloan Foundation, an Olin Fellowship, and the National Bureau of Economic Research. Roubini gratefully acknowledges support from Yale University and the Stern School of Business of New York University. Cohen acknowledges the support of the National Science Foundation for a fellowship in the Harvard-MIT Research and Training Program in Political Economy.

For research assistance we thank Joanna Barnish, Jinee Kim, and Tae Kim. Roberta Gatti carefully read drafts of the manuscript and greatly helped us with the final editing. June Wynn did a wonderful job in typing a good portion of the manuscript since the first author (in alphabetical order) of this book types about five words per minute. Finally, Gerald Cohen would like to thank Elizabeth Brandwein for her love and support.

The views expressed in this book are those of the authors and do not necessarily reflect the position of the Federal Reserve Bank of New York or the Federal Reserve System.

1 Overview

This book studies how the timing of elections, the ideological orientation of governments, and competition among political parties influence unemployment, economic growth, inflation, and various monetary and fiscal policy instruments.

The topic of political cycles is one of the most widely studied subjects in political economics. Many believe that one can adequately explain political cycles with the simple observation that politicians artificially create unusually favorable economic conditions before an election and that voters reward incumbent governments for doing so, even though the economy will take a turn for the worse immediately after the election. We argue, instead, that the explanation is far more complex: In fact, this book explores a complex pattern of relationships between macroeconomic policies, timing of elections, ideological orientations of different governments, party structure, electoral laws, and degrees of central banks' political independence.

The literature on political and economic cycles developed in two clearly distinct phases. The first, which flourished in the mid-1970s, uses traditional macroeconomic models, in which, taking advantage of an exploitable Phillips curve, governments can systematically and predictably influence macroeconomic outcomes. The first strand of this literature (Nordhaus 1975, Lindbeck 1976) emphasizes policymakers' "opportunistic" motivation: Politicians have no policy preferences of their own, so they choose the policies that maximize their chances of

Table 1.1
Models of political cycles

	Opportunistic	Partisan
Models with an exploitable Phillips curve	Nordhaus (1975)	Hibbs (1977)
	Lindbeck (1976)	
Rational expectations models	Cukierman-Meltzer (1986)	Alesina (1987)
	Rogoff and Sibert (1988)	
	Rogoff (1990)	
	Persson and Tabellini (1990)	

electoral victory. The second strand of the literature (Hibbs 1977) emphasizes, instead, policymakers' partisan motivation. Specifically, according to this view, left-wing parties are relatively more concerned with unemployment than with inflation, and right-wing parties have opposite concerns. Moreover, parties stick to their electoral platform when in office.

The second phase of the literature evolved in the mid-1980s as a branch of the game-theoretic approach to macroeconomic policy, an approach pioneered by Kydland and Prescott (1977) and Barro and Gordon (1983a).[1] These models of political cycles incorporate rational expectations and emphasize how a rational public limits the extent to which policymakers can influence the economic cycle. Cukierman and Meltzer (1986), Rogoff and Sibert (1988), Rogoff (1990), and Persson and Tabellini (1990) develop opportunistic models with rational expectations. Alesina (1987) suggests a partisan model with rational expectations.

Table 1.1 frames the above-mentioned contributions in a simple two-by-two matrix. These models differ on two critical dimensions. First, they may be either "partisan" or "opportunistic." Partisan models focus on differences in policies and outcomes as a result of different governments' ideological orientations. On the other hand, opportunistic models claim that every government behaves in the same way: opportunistically, to win reelection. Second, they may be "traditional" or "rational." Traditional models theorize that governments exploit their abilities to predict and influence macroeconomic outcomes. Rational expectations models, on the other hand, emphasize the limits in the policymakers' ability to influence, permanently and predictably, the state of the economy. This rationality constraint affects both the policy (via voting behavior) and the economy (via the expectations-augmented Phillips curve).

Our first goal (which we pursue in the next two chapters) is to illustrate these four types of models. (Table 1.2 succinctly summarizes their empirical bearings.) We then test them on data drawn from the United States and almost all the other OECD countries. We analyze both policy outcomes (unemployment, output growth, and inflation), and policy instruments (monetary and fiscal variables), using evidence from financial markets as well as economic and political indicators such as preelectoral polls. We also discuss how opportunistic and partisan motivations interact with various institutional features, such as government structure (coalition versus single-party governments), electoral laws, and the degree of independence of central banks.

Based on our analysis, this book reaches a number of conclusions. First, the most recent theories of political cycles, based on the paradigms of rational choice and rational expectations, are empirically more successful than their predecessors. Second, the partisan model outperforms the opportunistic one as an explanation of macroeconomic fluctuations in output growth, inflation, and unemployment. Opportunistic effects are confined to short-run, occasional manipulations of policy instruments around elections; for instance, in election years, one might expect loose monetary and fiscal policies but not a significant surge in output growth or sharp reductions in unemployment. Third, although we do not observe a systematic surge of growth in election years, this does not imply that economic conditions are not an important determinant of election results. We argue, in fact, that these two observations are not inconsistent. Fourth, the characteristics of the political cycle depend upon the nature of the party system. A clear partisan

Table 1.2
Empirical implications of different models of political cycles

Opportunistic traditional models

• expansion in the year or two before the elections; GNP growth above normal, unemployment below normal in the election year;

• inflation begins to increase immediately before or immediately after the election;

• recession (or downturn) after the election, with gradual reduction of inflation;

• no differences in policies and outcomes between different governments;

• incumbents reappointed when growth is high and unemployment low in election years.

Rational opportunistic models

• short-run manipulations of policy instruments immediately before elections: increase in deficits, inflation, money growth in the two or three quarters before each election;

• tightening of monetary and fiscal policies after elections;

• no systematic, multiyear effects on growth and unemployment except for, possibly, some minor effects immediately before the election;

• incumbents reappointed when growth is high and unemployment low in election years.

Traditional partisan models

• unemployment permanently lower, growth and inflation permanently higher during the tenure in office of left-wing governments than that of right-wing governments.

Rational partisan models

• short-run partisan effects after elections: unemployment temporarily lower than normal and growth temporarily higher than normal for about two years after an electoral victory of the left; the opposite outcome after an electoral victory of the right;

• inflation permanently higher when the left is in office relative to when the right is in office.

cycle emerges in countries with two-party or two-bloc systems, which typically have majoritarian, or at least not strictly proportional, electoral laws. In contrast, partisan cycles are less clearly identifiable in systems with coalition governments, the typical product of proportional electoral systems. On the other hand, proportional electoral systems that produce coalition governments tend also to be associated with excessive deficits and deadlocks in policy making. Fifth, we discuss how explicit consideration of elected politicians' opportunistic and partisan behavior enhances the benefits of independent monetary institutions.

These points frame a consistent and rather clear picture. Our first result establishes the usefulness of the research efforts of economists and political scientists who have taken seriously the notion of rationality in political economy. However, even though we emphasize the role of rational behavior and expectations, we believe that wage-price rigidities are crucial ingredients for a realistic model of the economy. The combination of rational expectations and wage-price rigidities leads to models that exhibit short-run nonneutrality and medium- to long-run neutrality of aggregate demand policies. In fact, our empirical results on political cycles are consistent with a view of the economy based upon sticky wages and prices with rational expectations.[2] Thus, although our empirical results are primarily concerned with political cycles, they have broader implications concerning the relative merits of different macroeconomic models.

Our second set of results highlights the nature of party policies. We argue that political parties in industrial democracies are not all alike. Different parties follow distinct macroeconomic policies when in office, and therefore partisan differences have been important determinants of macroeconomic policies and outcomes in the last thirty years. Although the idea that parties are not all alike may strike many outside the field of political science as obvious, an established tradition in the field emphasizes the tendency of parties in two-bloc systems to converge to the middle.[3]

This observation raises several issues relevant to current events. For example, one may wonder whether partisan cycles will become less marked in the future. Both left- and right-wing parties may realize, looking back, that partisan cycles destabilize domestic and world economies. For instance, in the late 1970s the political barometer of OECD tilted toward the left: In the United States, Germany, and the United Kingdom, left-leaning governments pursued expansionary policy, leading to a temporary boom and a buildup of inflation (aggravated by the second oil shock). In the early 1980s, the same three major economies moved to the right of the political spectrum, leading to decisive anti-inflationary policies and sharp recessions. Of the largest economies, only France followed the opposite political cycle, turning to the left in May 1981. The Socialist government in France in 1982–83 followed typically partisan policies that were not very successful, partly as a result of the fact that the country was moving in the direction opposite to that of the world business cycle. In fact, France is a good example of an important theme of this book, namely how external constraints limit the influence of partisan governments in open, integrated economies.

A related question is whether governments in OECD countries are learning to be less partisan and follow more middle-of-the-road policies in macroeconomic management. For instance, the policies of the French and Spanish Socialist governments in the second half of the 1980s point in this direction. Also, the process of European integration will affect partisan cycles. Will a monetary union and economic integration prevent national partisan cycles? How will the domestic politics of macroeconomic policy interact with European-level politics?

Our third result highlights an apparent puzzle. The rate of economic growth is an important determinant of election results, but incumbent governments do not seem systematically to raise the rate of growth in election years. We address this puzzle directly by showing how recent theoretical developments, and particularly the work by Alesina and Rosenthal (1995), are consistent with this observation.

Our fourth result, which contrasts two-party systems with coalition governments, links our book to a recent literature on the impact of institutional design on macroeconomic policy. Both academics and legislators around the world are debating the relative merits of proportional versus majoritarian systems. We believe, and our results confirm, that one faces a trade-off between these two systems. Proportional systems, which lead to coalition governments, are likely to ensure moderation in policy making and reduce the magnitude of partisan cycles. Coalition governments are slow in reacting to shocks, however, because each member of the coalition has veto power over the choice of policies. In contrast, majoritarian systems exhibit the opposite features: They do not delay policies but emphasize partisan cycles. Theoretical results by Alesina and Drazen (1991) and Spolaore (1993), empirical results by Roubini and Sachs (1989a,b), Grilli, Masciandaro, and Tabellini (1991), and Alesina and Perotti (1995a), as well as the findings of this book support this view. Proportional systems achieve moderation, but create potentially inefficient delays in policy making and fiscal imbalances. Majoritarian, single-party governments do not delay policy implementation but create partisan cycles.[4]

A second institutional variable that we emphasize is the degree of central bank independence. A vast literature has discussed the advantages and disadvantages of this institution and pointed out empirical regularities and puzzles.[5] Developing the recent work by Alesina and Gatti (1995) and Waller (1995), we extend the discussion of central bank independence to an explicitly political model that accounts for politicians' partisan and opportunistic motivations. This model resolves several empirical puzzles and shows that the benefits of central bank independence may be even larger when political incentives are explicitly taken into account.

The attentive reader may have noted that in summarizing our results, we have not made a distinction between those that apply to the United States and those that hold for other countries. In fact, one of our most striking results is that the United States is not exceptional.

The same correlations between macroeconomic policies and outcomes on one side and elections and government changes on the other are remarkably similar in the United States and in other democracies, particularly those with two-party systems. A widely held view in political science suggests, instead, that the polity in the United States is unique and hardly comparable with that of other parliamentary democracies.[6] On the contrary, we argue that at least as far as macroeconomics and politics are concerned, the similarities between the political economy of the United States and that of other OECD democracies are much more important than the differences. In fact, the key differences are not those between the United States and other parliamentary democracies as a whole but those between two-party systems and systems of large coalition governments.

1.1   Organization of the Book

This book is organized in ten chapters, including this introduction. Chapters 2 and 3 illustrate different theories of political cycles. Chapters 4 through 7 discuss empirical evidence on political cycles from both the United States and other OECD economies. Chapters 8 and 9 explore questions of institutional design and their relationship with partisan and opportunistic incentives. The last chapter concludes and summarizes our results. We now provide a brief overview of each chapter's content so that the reader has a sense of how the book unfolds.

Chapter 2 discusses opportunistic models. We begin with what we define as traditional approaches, and specifically with the Nordhaus (1975) model, the most widely cited in this area. We then move to "rational" opportunistic models, in which voters are rational, rather than naive as in Nordhaus's model, but are imperfectly informed about some characteristics of the policymakers. Because of this information asymmetry, politicians have incentives to be strategic and opportunistic. These models also rationalize the widely observed phenomenon of "retrospective voting" (Fiorina 1981). That is, they suggest why a rational electorate should evaluate the incumbent politician by looking at the state of the economy immediately before elections. This chapter ends with a discussion of the relationship between politicians' opportunistic behavior and rational opportunistic voting, which is quite important for interpreting the following empirical evidence.

Chapter 3 discusses partisan models. We begin again with what we refer to as the traditional approach by Hibbs (1977) and discuss party motivations and preferences. Then we proceed to a "rational" version of the partisan model, originally proposed by Alesina (1987 and 1988b). This model features rational expectations with wage stickiness rather than a Phillips curve with adaptive expectations as in Hibbs (1987a). This chapter also includes an extension of the partisan model to incorporate retrospective voting behavior. We conclude with a summary of the empirical implications of all the theoretical models, which we then test in the subsequent three chapters.

The empirical chapters begin with a comprehensive study of the United States on both macroeconomic policies and outcomes as a function of the electoral cycle. Chapters 4 and 5 present several tests of political cycles on U.S. data from 1947 to 1993. We reach several conclusions that our study of all the other OECD countries then broadly confirms. We devote two chapters to the United States not, as we argued above, because the results for this country are special, but because we can study this country in more detail than any other country, and we can compare our results with those of the previous literature on the subject, which has largely focused on the United States. For instance, chapter 5 includes several tests using financial market data and preelectoral polls; we do not perform the same tests for all the other OECD countries because of both data availability problems and other technical problems, in addition to a budget constraint on our energies! Chapter 5 is probably the most demanding technically of the book, particularly for those not familiar with basic notions of finance theory. Readers not interested in this subject may skip this chapter without losing trace of the main line of the book's argument.

The next two chapters consider a sample of almost all the OECD countries. Chapter 6 tests the implications of all the different models of political cycles on macroeconomic outcomes, namely unemployment, growth, and inflation. We study whether the timing of elections and the partisan nature of different governments systematically affects the cyclical movements of these three variables. Our sample includes quarterly observations on inflation, unemployment, and output growth in the last three decades for the following eighteen OECD democracies: Australia, Austria, Belgium, Canada, Denmark, Finland, France, Germany, Japan, Ireland, Italy, the Netherlands, New Zealand, Norway, Sweden, Switzerland, the United Kingdom, and the United States.

Whereas the previous chapter considers evidence of political cycles by studying economic outcomes, chapter 7 follows a similar empirical methodology to test for the presence of political cycles in policy instruments. We conduct a detailed analysis of opportunistic and partisan cycles in monetary and fiscal policy.

Chapter 8 explores the interaction of central bank independence with party competition and economic policy making. In particular, we study the role of independent monetary institutions in a world of partisan and opportunistic politicians. This chapter emphasizes the costs and benefits of insulating monetary policy from direct political pressures.

Chapter 9 briefly touches on issues of institutional design in fiscal policy. First, we discuss which institutional features are more or less likely to promote fiscal discipline. Second, we illustrate how different institutional structures interact with the partisan and opportunistic behavior of politicians which create budget cycles. More specifically, we develop, in more detail, an idea that emerges in previous chapters, namely, that macroeconomic policies differ systematically in countries with a two-party system relative to countries with coalition governments. In particular, we document the trade-off between coalition governments and single-party governments discussed above.

The last chapter concludes by summarizing our main results and by discussing whether we should expect to see in the future more political cycles. In particular, we speculate on how certain institutional developments, European integration, increasing capital mobility and financial integration, learning from past experience, and ideological changes in attitude toward economic policy are likely to reduce or increase the magnitude of partisan and opportunistic cycles in the next decade.

1.2 How Does This Book Relate to Previous Research?

This book resulted from several years of joint and individual research of the three authors. Some of this research appeared in academic journals in the last decade, but this book is very far from merely a collection of previously published articles. First of all, the theoretical part of the book provides a comprehensive treatment of the theory of political cycles which is unavailable, as a whole, in any previously published work. Second, all of the empirical results presented in the book that were previously published have been updated to include the most recent available data. This procedure not only checks the robustness of our previous results but also allows us to study whether in recent years some systematic changes in governments' behavior have occurred. Third, we present several new tests never previously published. Fourth, and foremost, this book treats this area of research comprehensively, a goal that escapes any individual paper.

In recent years, several authors have published books on topics related to that of the present volume. In terms of coverage, the closest work to our own is probably Lewis-Beck 1988. Our book differs from his in two significant ways. First, Lewis-Beck focuses more on the effects of economic conditions on voting behavior rather than on the impact of elections on the economy, which is, instead, the main argument of our book. Second, at the time during which Lewis-Beck's volume was written, the new wave of rational expectation models had not appeared. Thus, his book deals only with the traditional models. In comparison, a critical point of the present volume is to show the usefulness of these more recent rational models as a guide to empirical research.

Alesina and Rosenthal (1995) present an original model of the political economy of the United States. Even though one of the authors of the present book is very sympathetic to Alesina and Rosenthal's message, the purpose, coverage, and goal of the two books are very different. First, Alesina and Rosenthal focus exclusively on the United States.[7] Second, their goal is not to test a broad range of models, which is our purpose here. They instead develop and test a specific politico-economic model with particular reference to American institutions and to the issue of divided government. Third, in this book we consider a much broader range of economic variables, whereas Alesina and Rosenthal focus almost exclusively on output growth.

Persson and Tabellini (1990) also discuss politico-economic models in the context of their review of recent developments in macro–political economy. They do not, however, discuss empirical evidence, whereas one of this book's main purposes is to evaluate different theories empirically.

Keech (1995) critically evaluates recent developments in the field of macro–political economy from the point of view of a political scientist. His book differs significantly from ours in many respects. First, he mainly focuses on the United States. Second, he addresses more normative issues than we do. Third, his book contains much less formal modeling than ours.

Tufte (1978) and Hibbs (1987a) discuss empirical evidence drawn almost exclusively on the United States concerning the opportunistic (Tufte) or the partisan (Hibbs) model. Both books, particularly the one by Hibbs, are richer in institutional details than ours. We draw evidence on a much larger sample of countries, however, and we use more economic variables. In addition, neither Tufte nor Hibbs discusses rational models, which are at the center of our attention.

1.3 Technical Level of This Book

We have tried to write a book that is at the same time rigorous and accessible to a much wider audience than the typical readership of academic journals. Our goal is to reach not only professional economists and political scientists but also the educated general reader with an interest in this field.

To achieve this goal, in the theoretical part of the book, we first develop the models intuitively, with very little use of mathematical tools. We believe that the basic assumptions and results of these models can be easily illustrated in this way. Then, we develop a more formal treatment of the models. The less technically inclined reader may skip these sections (and appendices). The empirical part of the book employs econometric techniques that for the most part, are fairly standard. A deep and detailed understanding of technical aspects is never essential to grasp the basic message that we want to convey.

2   Opportunistic Models

2.1 Introduction

Most people (except perhaps professional politicians) would agree that politicians love holding office. In fact, according to most formal models of politics, although voters care about policies, politicians care only about winning elections[1] and thus choose policies only to please the voters. We label this behavior "opportunistic" and illustrate in this chapter how opportunistic policymakers choose monetary and fiscal policies to remain in office.

We begin with the most popular politico-economic approach to macroeconomic policy: the political business cycle model developed by Nordhaus (1975) and Lindbeck (1976). In this model, opportunistic policymakers can take advantage of an exploitable Phillips curve and face naïve voters who forget the past, are unaware of the policymakers' incentives, and do not understand how the economy works, in particular, they do not take into account the trade-off between inflation and unemployment. This model implies that the incumbent government artificially stimulates the economy immediately before each election and eliminates the resulting inflation with a postelectoral downturn or recession. The voters reward this behavior because the election takes place when the economy is temporarily doing well and because they do not understand the nature of this opportunistic behavior so that they can be fooled time after time. They do not even learn from the past, and they have forgotten the previous postelectoral recession by the time the following election approaches.

These assumptions that the electorate is very naïve, incapable of learning, and prone to systematic mistakes in expectations are quite unsatisfactory from a conceptual point of view. Robert Lucas received the Nobel prize in Economics in 1995 for arguing that the standard notion of rationality of behavior should also be applied to expectation formation. Applying the idea of rational expectations to the Phillips curve and macroeconomics in general yields striking results in interpreting the effects of policy. Following these recent developments of the economic literature, several authors have recently proposed models which reconcile the Nordhaus-Lindbeck insights with voter rationality. All of these models emphasize the role of the policymakers' "competence," defined as their ability to reduce waste in the budget process (Rogoff and Sibert 1988 and Rogoff 1990), promote growth without inflation (Persson and Tabellini 1990) or insulate the economy from random shocks (Cukierman and Meltzer 1986). Each makes the critical assumption that the policymakers are more informed than the citizens about their own competence. By taking advantage of this informational asymmetry, and trying to signal as much competence as possible, politicians behave in ways leading to a political business cycle. Voters' rationality, however, limits how opportunistic politicians can be. Thus, the political cycles in these rational models are more short-lived, smaller in magnitude, and less regular than in traditional models. These rational opportunistic models are also consistent with retrospective voting behavior on the economy. In fact, they formalize precisely a "rational retrospective voting behavior" that can be contrasted with the naive voting behavior of the Nordhaus-Lindbeck model.

In summary, this chapter lays out the theory of opportunistic cycles. We develop, as much as possible, a coherent theoretical structure: We spell out the different models' underlying assumptions and emphasize their similarities and differences. Section 2.2 discusses the Lindbeck-Nordhaus model of political business cycles, and section 2.3

presents several rational versions of it. Section 2.4 discusses retrospective voting. The last section concludes, emphasizing the empirical implications.

2.2 The Traditional Opportunistic Model: The Political Business Cycle

The following assumptions underlie the Nordhaus-Lindbeck model.

2.2.1 *Assumptions*

A.1 *The economy is characterized by an expectation-augmented Phillips curve.* Specifically, we use the following formulation of the Phillips curve:

$$y_t = \bar{y} + \gamma(\pi_t - \pi_t^e); \qquad \gamma > 0 \tag{2.1}$$

where y_t is the rate of GNP growth, π_t is the inflation rate, π_t^e is the expected inflation and $\bar{y}$ is the natural rate of growth, and γ is a positive parameter. We could also write the Phillips curve in terms of unemployment:

$$u_t = \bar{u} - \gamma'(\pi_t - \pi_t^e); \qquad \gamma' > 0 \tag{2.2}$$

where u_t is the unemployment rate and $\bar{u}$ is the natural rate of unemployment. To further simplify matters, we assume that $\gamma = \gamma' = 1$, so that we will use a very simple equation:

$$y_t = \bar{y} + \pi_t - \pi_t^e \tag{2.3}$$

The appendix to this chapter illustrates a standard derivation of this equation based on a wage-contract model. The basic feature of this setup is that wage contracts are signed at discrete intervals and incorporate expected inflation at contract stipulation. If inflation exceeds expectation, the reduction in the realized real wage implies a higher labor demand, lower unemployment, and faster growth.[2] From an empirical standpoint, one would want to enrich (2.3) with a more realistic dynamic structure, for instance by allowing for one or more autoregressive terms of growth, namely, $y_{t-1}, y_{t-2}, \ldots, y_{t-m}$.[3] Although a careful dynamic specification is important for the empirical analysis, the simple equation (2.3) is sufficient to illustrate the theory.

A.2   *Inflation expectations are adaptive:*

$$\pi_t^e = \pi_{t-1} + \lambda(\pi_{t-1}^e - \pi_{t-1}); \qquad 0 < \lambda < 1 \tag{2.4}$$

Equation (2.4) states that expected inflation equals past inflation if past expectations are correct. Otherwise, current expectations adjust for past mistakes. The parameter λ captures the size of today's reaction to past mistakes in forecasting. For example, a low λ implies that current expectations are always almost identical to last period's inflation, regardless of past mistakes. The crucial point is that expectations depend only on past observations of inflation. They do not take into account all the available information; in particular, they do not depend on the public expectations of the policymakers' future policies. For this reason, expectations are not rational. Note that simple recursive substitutions lead to

$$\pi_t^e = (1 - \lambda)[\pi_{t-1} + \lambda \pi_{t-2} + \lambda^2 \pi_{t-3} \ldots] \tag{2.5}$$

From (2.5) and (2.2), it follows that

$$y_t = \bar{y} + \pi_t - (1 - \lambda) \sum_{j=0}^{\infty} \lambda^j [\pi_{t-j-1}] \tag{2.6}$$

Equation (2.6) shows that given past inflation, the policymaker can achieve the desired rate of growth by an appropriate choice of current inflation.

A.3   *Politicians are identical. They prefer to be in office rather than out of office.*

A.4   *In every election, only two candidates (parties) face each other: an incumbent and a challenger.*

A.5 *Voters like growth and dislike inflation and unemployment. They are retrospective: They vote in favor of the incumbent if the economy is doing well (low unemployment and inflation, high growth) during his term of office. Voters heavily discount the past. Thus, the economic performance immediately before an election affects voters' decisions much more than the economic performance in the more distant past.*

These last three assumptions imply that incumbent governments behave identically, because they all maximize the same objective function (the likelihood of reelection) and face an electorate that follows a predictable voting pattern. What exactly the politicians maximize depends on the model's specification. The most realistic approach holds that the incumbent maximizes the probability of being reelected, which is a function of, among other things, the economic performance while the incumbent was in office (as A.5 states). Thus we can write that the probability Q of reelecting the incumbent in the election held at the end of period t is

$$Q_t = Q(\pi_t, u_t, y_t, \pi_{t-i}, u_{t-i}, y_{t-i}, \dots, Z); \qquad i = 1 \dots n \qquad (2.7)$$

where n is the length of the appointment of the current government and Z is a vector of noneconomic variables that may influence the election and are uncorrelated to the state of the economy.[4] As argued above, the weights attributed by the voters to the economic performance are declining over time, so that past economic outcomes weigh less in their decisions than more recent ones.

Equation (2.7) emphasizes that policymakers face some uncertainty about electoral outcomes given certain economic conditions. If the incumbent knew how many votes he would receive for given policies, he would always choose the policy combination assuring victory. To allow for the possibility of an incumbent loss, one needs to introduce some form of uncertainty, either in the economy (i.e., in the links between policy choices and economic outcomes) or in the polity (i.e., in the electorate's response to economic outcomes). Equation (2.7) captures the case in which the electorate's preferences are not known with

Table 2.1
Assumptions of the traditional opportunistic model

A.1 The economy is characterized by an expectation-augmented Phillips curve. Specifically, we use the following formulation of the Phillips curve:

$y_t = \bar{y} + \pi_t - \pi_t^e;$

A.2 Inflation expectations are adaptive:

$\pi_t^e = \pi_{t-1} + \lambda(\pi_{t-1}^e - \pi_{t-1}); \qquad 0 < \lambda < 1$

A.3 Politicians are identical. They prefer to be in office rather than out of office.

A.4 In every election, only two candidates (parties) face each other: an incumbent and a challenger.

A.5 Voters like growth and dislike inflation and unemployment. They are retrospective: They vote in favor of the incumbent if the economy is doing well (low unemployment and inflation, high growth) during his term of office. Voters heavily discount the past. Thus, the economic performance immediately before an election affects voters' decisions much more than the economic performance in the more distant past.

A.6 The policymaker controls a policy instrument deterministically related to aggregate demand.

A.7 The timing of elections is exogenously fixed.

---

certainty, thus the electoral outcomes, given certain policies of the incumbent, cannot be predicted with certainty.

A.6 *The policymaker controls a policy instrument deterministically related to aggregate demand.*

The policy instrument used by the politicians may be either monetary or fiscal, and in the empirical part of this book we investigate both.

A.7 *The timing of elections is exogenously fixed.*

Although this assumption is appropriate for the United States, in almost all the other OECD countries the timing of elections is not fixed; elections can be called, according to procedures which differ among countries.

Table 2.1 summarizes the assumptions of this traditional opportunistic model.

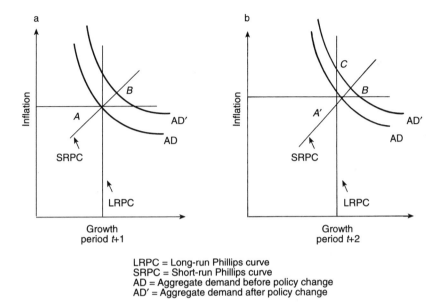

LRPC = Long-run Phillips curve
SRPC = Short-run Phillips curve
AD = Aggregate demand before policy change
AD′ = Aggregate demand after policy change

Figure 2.1
The Nordhaus-Lindbeck model at work

2.2.2   The Model at Work

A simple picture illustrates how the traditional opportunistic model works. Panel a of Figure 2.1 shows a long-run vertical Phillips curve (LRPC) for the case in which $\pi_t = \pi_t^e$; it also shows a short-run Phillips curve (SRPC) for the case of $\pi_t \neq \pi_{t-1} = \pi_t^e$. Let us consider point A where the long- and short-run curves cross, so that $\pi_t = \pi_{t-1} = \pi_t^e$. The downward sloping curve is the aggregate demand curve (AD), the position of which is shifted by monetary or fiscal policy. Suppose that elections take place at the end of period $t + 1$. By manipulating monetary and fiscal policy to expand aggregate demand, the incumbent can move to point B in period $t + 1$. In B, inflation is greater than expected, $\pi_{t+1} > \pi_t = \pi_{t+1}^e$, so that growth is above "normal," namely, $y_{t+1} > \bar{y}$. Thus, the election occurs at the end of a period with growth above normal and inflation rising only moderately. Note that the flatter the SRPC, the smaller the increase in inflation necessary to achieve a certain increase in growth.

Assume now that the incumbent is reappointed, partly (or largely) because of the good preelection outcome characterized by point B. Expectations at $t + 2$ begin to catch up, as shown in panel b because in $t + 1$ there was an expectation error, namely, $\pi_{t+1} > \pi_{t+1}^e$ (see equation (2.4)). If the policymaker does not further expand aggregate demand, the economy moves along the AD curve toward point C.[5] At point C growth is at its natural rate, $\bar{y}$, but inflation is higher than at A. The policymaker, after elections, can bring inflation back toward A by employing contractionary aggregate demand policies. Such policies will cause a downturn or recession, but by the time the next election approaches, the economy is back at point A, ready to move again to B. Nordhaus (1975) also shows that with certain specification of preferences, the policymaker may not return all the way to A, but to a point A' above A. Thus, with every electoral cycle one should also observe an increase in the average inflation rate, as panel b of Figure 2.1 shows.

In summary, this model implies that before each election one should observe growth above normal and unemployment below normal, with a moderate increase in inflation.[6] Immediately after the election, one should observe a more substantial increase in inflation which is soon reduced, however, with a downturn or recession. This economic cycle is clearly suboptimal because it creates economic fluctuations and variability with no gains in efficiency. Furthermore, this political business cycle may also increase average inflation with no gains in average growth or unemployment.

2.3   Rational Opportunistic Models

The Nordhaus-Lindbeck model is not based upon rational behavior on two grounds: (a) the Phillips curve embeds (nonrational) adaptive expectations; (b) voters do not act rationally. Several authors (Cukierman and Meltzer (1986), Rogoff and Sibert (1988), Rogoff (1990),

Persson and Tabellini (1990)) have proposed rational models consistent with the main thrust of the Nordhaus-Lindbeck model. In all of these models, voters behave rationally, that is, they maximize their expected utility and form expectations optimally, given their information.

All of these authors emphasize the idea of competence coupled with asymmetric information. Different governments handle the economy more or less competently. Competence is private information: The government knows its own ability; voters do not. Voters can assess government's competence only by observing economic outcomes. Under certain assumptions about when voters observe various economic variables, these models imply that generally, policymakers behave opportunistically to appear as competent as possible before each election. This behavior leads to cycles in economic outcomes that resemble, although with important differences, the Nordhaus-Lindbeck political business cycles.

Cukierman and Meltzer (1986) and Rogoff and Sibert (1988) independently proposed the first formalization of this idea. However, we begin in the next section with an overview of the model by Persson and Tabellini (1990), which is more directly related to the Phillips curve model discussed in the previous section.

2.3.1 A Model of Competence: The Phillips Curve

Persson and Tabellini (1990) modify Nordhaus's assumptions as follows:

A.1′ *The economy is described by a Phillips curve with a competence term:*

$$y_t = \bar{y} + \bar{\pi}_t - \pi_t^e + \varepsilon_t \tag{2.8}$$

where ε_t measures competence. The competence term (ε_t) is viewed as the government's ability to solve problems and handle the economy efficiently. A competent government can increase the natural rate of growth for given inflation and expected inflation. In Persson and Tabellini's words, "one candidate may be particularly able (or unable) to cope with a shock in the price of oil, or the effective labor market legislation, or to negotiate with the trade unions (80)." Competence has the following time structure:

$$\varepsilon_t = \mu_t + \mu_{t-1}$$

$$E(\mu_t) = 0 \qquad \text{for every } t.$$

(2.9)

Equation (2.9) embodies the assumption that competence is persistent. In fact, the moving average specification (MA(1)) implies that competence at time t contains both a contemporary portion and the realization of the preceding period. Competence does not carry over if after an election the challenger replaces the incumbent. The value of the challenger's competence is normalized at zero in the election period. Thus, if the challenger wins the election at the end of period t, $\varepsilon_{t+1} = \mu_{t+1}$ and $\mu_t = 0$.[7] The MA(1) specification is convenient because it does not allow competence to carry over for more than two periods. Below, we discuss the distribution of μ_t.

A.2′ *Inflation expectations are rational:*

$$\pi_t^e = E(\pi_t | I_{t-1})$$

(2.10)

where I_{t-1} is the information available to voters at the end of period $t-1$. What exactly voters' information set contains is crucial and is discussed below.

A.3 This assumption is changed only by the slight modification that the identical politicians not only care about reelection but also put some weight on social welfare.

Assumption A.4 is unchanged. For assumption A.5 is substituted:

A.5′ *Voters want to elect the policymaker who maximizes their expected utility. All voters have the same expected utility U, given by*

$$U = E\left\{ \sum_{t=0}^{\infty} \beta^t u(\pi_t, y_t) \right\}; \qquad 0 < \beta < 1$$

(2.11)

In (2.11) β is the discount factor, and we specify $u(\pi_t, y_t)$ as follows:

$$u(\pi_t, y_t) = -\frac{1}{2}(\pi_t^2) + by_t; \qquad b > 0 \tag{2.12}$$

Equation (2.12) states that the representative voter likes price stability and growth. In fact, the target rate of inflation is zero, and higher growth increases (linearly) the utility level. The parameter b captures the benefit of growth relative to the cost of higher inflation. This model totally ignores differences in preferences among voters. Although an electoral model with identical voters may appear somewhat peculiar, in chapter 3 we briefly discuss how these competence models can be extended to include differences in preferences.[8]

Assumption A.6 is simplified with no loss of generality to:

A.6′ *The policymaker controls inflation directly.*

Assumption A.7 is unchanged. Table 2.2 summarizes the assumptions of the rational opportunistic model.

Table 2.2
Assumptions of the rational opportunistic model

A.1′ The economy is described by a Phillips curve with a competence term:

$y_t = \bar{y} + \pi_t - \pi_t^e + \varepsilon_t;$

A.2′ Inflation expectations are rational:

$\pi_t^e = E(\pi_t | I_{t-1})$

A.3 Politicians are identical. They prefer to be in office rather than out of office.

A.4 In every election, only two candidates (parties) face each other: an incumbent and a challenger.

A.5′ Voters want to elect the policymaker who maximizes their expected utility. All voters have the same expected utility U, given by:

$$U = E\left\{ \sum_{t=0}^{\infty} \beta^t u(\pi_t, y_t) \right\}; \qquad 0 < \beta < 1$$

$$u(\pi_t, y_t) = -\frac{1}{2}(\pi_t^2) + by_t; \qquad b > 0$$

A.6′ The policymaker controls inflation directly.

A.7 The timing of elections is exogenously fixed.

To solve the model we must specify exactly what the voters know and when. First of all, we posit that competence can assume only two values: high ($\bar{\mu}$) or low ($\underline{\mu}$). Namely:

$$\mu_t = \bar{\mu} > 0 \text{ with probability } p$$
$$\underline{\mu} < 0 \text{ with probability } 1 - p \tag{2.13}$$

Therefore:

$$E(\mu_t) = p\bar{\mu} + (1 - p)\underline{\mu} = 0 \tag{2.14}$$

Voters know the distribution of μ_t, as in (2.13), and know that the unconditional expectation of μ_t is zero, namely (2.14); nonetheless they cannot observe competence (ε_t). In period t they observe y_t and, obviously, π_t^e, but they do not observe π_t: π_t becomes known at time $t + 1$. Because of this timing, voters learn competence with a one-period delay; in fact, in period $t + 1$, voters can compute ε_t. In other words, in any period t voters know μ_{t-1}, but not μ_t.

The assumption that inflation is observed with a one-period delay is crucial. If inflation were observed simultaneously with growth, competence would be observable by computing

$$\varepsilon_t = y_t - \bar{y} - \pi_t + \pi_t^e \tag{2.15}$$

As is clear from later discussion, if competence is observable, this model produces no political cycle. Persson and Tabellini (1990) write: "The assumption that [growth] can be observed before inflation may appear odd to some readers (82)." They justify the assumption by arguing that, in reality, policymakers do not directly control inflation but rather some monetary instrument that may not be immediately observable to the average voter.

This model can have two types of equilibrium (a) a separating equilibrium, and (b) a pooling equilibrium. In a separating equilibrium, the two types of policymakers choose policies revealing their competence, that is, voters know whether the incumbent has a high ($\bar{\mu}$) or a low ($\underline{\mu}$) level of competence μ_t in the election year t. In a pooling equilibrium, voters cannot infer from the policy the level of the incumbent's competence at time t. In the appendix to this chapter, we provide a formal solution of this model and describe both equilibria. Here we discuss intuitively the more interesting case of the separating equilibrium.

First of all, because voters are identical, what matters is the representative voter's perception of the incumbent government's expected competence, relative to the challenger's expected competence, which is normalized to zero. Clearly, because the voters prefer the more competent policymaker, the incumbent is reappointed if his expected competence is above zero, the challenger's expected level. Thus, the incumbent would like to appear as competent as possible. A competent policymaker (i.e., one who has a high realization of $\mu_t = \bar{\mu}$) would like to share this information with the voters. To do so, the competent policymaker needs to achieve a level of growth unattainable by an incompetent incumbent. Define this level of growth $y^s > \bar{y}$. Thus, the competent policymaker chooses a high level of inflation, above expectations, so as to achieve y^s. By definition, the incompetent policymaker cannot match y^s, thus he chooses the one-period optimal inflation rate. The public does not know ex ante which type of policymaker each is. Therefore, expected inflation is an average of the competent policymaker's high inflation and the lower inflation of the incompetent one. The average is computed using the voters' beliefs concerning the nature of the incumbent. Thus, the realized inflation rate in the election year is above expectation with the competent policymaker and below expectation with the incompetent one.

As a result, this model generates two important results: (a) a political business cycle with one type of policymaker; and (b) rational retrospective voting. In fact, the competent policymaker creates an expansion above normal immediately before an election. Voters, by observing this high growth, recognize the competent incumbent and choose to reappoint him. This political business cycle is, however, quite different from that in the traditional Nordhaus-Lindbeck model. In the Persson-Tabellini model, only one type of policymaker creates a preelectoral expansion; the other creates a downturn.[9] Furthermore, this model does not predict a postelectoral recession after the preelectoral boom.

The model also implies rational retrospective voting: Competent policymakers who create a preelectoral boom are reappointed. In other words, one should observe a correlation between the rate of growth before the election and the electoral results. Furthermore, it is rational for the voters to look at the economy in the election year when they vote, since the state of the economy reveals the policymaker's competence. The persistence of competence (2.9) is crucial to obtaining this result; otherwise the voters would have no reason to vote for an incumbent who appears competent today, since this information would have no bearing on future competence and therefore on future growth.

2.3.2 Political Budget Cycles

Rogoff and Sibert (1988), who (together with Cukierman and Meltzer (1986)) originally proposed the competence model, consider the government budget, rather than a Phillips curve. They write the following budget constraint:

$$g = \tau_t + s_t + \varepsilon_t \tag{2.16}$$

where g is an exogenously given level of government spending on goods and services or transfers which needs to be financed; τ_t is a lump-sum, nondistortionary tax; s_t is the seigniorage revenue raised at cost of distortions in the economy; ε_t is government competence. In this case competence must be interpreted as the ability to limit waste in the budget process, so that the required amount of spending can be financed with a smaller amount of total revenues. As in the preceding section, competence has a moving average structure. However, rather than assuming only two values for the competence shock μ_t, Rogoff and Sibert assume that μ_t can take any value between a minimum level (normalized at zero) and a maximum level.

The structure of information is analogous to the one in the model by Persson and Tabellini. Suppose that elections are held at the end of period t. Voters observe g and τ_t but not s_t and ε_t. The level of seigniorage (inflation) is observed with a one-period delay, exactly as in the previous model. All the assumptions concerning politicians' motivations, structure of elections, and voters' rationality are identical to those of the Phillips curve model. Here the representative voter utility function is as follows:

$$U = E\left\{ \sum_{t=0}^{\infty} \beta^t u_t \right\} \tag{2.17}$$

where

$$u_t = \bar{x} - \tau_t - s_t - \Delta(s_t) \tag{2.18}$$

where $\bar{x}$ is an exogenously given level of income and $\Delta(s)$ are the distortionary costs of seigniorage, so that $\Delta(0) = 0$, $\Delta'(\cdot) > 0$ for $s > 0$ and $\Delta''(\cdot) > 0$. This utility function makes it clear that a benevolent social planner would never use seigniorage to finance government spending, since seigniorage is distortionary and the lump-sum tax is not.[10]

Rogoff and Sibert show that a separating equilibrium always exists. In this equilibrium, for every realization of μ_t, the incumbent chooses some positive amount of seigniorage, except for the lowest realization of μ, namely for $\mu = 0$. In other words, every type of policymaker, except for the least competent, distorts preelectoral fiscal policies. The intuition is that all the other types are choosing enough seigniorage so that the lowest type cannot hide his lowest level of competence. Thus, he may as well choose the optimal policy. The intuition is similar to that in our previous discussion of the Phillips curve, except that here, with a continuum of types, generically everyone chooses distorted policies, except for one type, the most incompetent.[11] Without further assumptions, one cannot rule out the existence of pooling equilibria.[12]

In summary, this model's empirical implication is that in the preelectoral period, one should observe a level of taxation below the efficient
level and a level of inflation above optimal.[13] An alternative interpretation views s as the budget deficit, rather than seigniorage. With
this interpretation, however, the model would become analytically
much more difficult, because one would have to consider an intertemporal budget constraint. However, the basic intuition should persist: In the election year, one should observe lower taxes and higher
deficits.

Rogoff (1990) presents a related model that emphasizes the composition of government spending rather than seigniorage. He considers
the following budget constraint for the government:

$$g_t + k_{t+1} = \tau_t + \varepsilon_t \tag{2.19}$$

where g_t is government spending on goods and services and transfer
programs; k_{t+1} is public investment with a one-period production lag.
That is, public investment decided in period t becomes visible and
productive in period $t + 1$. Competence (ε_t), behaves exactly as before;
in particular, Rogoff presents the two-type model, in which the competence shock μ_t can assume only two values, high or low. The information asymmetry here is that the voters observe g_t and k_t at time t
but not k_{t+1}. Thus, when they vote at the end of period t, they do not
know ε_t and k_{t+1}.

The reader should by now see this model's implications. A separating equilibrium exists in which the competent incumbent signals his
administrative competence by cutting k_{t+1} below the full information-
efficient level and conversely raising g_t above (and cutting τ_t below)
the efficient level. Thus, the competent policymaker engineers a political budget cycle that shifts government outlays to favor transfers and
more visible programs instead of investment projects and possibly tax
cuts. Finally, Cukierman and Meltzer (1986) present another model of
competence that is also consistent with preelectoral policy distortions.
In their model, "governments differ from each other in their ability to

make ... forecasts of future states of nature (371)." Because of asymmetries of information between the government and the voters similar to those discussed above, the incumbent has an incentive to distort policy in the electoral period. Cukierman and Meltzer's focus is more on a general discussion of the "cost of democracy" in the absence of policy rules than on specific empirical implications for the political business cycle.

2.3.3 Discussion

Rational opportunistic models achieve two goals. First, they generate opportunistic policy cycles in models with rational expectations. Second, they rationalize retrospective voting behavior on the economy.

The first result hinges on an information asymmetry between the voters and policymakers and on a specific timing of information acquisition. How realistic are these assumptions? In the Phillips curve model, the assumption that voters can observe contemporaneous growth but can observe inflation only with a significant delay seems rather unrealistic. The asymmetries of information required in the budget models are more reasonable. The government budget, its composition, and the amount of projected deficits for the current fiscal year are sufficiently obscure and complicated that significant short-run informational asymmetries are quite likely. For example, suppose that in an election year the incumbent government raises certain transfers, claiming that no new taxes will be needed because a high expected growth rate will automatically increase revenues. Such a claim is quite hard for the average voter to check, certainly harder than observing inflation and unemployment in the election year. Particularly convincing is Rogoff's (1990) example focusing on the composition of government spending. Although aggregate macro variables, such as unemployment, growth, inflation, and the deficit, are relatively easily to observe, the composition of spending may be a more subtle and powerful way for incumbents to engineer opportunistic electoral cycles. Shifting spending to more visible programs that may favor key constituencies is a much easier policy to implement than reducing aggregate unemployment in an election year.

In summary, these rational opportunistic models reasonably predict short-run manipulations of the budget and, perhaps, monetary policy in the period immediately before and after an election. They are less powerful in providing a rationale for regular cycles of several years of inflation and unemployment.

These models have the unpleasant feature that, loosely speaking, the more competent politicians distort the economy, rather than the incompetent ones. This result follows from the nature of the separating equilibrium, in which, by distorting macroeconomic policy, the more competent policymakers signal their type. If competence were measurable (at least ex post) one should find that more competent policymakers exhibit the sharpest opportunistic cycles around elections, an implication that does not appear particularly realistic.

On the other hand, these models imply, rather intriguingly, that rational opportunistic cycles are the price for selecting the most competent politicians. In the Nordhaus-Lindbeck approach, elections are, from a purely economic perspective, just a cost; in these rational models of competence, elections do imply economic distortions but serve a useful purpose (choosing competent policymakers) explicitly accounted for within the model. Thus, competence models could address normative questions, such as the optimal frequency of elections, the introduction of term limits, and the choice of fixed versus flexible timing elections.[14]

These models' second important implication is that even rational voters should be retrospective: namely, they should judge the incumbent based on the election year's rate of growth. However, note that rational retrospective voting does not require the same informational asymmetries that generate rational opportunistic cycles. Rational voters would be retrospective on the economy, and specifically on growth and unemployment, even without the rather artificial assumptions about the timing of information discussed in the Phillips curve model by Persson and Tabellini. Furthermore, the rationality assumption imposes (potentially testable) conditions on to what degree and in what way rational voters should be retrospective. These points require a more detailed treatment presented in the next section, which draws on work by Alesina and Rosenthal (1995). The reader not particularly interested in the formalization of this problem may proceed directly to the chapter's conclusions.

2.4 Rational Retrospective Voting

Consider a generalization of the competence model by Persson and Tabellini (1990), where output growth is given by

$$y_t = \bar{y} + \pi_t - \pi_t^e + \eta_t \qquad (2.20)$$

where

$$\eta_t = \varepsilon_t + \xi_t \qquad (2.21)$$

The shock of η_t is composed by competence (ε_t) as before and by a second element (ξ_t) capturing various exogenous shocks beyond government's control. Competence has the same dynamic structure as above,

$$\varepsilon_t = \mu_t + \mu_{t-1} \qquad (2.22)$$

where all the random shocks (μ_t, ξ_t), have zero means and finite variances (σ_μ^2 and σ_ξ^2). The competence shock can assume any value, and the challenger's competence is normalized to zero. As before, voters do not observe competence directly. However, they observe growth and inflation at the same time, together with expected inflation. Therefore, there is no room for signaling and for strategic and opportunistic preelectoral manipulations. In fact, voters can observe η_t, because they observe $\bar{y}$, y_t, π_t and π_t^e.

Even though opportunistic cycles disappear, meaningful rational retrospective voting remains. In fact, suppose that, with elections held at the end of period t, growth is high in period t, namely:

$$\bar{y}_t - \bar{y} = \varepsilon_t + \xi_t = \eta_t > 0 \qquad (2.23)$$

Growth is above its average value, $\bar{y}$. Voters cannot distinguish competence (ε_t) from luck (ξ_t). If growth is high, however, there is a good chance that competence is high. In other words, if growth is above $\bar{y}$, voters learn something about the competence of the incumbent government, and thus, because of (2.22), about future competence, if the incumbent is reelected. More specifically, voters are interested in the best estimate of ε_{t+1}, having observed y_t and π_t. Remembering that $E(\mu_{t+1})$, the expected value of ε_{t+1} is, at time t:

$$E(\varepsilon_{t+1}) = E(\mu_{t+1}) + E(\mu_t|y_t) = E(\mu_t|y_t) \qquad (2.24)$$

Thus, the voters must evaluate μ_t, having observed a noisy signal of it, namely y_t, or equivalently, η_t. Assuming that voters observe μ_{t-1}, that is, competence is learned with a one-period delay, as in Persson and Tabellini 1990, the solution of a standard signal extraction problem leads to the following result:[15]

$$E(\varepsilon_{t+1}) = E(\mu_t/y_t) = \frac{\sigma_\mu^2}{\sigma_\mu^2 + \sigma_\xi^2}(y_t - \bar{y} - \mu_{t-1}) \qquad (2.25)$$

The voters know or observe all the components of the right-hand side of (2.25). It follows that if y_t is high, they favor the incumbent, because they assign some probability to the fact that high growth is the result not of luck but of competence. Thus, the voters are retrospective. They are rationally retrospective because they use their knowledge of the model to compute their optimal forecast of competence, which is the unique driving force of their electoral behavior. One interesting feature of (2.25) is that the forecast of competence depends intuitively on the relative variance of competence (σ_μ^2) and of exogenous shocks (σ_ξ^2). In an economy where the variance of exogenous shocks greatly exceeds (is below) that of competence, the voters place very little (*high*) weight on the observation of preelectoral growth when voting. The crucial point is that a rational voter disentangles luck from competence in the *best* possible way. A naive voter cannot achieve that: He simply votes for the incumbent when growth is high, without any further thought. Thus, a naive voter would punish an unlucky incumbent, whereas a rational voter would, at least in part, take bad luck into consideration. In summary, rational retrospective voting survives, even in a model without any opportunistic cycle. This is an important result. In fact, anticipating the next chapters, we find virtually no evidence of opportunistic cycles in growth or unemployment, although a large body of literature reports that the level of growth and unemployment in the election year strongly influences electoral results.[16]

Rational retrospective voting does not require specific assumptions about the dynamic behavior of competence and the delay in the voters' observation of competence. It requires only that competence be persistent, hardly a questionable assumption. For instance, even if, in the above model, competence were observable with no delay, it would still be rational for voters to look at the election year growth rate to decide how to vote. In this case, they could perfectly disentangle luck from competence, but one would still observe a positive statistical correlation between preelectoral growth and electoral results; obviously, past value of growth, beyond the election year, would bear no information for rational voters.

The opposite assumption is that the voters learn competence with several periods of delay, or perhaps never. In this case, not only the election year growth is relevant to form the optimal forecast of future competence, but also past observations of growth. Similar considerations apply if competence is persistent for more than one period, for instance, because it has a moving average structure of a high degree. In these cases, rational voters should look further into the past beyond the election year. If past values of competence have decreasing weights, then it is also rational for the voters to place less weight on

Table 2.3
Empirical implications of opportunistic models

Traditional models	Rational models
• regular multiyear cycle in growth and unemployment: growth is above normal (unemployment below normal) in the year or two before an election; growth falls (unemployment increases) after the election.	• no regular multiyear cycle in growth and in unemployment.
• monetary and fiscal policy are expansionary in the year or two before the election and contractionary in the year or two after the election.	• monetary and fiscal policy are expansionary two to three quarters preceding an election and contractionary two to three quarters after the election; smaller and shorter-lived effects than in the traditional model.
• inflation begins to increase immediately before an election, continues to increase for a few quarters after the election, then falls.	• same as for the traditional model, but smaller and shorter-lived effects on inflation.
• the vote share of the incumbent is increasing in the rate of growth in the election year (and decreasing in the unemployment rate).	• the vote share of the incumbent is increasing in past growth (and decreasing in past unemployment); the specific pattern of this relationship depends on voters' information.

past observations of growth. Therefore, empirical observations on the time horizon of retrospective voters and the relative weights of recent to past observations are not a satisfactory test of rationality. It may be perfectly rational to ignore any observation of the economy before the election year if, for instance, the previous years' growth rate reveals no information about competence.

2.5 Conclusions

Table 2.3 summarizes the empirical implications of the various models we have illustrated; in particular, it contrasts the predictions of the traditional opportunistic model with the rational versions of it. This comparison will be a major theme of our empirical analysis. Although the two types of models have reasonably similar implications for policy instruments and inflation, they sharply differ in their predictions of growth and unemployment. Furthermore, one should expect more regular and longer-lasting electoral effects on policy instruments in the traditional model, since in that model monetary and fiscal policy are more effective in generating the desired macroeconomic outcomes. Also, whereas in the traditional model every government acts identically, in the rational version some incumbents have little incentive to behave opportunistically. These two differences, outcomes versus instruments and size and regularity of the cycles, are crucial for our empirical comparison of these two approaches.

Appendix

1 Derivation of Equation (2.3)

Consider a production function, without capital, where Y is output and N is labor input, for example, employment:

$$Y_t = F(N_t); \qquad F'(\cdot) > 0, \qquad F''(\cdot) < 0 \tag{A.2.1}$$

From the profit maximization of competitive firms, taking output price (P) and wages (W) as given, we obtain a downward sloping labor demand (N^d):

$$N_t^d = G\left(\frac{W_t}{P_t}\right); \qquad G'(\cdot) < 0 \tag{A.2.2}$$

With a horizontal labor supply (to make things simple), from (A.2.2) it follows that

$$N_t^d = N_t = G\left(\frac{W_t}{P_t}\right) \tag{A.2.3}$$

Using (A.2.3) in (A.2.1), and assuming linearity, one obtains

$$Y = \gamma(P/W); \qquad \gamma > 0 \tag{A.2.4}$$

Setting $\gamma = 1$ and taking logarithms:

$$\log Y_t = \log P_t - \log W_t \tag{A.2.5}$$

Subtracting $\log Y_{t-1}$ on both sides of (A.2.5), and using (A.2.5) lagged:

$$\log Y_t - \log Y_{t-1} = \log P_t - \log P_{t-1} - \log W_t + \log W_{t-1} \tag{A.2.6}$$

Thus, using the same notation in the text and differences in logarithms as measures of rates of growth:

$$y_t = \pi_t - w_t \tag{A.2.7}$$

In (A.2.7), w_t is the rate of growth of nominal wages. If nominal wages are set one period in advance, they are based on expected, rather than actual, inflation, thus

$$w_t = \pi_t^e \tag{A.2.8}$$

Substituting (A.2.8) in (A.2.7) we get (2.3), with the constant $\bar{y}$ normalized at zero.

2   Rational Opportunistic Cycles: The Persson-Tabellini Model

Because of the assumption that competence has an MA(1) structure, the Persson-Tabellini (1990) model can be solved as a two-period model. Call the two periods t and $t + 1$, with elections occurring at the end of period t but not at the end of period $t + 1$. That is, a term of office lasts at least two periods. Purely for notational convenience, we will posit that

$$y_t = \bar{y} + \pi_t - \pi_t^e + \mu_t \tag{A.2.9}$$

In other words, we are ignoring μ_{t-1}, or we are assuming that $\mu_{t-1} = 0$. This is completely inconsequential if we assume, as Persson and Tabellini do, that μ_{t-1} becomes known in period t, thus before the voters go to the ballot box. Because μ_{t-1} is common knowledge, and it does not affect the value of μ_{t+1}, it does not affect in any way strategies or expectations and can be ignored. Alternatively, one can assume that t is the first period, that is, $t = 1$. Define $E(U_{t+1}^i)$, the expected utility for the generic voter, with $i = c$ if the competent policymaker wins or $i = nc$ if the incompetent one wins. Assume that, according to A.3 in section 2.2.1, the policymaker's is utility function is the same as that of the generic voter, but in addition, the policymaker enjoys a benefit denoted by H if he is in office. Let us begin from period $t + 1$, when the policymaker has no incentive to signal, because there are no elections at the end of the period and the asymmetry of information lasts only one period. Thus, using (2.12):

$$\pi_{t+1} = \pi_{t+1}^e = b \tag{A.2.10}$$

Equation (A.2.10) also implies that the voters know that in a non–election year, no signaling occurs. Thus:

$$y_{t+1} = \bar{y} + \varepsilon_{t+1} \tag{A.2.11}$$

The expected utility for the generic voter is

$$E(U_{t+1}) = -\frac{1}{2}b^2 + b\bar{y} + bE(\varepsilon_{t+1}) \tag{A.2.12}$$

Consider the incumbent net gain (W) from winning the election:

$$W(\mu_t^i) = [U_{t+1}^i - U_{t+1}^0 + H]; \qquad i = c, nc \tag{A.2.13}$$

The net gain for a policymaker of type i equals the difference in his utility if he wins minus his utility if the opponent wins, that is, U^0, plus *some personal* gain from the victory (H). Using (A.2.12) and (2.10) one obtains

$$W(\mu_t^i) = b\mu_t^i + H \tag{A.2.14}$$

In (A.2.14) we used the fact that the expected value of competence for the opponent is zero, that is, $E(\mu_{t+1}^0) = E(\mu_t^0) = 0$. We assume that H is sufficiently large so that even the incompetent incumbent prefers to be in office rather than out, so that

$$H > -b\underline{\mu} \tag{A.2.15}$$

If (A.2.15) did not hold, the incompetent policymaker would always reveal his identity to lose the election. In this (uninteresting) case, he would care more about his incompetence than about his rewards of office holding. In period t the incumbent policymaker knows that his reelection probability depends on whether the voters perceive him as competent. Thus, both the competent and the incompetent policymakers would like to be perceived as competent. This implies that the incumbent wishes to increase the level of growth in period t, to convince the electorate that he is competent. To do so, the incumbent must choose an inflation rate above expectation, setting π_t equal to

$$\pi_t(\mu_t^i) = \pi_t^e + y_t - \mu_t^i - \bar{y} \tag{A.2.16}$$

Given (A.2.16), the net costs of signaling (C) can be defined as follows:

$$C(\mu_t^i, y_t) = -\frac{1}{2}b^2 + b[\bar{y} + b - \pi_t^e + \mu_t^i]$$

$$- \left\{ -\frac{1}{2}[\pi_t(\mu_1^i)]^2 + b[\bar{y} + \pi_t(\mu_t^i) - \pi_t^e + \mu_t^i] \right\} \tag{A.2.17}$$

Equation (A.2.17) is the difference between the utility achieved when inflation is set equal to the time consistent level b and the level of utility when the incumbent signals, choosing $\pi_t(\mu_t^i)$. Note that the net cost of signaling depends on μ_t^i: The cost is lower for the competent policymaker because he has to inflate less to achieve the same level of growth.

This game can have two types of equilibrium: separating or pooling.

Separating Equilibrium

In this type of equilibrium the two types of policymakers achieve two different levels of growth. Thus, voters learn the type of incumbent and vote with complete information. If the incumbent is competent, he is reelected; if not, the challenger wins. Define $p_{t+1} = \text{Prob}(\mu_t^i = \bar{\mu}|y_t)$; that is, p_{t+1} is the posterior probability that voters attribute to the incumbent's being competent once they have observed y_t. Define y_t^s such that

$$p_{t+1} = 0 \quad \text{if} \quad y_t < y_t^s$$
$$p_{t+1} = 1 \quad \text{if} \quad y_t \geq y_t^s \tag{A.2.18}$$

where y_t^s is an appropriate threshold. Thus if the incumbent manages to achieve a level of growth not below y_t^s, his identity is revealed. If this threshold exists, and we are in a separating equilibrium, the competent policymaker can achieve y_t^s, the incompetent cannot. Thus, the incompetent one chooses $\pi_t = b$, because there is no point in distorting his policy. Two conditions for equilibrium must apply. First, expectations must be rational. This implies

$$\pi_t^e = (1 - p)b + p\pi(\bar{\mu}) = b + p\frac{(y^s - \bar{\mu} - \bar{y})}{1 - p} \tag{A.2.19}$$

In obtaining the right-hand side of (A.2.19), we made use of (A.2.16). The second condition for an equilibrium is that for the competent policymaker, the discounted net gain from reelection must be greater than the costs of signaling. The reverse must hold for the incompetent policymaker. Thus:

$$\beta W(\bar{\mu}) > C(y^s, \bar{\mu}) \tag{A.2.20}$$

$$\beta W(\underline{\mu}) \leq C(y^s, \underline{\mu}) \tag{A.2.21}$$

where $W(\cdot)$ and $C(\cdot)$ are defined by (A.2.14) and (A.2.17) respectively. These conditions do not identify a unique y^s but a range of values all consistent with equilibrium. Elimination of weakly dominated strategies, however, delivers a unique equilibrium in which the competent incumbent signals at the lowest possible level, achieving exactly y^s. This implies that, in equilibrium, (A.2.21) holds with equality.

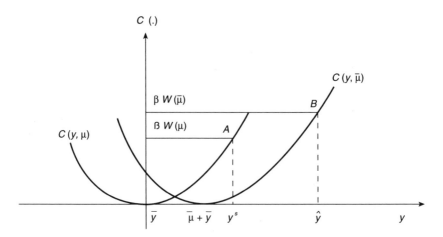

Figure 2.A.1

Figure 2.A.1, adapted from figure 5.1 of Persson and Tabellini 1990 (p. 85), illustrates this equilibrium. The two curves represent the costs of signaling. The curve for the competent government is shifted to the right of that of the incompetent one because it is less costly for the competent one to signal. The equilibrium must be on the left of point B, where condition (A.2.20) holds with equality. In this range, the cost of signaling for the competent policymaker is below the benefit. On the left of point A, the incompetent policymaker could also signal, so that the equilibrium would not be separating. The lowest amount of signaling necessary for the competent policymaker to identify himself occurs at A, where (A.2.21) holds with equality. On the right of A, the competent policymaker signals excessively, incurring unnecessary costs. Strategies leading to outcomes on the right of A are weakly dominated.

Pooling Equilibrium

In a pooling equilibrium, both the competent and incompetent policymaker choose the same level of growth. Thus the voters cannot learn anything about the incumbent. The voters' beliefs are as follows:

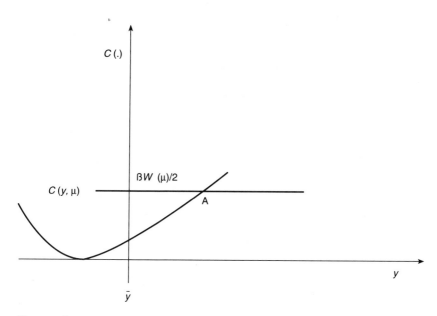

Figure 2.A.2

$$\rho_{t+1} = \rho \quad \text{if} \quad y_t \geq y^p$$
$$\rho_{t+1} = 0 \quad \text{if} \quad y_t < y^p \tag{A.2.22}$$

where y^p is a threshold to be determined. Note that since voters do not learn anything about the incumbent, his probability of reappointment is $\frac{1}{2}$.[17] In this equilibrium, competent policymakers choose inflation without signaling, thus setting $\pi_t = b$, which implies

$$y_p = b - \pi_t^e + \bar{\mu} + \bar{y} \tag{A.2.23}$$

The incompetent policymaker chooses enough inflation to achieve y^p:

$$\pi(\underline{\mu}, y^p) = y_p + \pi_t^e - \bar{y} - \underline{\mu} \tag{A.2.24}$$

Rationality of expectations in equilibrium implies

$$\pi_t^e = \rho b + (1 - \rho)\pi(\underline{\mu}, y^p) = b + \frac{(1 - \rho)}{\rho}(y^p - \bar{y} - \underline{\mu}) \tag{A.2.25}$$

Using (A.2.25) in (A.2.23), rearranging, and remembering that $\rho\bar{\mu} +$ $(1 - \rho)\underline{\mu} = 0$, we obtain $y^p = \bar{y}$. An incompetent policymaker chooses $y^p = \bar{y}$ if the cost of mimicking is lower than the benefit. Remembering that the probability of reelecting the incumbent is $\frac{1}{2}$, this condition implies:

$$C(\bar{y}, \underline{\mu}) \leq \frac{1}{2}\beta W(\underline{\mu}) \qquad\qquad (A.2.26)$$

Figure 2.A.2, adapted from figure 5.2 of Persson and Tabellini 1990 (p. 88), illustrates this equilibrium at point A. Persson and Tabellini show that for some parameter values, the pooling equilibrium can be ruled out by appealing to the "intuitive criterium" of Cho and Kreps (1987).

3   Partisan Models

3.1   Introduction

Most people (excluding some political scientists) would agree that different parties have different goals. We label as "partisan" those politicians, who, when in office, act as if they pursue certain ideological goals, and we focus upon differences in preferences over macroeconomic policies. Clearly, even partisan policymakers prefer to be in office rather than out of office. But although opportunistic policymakers choose policies solely to win elections, partisan policymakers want to win in order to implement their desired policies.[1]

This chapter examines the macroeconomic implications of electoral cycles in which different parties care more about inflation relative to growth and unemployment. Hibbs (1977) contrasted his partisan model to Nordhaus's political business cycle and argued that in OECD countries, left-wing parties typically choose combinations of inflation, unemployment and growth systematically different from those chosen by right-wing parties. In other words, left- and right-wing parties choose different points on the exploitable trade-off between inflation and unemployment; in particular, left-wing parties more willingly bear the costs of inflation to fight unemployment.

A more recent literature started by Alesina (1987) incorporates partisan preferences into a rational expectation model with wage (or price) rigidities. This theory, labeled rational partisan theory, emphasizes how policy uncertainty arising from electoral uncertainty interacts with rational expectations. Only unexpected inflation (deflation) shocks can influence real variables. But since electoral outcomes are not perfectly predictable, each election can produce policy shocks with temporary real effects. The rational partisan theory has two critical implications for Hibbs's model. First, according to the rational partisan theory differences in real economic outcomes are transitory rather than persistent, because rational expectations adjust after the postelectoral surprise. Second, the degree of surprise in the electoral result, by influencing the amount of unexpected inflation (deflation) after each election, influences the macroeconomic outcomes.

This chapter is organized as follows. Section 3.2 describes Hibbs's model. Section 3.3 illustrates the rational partisan theory. Section 3.4 discusses some welfare properties of partisan cycles. Section 3.5 examines how retrospective voting can be incorporated into a partisan model. The last section concludes. A brief appendix summarizes the basic time inconsistency problem in monetary policy. Readers not familiar with this issue may want to read the appendix before they begin section 3.3.

3.2   The Traditional Partisan Model

In a very influential article published in 1977 and in a successful book published ten years later, Hibbs (1977, 1987a) lays out his partisan model of macroeconomic policy. Hibbs's interests were mostly empirical, so he never spelled out a formal theoretical derivation of his empirical model. One can, however, clearly place his model within the exploitable Phillips curve approach to macroeconomics, dominant in the 1960s and 1970s. Table 3.1 summarizes Hibbs's assumptions in the context of our notation. Assumptions A.1 and A.2 are unchanged from the versions introduced in Section 2.2.1. In his 1977 and 1987a publications, Hibbs is never explicit about his assumptions concerning the Phillips curve, but assumptions A.1 and A.2 are the theoretical

Table 3.1
Assumptions of the traditional partisan theory

A.1 The economy is characterized by an expectation-augmented Phillips curve:

$y_t = \bar{y} + \pi_t - \pi_t^e$

A.2 Inflation expectations are adaptive:

$\pi_t^e = \pi_{t-1} + \lambda(\pi_{t-1}^e - \pi_{t-1}); \qquad 0 < \lambda < 1$

A.3' Politicians are not identical. Members of left-wing parties are more concerned with unemployment and growth and relatively less concerned with inflation. Members of right-wing parties have opposite preferences.

A.4 In every election, only two candidates (parties) face each other: an incumbent and a challenger.

A.5″ Different voters have different preferences over inflation and unemployment (or growth). Voters choose the left- or the right-wing parties, according to their preferences.

A.6 The policymaker chooses a policy instrument deterministically related to aggregate demand.

A.7 The timing of elections is exogenously fixed.

basis for his empirical tests. Furthermore, his relative silence on the role played by expectation adjustment suggests that he had in mind a model where λ is low, that is, expectations are quite static.[2]

The key change from the Nordhaus-Lindbeck models concerns assumption A.3, for which is substituted:

A.3' Politicians are not identical. Members of left-wing parties are more concerned with unemployment and growth and relatively less concerned with inflation. Members of right-wing parties have opposite preferences.

Hibbs's model sees political parties as the representatives of different constituencies with different preferences. In particular, the right-wing constituency includes the upper middle class and the business and financial community; the left-wing constituency includes the lower middle class and the union movement. Inflation and unemployment have distributional consequences that explain these different preferences. Hibbs (1987a) provides unambiguous evidence about unemployment's effect on income distribution in the United States: an increase in unemployment reduces the income shares of the populations's two poorest quintiles and increases those of the two richest quintiles. Hibbs calculates that a one-year increase in the unemployment rate from 6 to 10 percent shifts about one percentage point of income from the poorest two quintiles to the richest two. It may not seem much, but even small changes in income distribution can have important sociopolitical effects. Inflation's distributional effects are harder to pinpoint with precision. Inflation influences income and wealth distribution through a variety of channels: the effects of nonindexed tax brackets; the interaction between inflation and firms' balance sheets; the effects on nominally denominated assets and liabilities; changes in relative prices, and so forth. After an extensive discussion and review of the literature, Hibbs concludes that in the United States, "inflation, although essentially neutral in its impact on money income distribution, may actually have improved somewhat the relative income position of low income households (87)." Inflation may also result from government spending programs that generally are redistributive toward the less well off.[3] Therefore, these considerations suggest that the political left should be particularly concerned with reducing unemployment and avoiding recessions, even at the cost of some inflation, and the right-wing parties should be relatively more concerned with the costs of inflation and relatively less with unemployment.

Hibbs also examines the platforms of the two main American parties and the publicly expressed preferences of union leaders, businessmen and various individuals with different income levels. Both his informal evidence and his statistical analysis confirm his basic hypothesis on preferences.

Assumption A.4 is unchanged. Assumption A.5 changes as follows:

A.5″ *Different voters have different preferences over inflation and unemployment (or growth). Voters choose the left- or the right-wing parties, according to their preferences.*

For instance, we can imagine a distribution of voter preferences on the inflation-unemployment trade-off with two peaks corresponding to the two parties positions on the issue. Hibbs also argues that the electorate's concerns over inflation and unemployment vary with the actual level of these variables. Voters are retrospective: they look at the economy, and based on their preferences, favor one party or the other. Voters are backward looking and do not use past observations to make rational forecasts of the future.

For the partisan model to hold true the two parties must act differently when in office. Having different preferences (assumption A.3) is a necessary but not a sufficient condition for this to happen. In fact, in two-party elections, the candidates may converge toward the middle in order to win: Even a partisan politician cannot implement his desired policies if he loses. A full discussion of policy convergence in a two-party system with partisan policymakers would require an entire chapter. For our purposes it is sufficient to recall that as long as the electoral results remain uncertain, the two parties adopt different policies. In fact, they trade off the potential gain in probability of victory if they converge to the middle against the potential loss in their preference dimension if they move away from their preferred position. In general, the two parties choose distinct policies and act differently when in office. Note that this result holds even if, in addition to their partisan inclination, the candidates of the two parties also love office holding per se. For more discussion of these and related issues, see Wittman 1977, 1983; Calvert 1985; and chapter 2 of Alesina and Rosenthal 1995.

Assumptions A.6 and A.7 are unchanged.

Figure 3.1 is analogous to figure 2.1, except that, in line with Hibbs's emphasis, we consider the inflation-unemployment trade-off, rather than that between inflation and growth. Assume that we start from point A, and a left-wing government is elected. This government has the goal of achieving point B, with lower unemployment, moving along the short-run Phillips curve. As argued above, Hibbs does not seem overly concerned about shifts of the short-run Phillips curve because of expectation adjustments, so that the SRPC is relatively

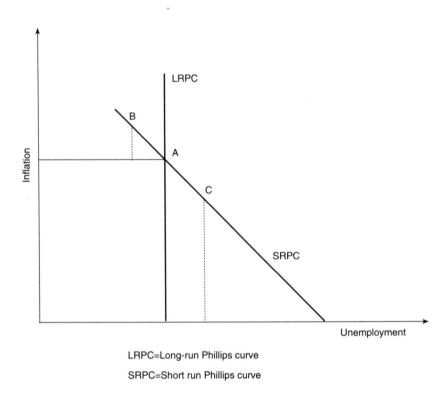

LRPC=Long-run Phillips curve

SRPC=Short run Phillips curve

Figure 3.1

stable, at least within the time horizon of one or two terms of office, say, up to eight years. Thus, he argues that a left-wing government can keep the economy at the target level of unemployment (point B) for several years with a reasonably stable inflation. Rather than shifts in the short-run Phillips curve because of expectation adjustments, Hibbs is more concerned with the lags between policy choices and the effects of policy on the real economy, so that he argues that it may take several years for the economy to move from A to B along the short-run Phillips curve after a left-wing electoral victory.

Suppose now that, while the economy is at point B, the right-wing party wins the election. The right-wing objective is to move the economy to point C with lower inflation. To do so, the new government adopts deflationary policies that more or less slowly move the econ-

Table 3.2
Assumptions of the rational partisan theory

A.1 The economy is described by an expectation-augmented Phillips curve:

$y_t = \bar{y} + \pi_t - \pi_t^e$

A.2' Inflation expectations are rational:

$\pi_t^e = E(\pi_t | I_{t-1})$

A.3' Politicians are not identical. Members of left-wing parties are more concerned with unemployment and growth and relatively less concerned with inflation. Members of right-wing parties have opposite preferences.

A.4 In every election, only two candidates (parties) face each other: an incumbent and a challenger.

A.5''' Different voters have different preferences over inflation and unemployment. Based on their preferences, they vote for the party that delivers the highest expected utility.

A.6' The policymaker controls inflation directly.

A.7 The timing of elections is exogenously fixed.

---

omy from A to C. Shifts in the short-run Phillips curve may complicate this picture a bit, but the basic message is unchanged. The two parties can achieve and sustain, with relatively stable inflation, two different levels of unemployment. Analogous arguments hold for output growth. In summary, this model's basic point is that the two parties can achieve two different levels of real economic activity for their entire term of office with relatively stable inflation.

3.3   The Rational Partisan Model

Alesina (1987) proposes a model that incorporates rational expectations into a partisan model of macroeconomic policy. Table 3.2 summarizes the model's assumptions.

Assumption A.1 is unchanged. Expectations are rational, as in A.2'. Political parties are partisan, as stated in A.3'. The assumption about voter behavior is a combination of A.5' (rationality) and A.5'' (partisanship):

A.5′′′ *Different voters have different preferences over inflation and un-*
employment. Based on their preferences, they vote for the party that delivers
the highest expected utility.

Assumptions A.6 and A.7 are unchanged;[4] with no loss of generality, Alesina adopts the simplified version of A.6, namely A.6′.

To better describe the model, it is worth emphasizing the specific
wage-contract interpretation of the Phillips curve.[5] Real output growth
is inversely related to the growth of real wages (here we ignore
physical capital and productivity growth):

$$y_t = \bar{y} + \pi_t - w_t \tag{3.1}$$

where w_t is the rate of growth of nominal wages. Contracts specifying
nominal wages are signed at the beginning of each period and last the
entire period. Thus, wages are fixed in nominal terms. The labor market
can be either competitive or not. In a competitive market, the rate of
growth of nominal wages equals the inflation rate to keep the real wage
constant at the level that clears the labor market.[6] In a noncompetitive
market, labor unions set the real wage at the level that maximizes
union members' welfare.[7] In either case, we have:

$$w_t = \pi_t^e = E(\pi_t | t_{-1}) \tag{3.2}$$

Substituting (3.2) into (3.1), we obtain:

$$y_t = \bar{y} + \pi_t - \pi_t^e \tag{3.3}$$

The left-wing party (*L*) and the right-wing party (*R*) have the following preferences:

$$u^L = \sum_{t=0}^{\infty} \beta^t [-(\pi_t - \bar{\pi}^L)^2 + b^L y_t] \tag{3.4}$$

$$u^R = \sum_{t=0}^{\infty} \beta^t [-(\pi_t - \bar{\pi}^R)^2 + b^R y_t] \tag{3.5}$$

where:

$$\bar{\pi}^L \geq \bar{\pi}^R \geq 0 \tag{3.6}$$

$$b^L > b^R \geq 0 \tag{3.7}$$

The first part of (3.4) and (3.5) implies an inflation target that may be positive if the optimal inflation rate is not zero. This may indeed be the case because of an optimal taxation argument: inflation is a tax that may play a role in a menu of optimal tax rates.[8] The second term in (3.4) and (3.5) represents the benefits of higher growth. Growth enters linearly for analytical simplicity and with no loss of generality. The partisan assumption (A.3) is embodied in (3.6) and, in particular, (3.7): the left cares relatively more about growth (and unemployment) than the right. In addition (but this is not necessary), the first inequality in (3.6) may hold strictly, namely, the optimal inflation tax for L may be higher than that for R. This may occur if, for instance, L favors a larger government and needs more tax revenues or if the inflation tax hurts more the constituency supporting the right.

The incentive to increase growth above its natural level $\bar{y}$ can be related to distortions in the labor market.[9] One source of distortion may be, for instance, labor taxation that keeps the level of economic activity below the undistorted full employment level. A second source may be labor unions that keep the real wage too high because they care only about union members. In either case, the level of economic activity is below the first best, that is, the undistorted full employment level. As a result, policymakers have an incentive to increase the level of economic activity.

Voters have preferences analogous to those of the parties; thus the generic voter has the following utility function (see also (2.12)):

$$u_i = \sum_{t=0}^{\infty} \beta^t [-(\pi_t - \bar{\pi}^i)^2 + b^i y_t] \tag{3.8}$$

In general, voters differ in their views over the optimal inflation tax $\bar{\pi}^i$ and the costs of inflation versus the benefits of growth b^i. The parameters $\bar{\pi}^i$ and b^i are distributed over the population; we do not need any specific assumption over this distribution, except that nobody, including the political parties, knows with certainty the distribution of voter preferences (i.e., of $\bar{\pi}^i$ and b^i).[10]

Finally, let us assume, for concreteness and without loss of generality, that elections take place every other period; thus a term of office lasts two periods.[11] Consider the term of office beginning in period t. The model needs to be solved by backward induction to ensure time consistency.[12] If party L wins the elections, it sets:

$$\pi_t = \pi_{t+1} = \bar{\pi}^L + \frac{b^L}{2} \equiv \hat{\pi}^L \tag{3.9}$$

If party R wins, it sets:

$$\pi_t = \pi_{t+1} = \bar{\pi}^R + \frac{b^R}{2} \equiv \hat{\pi}^R \tag{3.10}$$

Equations (3.9) and (3.10) can be easily derived by substituting (3.3) in (3.4) and (3.5) and by maximizing with respect to π_t, taking π_t^e as given. Expectations must be taken as given because they are formed before the policymaker chooses policy. In equations (3.9) and (3.10) the first term ($\bar{\pi}^L$ and $\bar{\pi}^R$) represents the target inflation rate for the two parties, regardless of growth considerations. The second term ($b^L/2$ and $b^R/2$) is the effect on inflation of the parties' attempt at increasing growth above the "natural" rate, namely above the level achieved with no inflation shocks.

Given our assumptions on preferences:

$$\hat{\pi}^L > \hat{\pi}^R \tag{3.11}$$

Inflation is permanently higher with the left-wing party in office than with the right-wing party in office.

This result holds, even if $\bar{\pi}^L = \bar{\pi}^R$, as long as $b^L > b^R$: The target inflation rates need not be different as long as one party cares relatively more about growth relative to inflation than the other party.

Voters, who are rational and forward looking, know the two parties' objective functions, and know the policies $\hat{\pi}^L$ and $\hat{\pi}^R$; thus they can solve the parties' optimization problem and find the equilibrium policies. Even though the policies are known, however, the electoral results are uncertain, since the distribution of voters' preferences is unknown. Denote P the probability that party R wins the election, and $1 - P$ the probability that party L wins. We will discuss the derivation of P below. The electorate knows the value of P. This assumption implies the following: First, we must impose that, realistically, the distribution of voter preferences is not known with certainty. This is equivalent to saying that even though the policies of the two contending parties are known in advance, the electoral results are not predictable with certainty. Second, we assume that "the distribution of the distribution of voter preferences" is known by everybody. In other words, everybody can compute the probability of the two possible electoral outcomes, given the knowledge of the two parties policies.[13]

Given P, expected inflation is:

$$\pi_t^e = P\hat{\pi}^R + (1 - P)\hat{\pi}^L \tag{3.12}$$

$$\pi_{t+1}^e = \hat{\pi}^R \qquad \text{if } R \text{ is in office} \tag{3.13a}$$

$$\pi_{t+1}^e = \hat{\pi}^L \qquad \text{if } L \text{ is in office} \tag{3.13b}$$

These equations are crucial for the rational partisan theory. The first, (3.12), emphasizes that before elections, expectations concerning inflation are an average of $\hat{\pi}^L$ and of $\hat{\pi}^R$ weighted by the probabilities of the two electoral outcomes. Afterwards, expectations adjust to the policy of whichever party is in office. Using (3.3) and (3.12), we can compute output growth with the left and the right, y^L and y^R respectively:

$$y_t^L = \bar{y} + P(\hat{\pi}^L - \hat{\pi}^R) \tag{3.14}$$

$$y_t^R = \bar{y} - (1 - P)(\hat{\pi}^L - \hat{\pi}^R) \tag{3.15}$$

$$y_{t+1}^L = y_{t+1}^R = \bar{y} \tag{3.16}$$

Thus, in the first period of a left-wing government, growth is above its natural rate, and in the first period of a right-wing government, growth is below the natural rate. In the second period, growth is at its natural rate with both types of government.

Several observations are in order.

i. The magnitude of the deviations of output growth from its natural rate is increasing in the difference between the two parties preferences, reflected in the difference between $\hat{\pi}^L$ and $\hat{\pi}^R$. In more colorful terms: more political polarization implies wider economic fluctuations;

ii. The degree of surprise of the electoral result influences the magnitude of the fluctuations in growth; for instance, the lower is P, the probability of electing the R government, the larger the recession caused by the latter.

iii. The right-wing party causes recessions (or at least downturns) even if $b^R > 0$, that is, even if this party likes growth above the natural rate, because the possibility of a victory by the left keeps expected inflation high.

iv. The model can be easily extended to the case of terms of office lasting more than two periods. In this case, output deviations from $\bar{y}$ would still occur only in the first period.

We can now turn to the determination of P. The generic voter i votes for party R if his expected utility is higher if party R wins than if party L wins. This condition is as follows:

$$
\begin{aligned}
-(\hat{\pi}^R - \bar{\pi}^i)^2 + b^i y_t^R + \beta[-(\hat{\pi}^R - \bar{\pi}^i)^2 + b^i \bar{y}] > \\
-(\hat{\pi}^L - \bar{\pi}^i)^2 + b^i y_t^L + \beta[-(\hat{\pi}^L - \bar{\pi}^i)^2 + b^i \bar{y}]
\end{aligned}
\tag{3.17}
$$

Recalling that $y_t^L > \bar{y} > y_t^R$, it is clear that "high b^i" voters prefer L to R; similarly, "high $\bar{\pi}^i$" voters prefer L. Remember that the distribution of $\bar{\pi}^i$ and b^i is uncertain, that is, it is perturbed by random shocks. *P is the probability that condition (3.17) holds for more than 50 percent of the voters.* Given $\hat{\pi}^R$ and $\hat{\pi}^L$, P depends only on the model's parameters and is a constant that can be computed. Note that, although policy is unidimensional, voting occurs on two dimensions, since voters differ on two parameters. However, voting cycles are not a factor because the electorate faces a binary choice. Although we do not need any assumption about the distribution of voter preferences,[14] it may be natural to assume that high b^i voters are also high $\bar{\pi}^i$ voters, and the other way around.

In summary, this model predicts a partisan cycle in which partisan effects on real aggregates are short-lived and confined to the post-electoral period. Inflation, on the other hand, is permanently different and is higher with the left-wing party in office.

The next two sections address two related issues. First, we discuss this equilibrium's welfare properties, then retrospective voting. In fact, a rather unappealing feature of this model is that it is not consistent with "voting on the economy," because electoral results depend only on exogenous shocks to voters' preferences and therefore are independent of the economy's preelectoral state. The reader less interested in formalization and more interested in the empirical tests can skip the next two sections and move directly to the chapter's conclusions.

3.4   Welfare Properties of Partisan Cycles

The cycle described in the section 3.3 is suboptimal in that both parties would be better off if they could agree to follow the same policy and eliminate fluctuations in inflation and growth.[15] Suppose that the two parties can agree to follow, when in office, the same policy π^*, such that:

$$\bar{\pi}^R < \pi^* < \bar{\pi}^L \tag{3.18}$$

Becasue the two parties' utility functions are concave in inflation, one can find a range of values for π^* for which both parties would be better off if they followed π^* rather than $\hat{\pi}^R$ and $\hat{\pi}^L$. With a common π^* the two parties avoid costly fluctuations in the inflation rate and the growth rate. This claim can easily be grasped intuitively with an example. Suppose that $b^R = b^L = 0$. (This is in fact not necessary but keeps the intuition as simple as possible.) Suppose also that $\bar{\pi}^R = 0$, $\bar{\pi}^L = 1$ and $P = \frac{1}{2}$. If the two parties follow the same policy $\pi^* = \frac{1}{2}$, expected utility in each period (U^*) is given by $U^* = -\frac{1}{4}$ for both. If instead they follow their individually most-preferred policies ($\hat{\pi}^L = 1$, $\hat{\pi}^R = 0$), their expected utility is, in each period, given by $U^L = U^R = -\frac{1}{2}$. Thus $U^* > U^L$ and $U^* > U^R$. This argument is unaffected if $b^L > b^R > 0$ and would be strengthened if output growth entered quadratically rather than linearly in the two parties' objective functions.[16]

How a policy like π^* may be chosen depends on the bargaining between the parties. Alesina (1987) computes the Nash bargaining solution and finds that π^* is decreasing in P. The intuition is that as P increases, the noncooperative solution is progressively more favorable to party R, so party R is stronger at the bargaining table and π^* is closer to $\hat{\pi}^R$.[17] The problem is how to enforce the credibility of π^*. In fact, consider, in particular, party L. If a policy rule π^* is agreed upon before the election and this rule is expected ($\pi^* = \pi^e$), if party L wins, it has an incentive to follow $\hat{\pi}^L$ instead of π^*. By doing so this party achieves a desirable burst of growth caused by unexpected inflation ($\hat{\pi}^L - \pi^*$). Analogous considerations apply to R because, in general, $\pi^* \neq \hat{\pi}^R$. The more intuitive case is the one in which $\pi^* > \hat{\pi}^R$, that is, b^R is low. In this case party R has an incentive to deviate from the rule in the opposite direction from L.

The rule π^* can be made credible in three ways:

i. The repeated interaction between the two parties in an infinitely repeated game (Alesina 1987) could make π^* credible. In this case, the cost of breaking the rule π^* arises because, as a result of the breakdown of cooperation, the system reverts to the noncooperative equilibrium ($\hat{\pi}^L$ and $\hat{\pi}^R$). For this mechanism to be effective, the two parties face to have a long time horizon (i.e., technically infinite) and not discount the future too heavily.

ii. The two parties could agree to a constitutional law that establishes π^* and requires unanimity to be changed. This arrangement has, of course, the drawback of imposing rigidity in policy making. Although in this simple model policy flexibility is irrelevant, it would be important in a more realistic scenario with various exogenous shocks to which the policymaker would like to react. The discussion of the benefits of flexibility versus those of commitments to fixed rules is wide-ranging and goes beyond the scope of this volume.[18]

iii. The two parties could agree to appoint an independent central banker and let him choose policy independent of partisan pressures. This arrangement would eliminate policy-induced cycles without eliminating the capability of reacting to economic shocks. In chapter 8 we develop in more detail the issue of central bank independence from political pressures in a partisan model.

3.5   A Rational Partisan Model with Retrospective Voting

The model described in the previous sections has the drawback that voting is not retrospective, namely, preelectoral economic conditions do not influence electoral outcomes. In fact, the voters are forward looking and are perfectly informed about the economy and the two parties' objectives. Thus, observing the state of the economy in the preelection period reveals no information concerning the future course of policy. This feature of the model is clearly inconsistent with a large body of empirical evidence that shows, rather conclusively, that the state of the economy before elections is a very important determinant of voting behavior.[19]

Alesina and Rosenthal (1995) extend the rational partisan model to encompass rational retrospective voting on the economy. This extension involves adding an element of competence to the rational partisan setup explored in this chapter. Specifically, consider exactly the same model of competence as in section 2.4, where competence (ε_t) has the following structure:

$\varepsilon_t = \mu_t + \mu_{t-1}$

and μ_t, μ_{t-1} are random shocks with zero mean and variance σ_μ^2. The reader will recall that, given the assumptions on the information structure, in that model there is no room for opportunistic behavior, but competence is not immediately distinguishable from other exogenous shocks. The persistence of competence gives rise to rational retrospective voting.

Suppose that party R is in office at time $t-1$, and consider the elections held at the beginning of the period t. The generic voter i votes R if his expected utility with party R in office in periods t and $t+1$ is higher than with party L in office. Let us review what voter i knows:

$$\pi_t^L = \pi_{t+1}^L = \hat{\pi}^L \qquad\qquad\qquad \text{if } L \text{ wins} \qquad\qquad (3.19)$$

$$\pi_t^R = \pi_{t+1}^R = \hat{\pi}^R \qquad\qquad\qquad \text{if } R \text{ wins} \qquad\qquad (3.20)$$

$$E(y_t^L) = \bar{y} + P(\hat{\pi}^L - \hat{\pi}^R) \qquad\qquad \text{if } L \text{ wins} \qquad\qquad (3.21)$$

$$E(y_t^R) = \bar{y} - (1 - P)(\hat{\pi}^L - \hat{\pi}^R) + E(\varepsilon_{t+1}) \qquad \text{if } R \text{ wins} \qquad\qquad (3.22)$$

$$E(y_{t+1}^L) = E(y_{t+1}^R) = \bar{y} \qquad\qquad\qquad\qquad\qquad\qquad (3.23)$$

$$E(\varepsilon_{t+1}) = E(\mu_{t+1}) + E(\mu_t|y_t) = E(\mu_t|y_t) \qquad\qquad\qquad (3.24)$$

The asymmetry between (3.21) and (3.22) arises because R is the incumbent. The expected competence for L is normalized at zero, since L is the challenger. The expected competence for R is generally not zero and depends on the observation of competence during R's term of office. In fact, equation (3.22) embodies the notion that expected competence for period $t+1$ depends on the realization of today's competence: Remember that $E(\mu_{t+1}) = 0$ and that $E(\mu_t|y_t)$ can be computed as a signal extraction problem (recall equation 2.25). Thus, voter i votes for R if:

$$-(\hat{\pi}^R - \bar{\pi}^i)^2 + b^i E(y_i^R) + \beta[-(\hat{\pi}^R - \bar{\pi}^i)^2 + b^i \bar{y}] >$$
$$-(\hat{\pi}^L - \bar{\pi}^i)^2 + b^i E(y_t^L) + \beta[-(\hat{\pi}^L - \bar{\pi}^i)^2 + b^i \bar{y}]$$
$$\qquad\qquad\qquad\qquad\qquad\qquad\qquad\qquad\qquad (3.25)$$

which simplifies to:

$$
\begin{aligned}
&- (\hat{\pi}^R - \bar{\pi}^i)^2 (1 + \beta) + b^i E(\mu_t | y_t) > \\
&- (\hat{\pi}^L - \bar{\pi}^i)^2 (1 + \beta) - b^i (\hat{\pi}^L - \hat{\pi}^R).
\end{aligned}
\tag{3.26}
$$

Equation (3.26) highlights that the fraction of R voters is increasing in the perceived competence of the incumbent R government for a given distribution of preferences. Thus, in this example, if $E(\mu_t | y_t)$ is high, some moderate left-of-center voters who would normally vote L actually choose R because the perceived competence outweighs the ideological preferences. On the other hand, some left-leaning voters would still vote L, because their ideological preferences are stronger. Under some general assumptions about the distribution of $\bar{\pi}^i$ and b^i and about the nature of the shocks over this distribution, Alesina and Rosenthal find a closed-form solution for this problem. Remember that calculating $E(\mu_t | y_t)$ implies rational retrospective voting: Voters optimally gather information on future competence by observing the state of the economy before elections.

In summary, in this model the voters consider both their preferences and the incumbent's competence. To evaluate the latter they have to look at the economy; thus, they have to be retrospective. Elections here serve two purposes: They indicate the electorate preferences among competing polarized parties and help in selecting, on average, the more competent policymakers.

3.6   Discussion and Conclusions

This chapter has considered partisan models of political cycles. As in chapter 2, we conclude with a summary of the empirical implications of the traditional versus the rational models. Table 3.3 summarizes our results.

Before proceeding to the empirical tests, we need to address two issues. With reference to the first, Hibbs (1992) summarizes several

Table 3.3
Empirical implications of partisan models

Traditional models	Rational models
1. Growth permanently higher, unemployment permanently lower when the left is in office.	1. Growth is temporarily higher, unemployment temporarily lower than the natural rate after a left-wing electoral victory; the opposite is true after a right-wing electoral victory.
2. Inflation permanently higher with the left in office.	2. Deviation of growth and unemployment from natural rates is correlated with the amount of electoral surprise.
	3. Unemployment and growth return to their natural rates in the second part of both right- and left-wing terms of office.
	4. Inflation permanently higher when the left is in office.

criticisms raised against the rational partisan theory. He raises three points in particular:

i. First, why would optimizing agents lock themselves into long-term contracts?

Wage stickiness is an important feature of the neo-Keynesian approach to macroeconomics.[20] The basic point is that for a variety of reasons, as pointed out by Alesina and Rosenthal (1995, 185), "the complexity of real-world inflation shocks makes it very difficult to write wage contracts that correctly adjust for what they should and do not adjust for what they should not," such as supply shocks. A second response comes from the literature on "menu costs," that is, costs of changing prices in monopolistically competitive markets (Mankiw 1985, Blanchard and Kyotaki 1987). For instance, if a monopolistic union sets the wage that maximizes its profit function, then even a small cost of adjusting the nominal wage in response to inflation may prevent adjustment even for relatively large fluctuations of the real wage, because the profit function is concave and reaches a maximum (with a zero first derivative) at the target real wage.

ii. The second criticism is that if all the wage contracts were signed after the election, political uncertainty would bring about no real effect.

The assumption that all contracts are signed before the election is an obvious simplification necessary only for analytical simplicity. In reality, wage contracts have an overlapping structure and are signed in staggered terms, as, for instance, in Taylor 1979. Accounting explicitly for staggered contracts would maintain the same qualitative feature of the simple model described in this chapter, although it would enrich the dynamics.[21] Garfinkel and Glazer (1994) present some interesting evidence precisely on this point. They show that the timing of elections influences the timing of wage contracts: namely, the stipulation of a fraction of wage contracts is moved after the November election in presidential election years, but the timing of contracts is unaffected in nonelection years.[22] This result shows two things. First, wage setters see the presidential elections as an important moment in resolving uncertainty concerning future inflation. Second, not all contracts adjust, so that real effects of electoral results can remain significant. Both implications are strikingly consistent with the spirit of the rational partisan theory.[23]

iii. The third criticism is that the correlation between electoral surprise and size of real economic fluctuations, critical for the model, would not survive close empirical scrutiny.

We tackle this point, at least for the United States, in chapter 5, and, contrary to Hibbs' suggestion, we find evidence broadly supportive of the model on this point.

The second general issue concerns the possibility of joining partisan and opportunistic models. Section 3.5 and Alesina and Rosenthal 1995 make some progress in this direction by merging the competence model and the partisan model. Building upon this foundation, one can consider the opportunistic incentives à la Rogoff and Sibert and Persson and Tabellini reviewed in chapter 2 and the partisan incentives emphasized in this chapter. Frey and Schneider (1978) follow a different approach. They suggest that partisan politicians, when in office, become opportunistic when elections approach if they are relatively unpopular. Although this insight is quite intriguing, it still awaits a formalization in a fully rational model.

Finally, it is worth noting that partisan politicians' opportunistic behavior may imply a run toward the middle with implications considerably different from the standard opportunistic models reviewed in chapter 2. For example, consider a left-wing government approaching an election with high inflation and, in the course of its tenure in office, a relatively low level of unemployment. It would be fruitless and electorally counterproductive for this government to follow even more expansionary policies in the election year. On the contrary, a show of anti-inflation concerns might be the most efficient way of attracting more electoral support. A Nordhaus-type preelectoral expansion may therefore actually be the wrong opportunistic policy for a left-wing government. Thus, the opportunistic policies of left- and right-wing parties may have opposite characteristics.

Appendix

In this appendix, we review the basic time inconsistency problem in monetary policy. Kydland and Presott (1977) produced the path-breaking work on the general point of time inconsistency, including an example on monetary policy. Barro and Gordon (1983a) developed this model in a "repeated game" framework and introduced the concept of credibility. For a more extensive review of the related theoretical literature, see Persson and Tabellini 1990.

Consider a supply function as in the text:

$$y_t = \bar{y} + \pi_t - \pi_t^e \tag{A.3.1}$$

Suppose that the social planner has the following objective function, which is the analog of (3.4) and (3.5) in the text:

$$U = \sum_{t=0}^{\infty} \beta^t [-(\pi_t - \bar{\pi})^2 + by_t] \qquad (A.3.2)$$

In (A.3.2), $\bar{\pi}$ is the optimal inflation rate for the social planner, and b is the relative benefit of higher output growth relative to inflation. Substituting (A.3.1) into (A.3.2), one obtains

$$U = \sum_{t=0}^{\infty} \beta^t [-(\pi_t - \bar{\pi})^2 + b(\bar{y} + \pi_t - \pi_t^e)] \qquad (A3.3)$$

The social planner maximizes his objective function, taking expectations as given, because they are not under his direct control. The solution is

$$\pi_t = \bar{\pi} + \frac{b}{2} \quad \text{for} \quad t = 0, 1 \ldots \infty \qquad (A.3.4)$$

The public knows the objective function of the social planner, thus it can compute the solution in (A.3.4). Therefore

$$\pi_t^e = \pi_t = \bar{\pi} + \frac{b}{2} \quad \text{for} \quad t = 0, 1 \ldots \infty \qquad (A.3.5)$$

and

$$y_t = \bar{y} \quad \text{for} \quad t = 0, 1 \ldots \infty \qquad (A.3.6)$$

This is often referred to as the "discretionary solution." The critical point is that inflation is above the optimal level ($\bar{\pi}$) without any benefit in terms of more output growth. The term $b/2$ in (A.3.5) represents the "inflation bias," namely, the part of the realized inflation rate that is above the optimal target and does not generate any real benefits.

The social planner (and therefore society as a whole) would be better off if he could commit ex ante to the following policy rule:

$$\hat{\pi}_t = \bar{\pi} \quad \text{for} \quad t = 0, 1 \ldots \infty \qquad (A.3.7)$$

With this policy, inflation is at its optimal level, and output growth is still at its natural rate, $\bar{y}$. In fact, the utility level with this rule is equal, using (A.3.3), to $b\bar{y}$ in every period. Instead, with the discretionary outcome, utility is equal to $(b\bar{y} - (b^2/4))$ in every period.

The time inconsistency problem arises because if the public expects the rule given in (A.3.7) then, ex post, the social planner would prefer to deviate from the rule itself. In fact, if $\pi^e = \bar{\pi}$, then from (A.3.3) it follows that the social planner would be better off by cheating, that is, by creating an inflation rate equal to the discretionary outcome given in (A.3.5). In the cheating solution, $\pi_t^e = \bar{\pi}$; $\pi_t = \bar{\pi} + b/2$; and $y_t = \bar{y} + b/2$. Again, using (A.3.3) one can easily verify that this cheating solution delivers a utility level of $b\bar{y} + b^2/4$ in every period.

Clearly, the cheating solution is not an equilibrium, otherwise expectation would not be rational: The public would be systematically incorrect in its forecast. Also, the possibility of reverting to the cheating solution renders the rule (A.3.7) not credible without some form of commitment that cannot be broken.

One can think of different ways to make the rule in (A.3.7) credible. One is to consider the role the incentives to cheat and the loss of reputation for truthfulness play in a repeated version of this game. A second way is to appoint independent central bankers who dislike inflation more than the social planner, so that they have a smaller incentive to create unexpected inflation and the credibility problem is reduced. Third, one can write a law (perhaps a constitutional law) that prescribes a monetary rule such as (A.3.7). We refer the reader to Barro and Gordon 1983a and Persson and Tabellini 1990 for a discussion of the credibility mechanism. In chapter 8, we discuss the other two solutions on models that take political incentives explicitly into account.

4   Political Cycles in the United States

4.1   Introduction

Do American politicians manipulate the economy before elections to maximize their re-election chances? Is this manipulation successful in stimulating growth and reducing unemployment before elections? Are there systematic differences in the macroeconomic performance of Democratic and Republican administrations? Are these differences transitory or permanent? In this chapter, we answer these questions.

Politicians' incentive to manipulate monetary and fiscal policy to stimulate the economy arises because the economic performance in the election year significantly affects the outcome of presidential elections: Clear evidence suggests that the American voter punishes the party of the incumbent President when the economy is in a recession and rewards the incumbent and his party if the economy is growing at a healthy rate.[1] Richard Nixon's comments about how he lost the 1960 presidential election are emblematic: "The bottom of the 1960 dip did come in October and the economy started to move in November—after it was too late to affect the election results. In October, usually a month of rising employment, the jobless rolls increased by 452,000. All the speeches, television broadcasts, and precinct work in the world could not counteract that one hard fact."[2]

A different view of political cycles in the American economy suggests that American politicians are partisan. Hibbs (1987a) provides convincing evidence that the Democratic and Republican parties in the United States represent distinct economic constituencies that care to a different extent about inflation and unemployment. This discrepancy in economic interests suggests that Democratic and Republican administrations might follow different macroeconomic policies leading to differences in the economy's performance as measured by growth, unemployment and inflation.

In this chapter and the next, we consider the empirical evidence on opportunistic and partisan cycles in the United States for 1947–94. In particular, we present evidence on partisan and opportunistic models, both in their traditional and rational versions. We will interchangeably refer to the opportunistic models as political business cycle models, as they are also known in the literature.

This chapter's main results are as follows. First, we find systematic differences in the rates of growth of output and the unemployment rate between Democratic and Republican administrations, but these partisan effects are concentrated in the first half of each administration; this evidence is consistent with the rational partisan theory.

Second, as the partisan theory predicts, we find small but systematic differences in the average inflation rate between Democratic and Republican administrations.

Third, our analysis of macroeconomic policy instruments also supports the evidence in favor of the partisan model. Monetary growth rates show systematic partisan differences, at least until the middle of the 1980s. Afterward these differences tend to vanish, probably because of the instability of money demand in the United States following the financial innovations of the 1980s. The evidence from short- and long-term interest rates confirms the hypothesis that the more inflation-prone Democratic administrations experience systematically higher nominal interest rates.

Fourth, we find no evidence of partisan differences in government spending or fiscal deficits. In particular, there is no evidence of a systematic bias toward fiscal deficits during Democratic administrations:

Although Democrats may be more likely to increase government spending, they are also more likely to raise revenues so that they do not appear to experience a greater propensity toward fiscal deficits than Republican administrations. The large fiscal deficits during the Republican administrations in 1981–92 explain the absence of significant partisan differences in fiscal deficits.

Fifth, in spite of the macroeconomy's importance for presidential electoral outcomes, we find little evidence of a pre-electoral cycle in macroeconomic variables in the United States' postwar experience. There is no evidence that the economy grows faster than average and that the unemployment rate is lower than average in election years; consistently with these observations, there is no postelectoral increase in the inflation rate. Similarly, we find no evidence that monetary policy is more expansionary before elections: Neither monetary aggregates nor interest rate data show any evidence of pre-electoral expansionary monetary policies.

Sixth, there is no evidence of a preelectoral opportunistic manipulation of fiscal policy, as fiscal deficits are not significantly higher during election years. Also, we find no systematic evidence that government spending in the form of transfers to individuals is greater in the quarters close to U.S. presidential elections. The lack of opportunistic cycles in macroeconomic variables, coupled with the evidence of a strong effect of election year economic conditions on electoral results, is consistent with the models of (rational) retrospective voting discussed in sections 2.4 and 3.5.

The chapter is organized as follows. Section 4.2 surveys the previous empirical literature on macroeconomic political cycles in the United States. In section 4.3, we describe the data and present some stylized summary statistics on partisan and electoral cycles. In section 4.4, we describe the empirical methodology used in our econometric analysis. Sections 4.5 and 4.6 present the results on economic outcomes for, respectively, the partisan models and the political business cycle models; section 4.7 presents the results on monetary policy for those same models; and section 4.8 tests the implications of those models on fiscal policy instruments, transfers and budget deficits. Section 4.9 discusses the results on the rational partisan model. The last section concludes.

4.2   Previous Empirical Results

Most of the empirical studies on political cycles in the United States use postwar U.S. data.[3] Generally, the evidence in favor of the rational partisan theory is relatively strong, but evidence of opportunistic political business cycles is found only for certain policy instruments (particularly government transfers) and for limited subsamples. We distinguish empirical results on economic outcomes (growth, unemployment and inflation) and results on monetary and fiscal policy instruments, and between partisan and opportunistic outcomes.

The original work on partisan effects in economic performance is by Hibbs (1977, 1987a), who showed strong partisan differences in growth rates and unemployment rates in the United States between Democratic and Republican administrations. The implications of the rational partisan theory were tested for the United States by Alesina (1988b), Alesina and Sachs (1988) for the postwar period, and Alesina and Rosenthal (1995) on a 1914–88 sample: they find evidence of transitory partisan effects in GNP growth and unemployment. Klein (1996), who considers more than a century of U.S. data, also provides favorable evidence

More limited attempts have been made at testing explicitly how temporary output effects relate to the degree of electoral surprise, as the rational partisan theory implies. Chappell and Keech (1988) show that deviations of the unemployment rate from its trend are related to errors in forecasting money growth; money growth forecasts are based upon a measure of electoral probabilities. Cohen (1993) implements a model of partisan differences that depends on an explicit measure of electoral surprise; he finds evidence that U.S. growth is related to the degree of partisan electoral surprise. The analysis in chapter 5 builds upon Cohen's work and tests formally for electoral surprise's effects on partisan growth effects.

Recently, Hibbs (1994) has suggested an alternative explanation to the rational partisan theory for the observed temporariness of the partisan growth effects in the United States. He argues that time-varying weights that Democratic and Republican administrations attach to growth and inflation targets and a time-varying Phillips curve trade-off between growth and inflation may explain why partisan effects are temporary even in a model where expected (as well as unexpected) aggregate demand policies affect economic activity.

The empirical literature generated by the Nordhaus political business cycle model yielded, at best, mixed results on growth, unemployment, and inflation. McCallum (1978), Golden and Poterba (1980), Hibbs (1987a), Alesina (1988b), and Klein (1996), among others, reject the Nordhaus model's implications on economic outcomes (such as GNP growth and unemployment) for the United States.[4]

Parallel to the literature on political cycles in macroeconomic targets, several authors have considered political influences on policy instruments. A number of studies have shown that political and special interest groups play an important role in influencing U.S. monetary policy. In particular, Havrilesky (1993) and Froyen, Havrilesky, and Waud (1993) have shown that the executive branch strongly influences the conduct of U.S. monetary policy. The study of political influences in fiscal policy goes back to the public choice school of Buchanan, who suggested that fiscal policy in democratic regimes is subject to systematic political biases (see Buchanan, Rowley, and Tollison 1986).[5]

Does this political influence on macro–policy making take a partisan or opportunistic form? The evidence on preelectoral manipulation of policy instruments is somewhat more favorable to the political business cycle models than the evidence on economic outcomes. Tufte (1978) shows examples of manipulation of the timing of fiscal instruments, in particular transfers, and evidence of monetary electoral cycles. His evidence is, however, confined to a few American elections. Alesina (1988b) also shows results on fiscal transfers in line with Tufte's for a sample that excludes the 1950s. Bizer and Durlauf (1990) report results on the dynamics of taxes in the United States. The authors claim that this evidence supports a political budget cycle, even though several caveats apply to this interpretation. Both Tufte (1978) and Hibbs (1987a) find evidence of political business cycles on disposable income. This observation, coupled with the lack of similar evidence on GNP, suggests the presence of fiscal cycles. McDonald (1991) finds evidence of public expenditure cycles by examining state level data in the United States. Grier (1987, 1989) reports results that identify an electoral monetary cycle in a sample from the early 1960s to the very early 1980s in the United States. When the sample is extended to include more of the 1980s, however, the results tend to vanish. Beck (1987) supports Grier's findings of a cycle in the money supply but shows that it disappears when one controls for fiscal policy. Thus, he suggests that the Fed may not be actively pursuing such policies but rather passively accommodating fiscal cycles. Allen (1986) finds no political business cycle in the growth of M1 or the monetary base; he argues, however, that the evidence suggests that the Fed "not only accommodates Treasury borrowing regardless of the electoral season, but also provides extra accommodation prior to presidential and congressional elections (90)." Finally, Frey and Schneider (1978) provide some evidence that preelectoral manipulation of fiscal instruments in the United States is more likely to occur when the incumbent administration is unpopular and concerned about its reelection chances.

For partisan models, Alesina (1988b) and Alesina and Sachs (1988) show partisan differences in U.S. monetary growth rates, whereas Lockwood, Philippopolous and Snell (1994) find some evidence of partisan differences in government spending levels for the United States. Because the partisan theory implies that inflation will be higher under Democratic administrations, Cohen (1993) tests whether changing probabilities of electing a Democrat, as derived by polling data before U.S. elections, affect short- and long-term interest rates.

Chapter 5 extends Cohen's work and tests formally for the effects of electoral probabilities on interest rates.

4.3 Data and Basic Statistics

4.3.1 Data

We consider U.S. data for 1947–1994. The economic data are quarterly observations on inflation rates, output growth, and unemployment rates as well as various measures of monetary and fiscal policy. Inflation is defined as the yearly rate change of CPI; output growth is the rate of change of seasonally adjusted real GNP; unemployment is also seasonally adjusted. Monetary policy data include money supply growth rates defined as the yearly rate change of M0 and M1, as well as short- and long-term interest rates. All data are from the Federal Reserve Board database; table 4.A.1 in the appendix to this chapter provides more details on the data.

The political data are election dates, dates of changes of administration, and the administrations' political orientation. We define an administration as Democratic or Republican according to which party controls the presidency. We therefore do not consider the party in control of Congress and midterm congressional elections. Table 4.A.2 in the appendix summarizes these data. Our definition of administration is precise when the same party controls both houses of Congress and the White House; in the presence of divided government, that is, when a party controls at least one house of Congress and the other the presidency, the definition of an administration is more complex.[6] This book does not, however, deal with issues of divided government and midterm elections.[7]

4.3.2 Stylized Facts on Political Cycles

According to the partisan hypothesis, economic growth should be higher (and the unemployment rate lower) during a Democratic administration than during a Republican one. According to the rational partisan theory, the growth effects will be transitory and concentrated in the first half of an administration. Hibbs's traditional partisan model says that these effects will last throughout an administration. The opportunistic political business cycle hypothesis predicts that growth will instead accelerate (and the unemployment rate will fall) around the end of every administration. As for the inflation rate, the partisan model suggests that the average inflation rate will be higher during a Democratic administration than under a Republican one, especially when exchange rates are flexible and the monetary authority has a larger degree of monetary autonomy. In the political business cycle model, the inflation rate tends to accelerate after an election as the lagged effects of the pre-electoral expansion are transmitted to the price level.

Table 4.1 shows the rate of GDP growth. The sample period runs from the beginning of the second Truman administration (1949:1) through the first half of the Clinton administration (1994:4). The average yearly growth rate of GDP for Democratic administrations was 4.2 percent and only 2.4 percent for Republican administrations. This difference is due mostly to the level of growth in the first half of Democratic and Republican administrations: The average growth is 4.5 percent in the first half of a Democratic administration and 1.5 percent in the first half of a Republican administration. The comparison of the second year's growth rates shows striking differences. On average, growth in the second year of a Democratic administration is close to 6 percent, whereas there is no growth on average in second years of Republican administrations; in fact, in a majority of cases, growth in second years of Republican administrations is negative. With reasonable lags between the changes of policies and their real effects, the second year more than the first should reflect partisan influences. In the second half of their terms, Democratic and Republican administration growth rates are relatively similar (4.1 percent versus 3.3 percent). This pattern is consistent with the implications of the rational partisan hypothesis and less consistent with Hibbs's traditional partisan model.

Table 4.1
Real GDP growth, 1949–1994

				Challenging		Incumbent	
	All	Republican	Democrat	Republican	Democrat	Republican	Democrat
Average	3.17%	2.41%	4.24%	2.59%	3.61%	2.27%	5.19%
Years 1 & 2	2.76	1.52	4.49	0.90	4.06	1.98	5.13
Years 3 & 4	3.59	3.30	4.09	4.28	2.94	2.56	5.25
Year 1	3.11	3.01	3.25	2.75	3.43	3.21	2.98
Year 2	2.40	0.03	5.73	−0.93	4.68	0.75	7.29
Year 3	3.52	2.79	4.80	4.13	3.32	1.78	6.27
Year 4	3.66	3.81	3.39	4.44	2.55	3.34	4.22

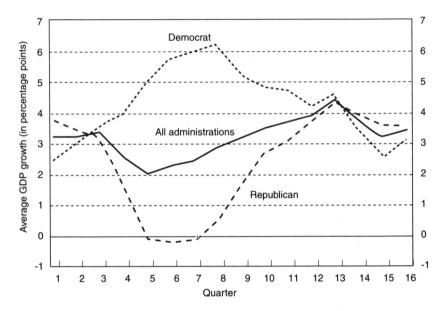

Figure 4.1
Real GDP growth

Figure 4.1 presents similar results by showing the average yearly
GDP growth rate in Democratic and Republican administrations over
their sixteen quarters. Growth rates start at very similar levels in
Democratic and Republican administrations; from the third quarter
through the eighth, the growth rate accelerates during Democratic
administrations and falls during Republican ones. After the midterm,
growth decelerates under Democratic administrations and accelerates
under Republican ones. The growth rates of Democratic and Republican administrations converge to about the same level by the administration's final six quarters.

Table 4.1 provides other indirect evidence in favor of transitory
effects when one compares administrations when the incumbent party
was reelected to those when the challenger won. According to the
rational partisan theory, the growth effects in the first half of the term
are stronger when the electoral surprise is greater. It is reasonable to
assume that a change in the party in power is generally more unex-

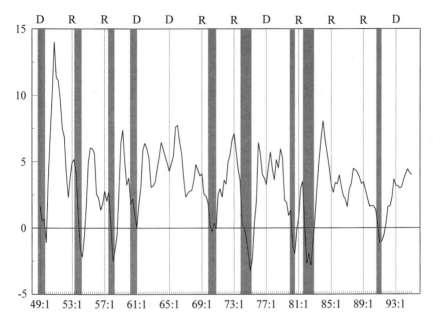

Figure 4.2
Real GDP growth

pected than the reelection of an incumbent administration. Table 4.1 shows that for both Republican and Democratic incumbent administrations, there is a relatively small difference in growth rates between the first half and the second half of their administrations. Conversely, in the case of administrations when a new party is in power, we observe the temporary partisan pattern: New Republican administrations experience a recession in their first half (0.9 percent growth) and a significant recovery in the second (4.3 percent growth). The reverse occurs for Democratic administrations, which experience a 4.0 percent growth in the first half and a 2.9 percent growth in the second. Chapter 5 tests more formally whether the partisan effects are related to the electoral surprise.

Figure 4.2, which plots the growth rate from 1949 until the end of 1994, provides further evidence. Shaded areas identify recessions, namely the period from the peak to the trough of each business cycle, and the administration in power is indicated by a vertical bar with an R (D) on top of it representing the beginning of a Republican (Democratic) administration. Of the nine postwar U.S. recessions, only two occurred during a Democratic administration (the 1949 brief recession at the beginning of the second Truman administration and that of 1980). The other seven occurred during Republican administrations: Of these, five occurred in the first half of a Republican administration (Eisenhower I, Eisenhower II, Nixon I, Nixon II, Reagan I), one in the second half (Eisenhower II), and one in the middle of the term (Bush).

Table 4.2 reports the unemployment rates for Democratic and Republican administrations. In evaluating this evidence, one must keep in mind the high level of persistence of this variable.[8] During Republican administrations, the unemployment rate reaches a peak in the second or third year and declines in the fourth. During Democratic administrations the trough is reached in the third year.

The inflation rate data reported in table 4.3 and figure 4.3 show a less clear pattern. Table 4.3 suggests that there is no significant difference in the average inflation rate of Democratic and Republican administrations—3.83 percent versus 4.16 percent—but these figures hide some substantial differences. As figure 4.3 shows, Democratic administrations start with inflation rates lower than those of Republican administrations, probably because new Democratic administrations inherit lower inflation rates from preceding Republican administrations that are less inflation-prone and new Republican administrations face the exact opposite scenario.[9] Starting from these initial conditions, however, the inflation rate significantly accelerates during a Democratic administration, reaching a peak at the end of the third year. In the election year of a Democratic administration, the inflation rate falls marginally, possibly because of increased concern about the electoral effects of high inflation. Republican administrations start instead with a higher level but experience a persistent fall in the inflation rate until their end. These observations do not take into account other impor-

Table 4.2
Unemployment rate, 1949–1994

	All	Republican	Democrat	Challenging Republican	Challenging Democrat	Incumbent Republican	Incumbent Democrat
Average	5.81%	6.10%	5.41%	5.95%	6.24%	6.22%	4.15%
Years 1 & 2	5.78	5.78	5.78	5.71	6.37	5.82	4.89
Years 3 & 4	5.80	6.43	4.69	6.19	5.95	6.62	3.42
Year 1	5.56	5.09	6.22	4.67	6.84	5.40	5.28
Year 2	6.00	6.47	5.34	6.76	5.90	6.25	4.50
Year 3	5.94	6.67	4.65	6.63	5.74	6.71	3.58
Year 4	5.66	6.19	4.73	5.74	6.16	6.53	3.29

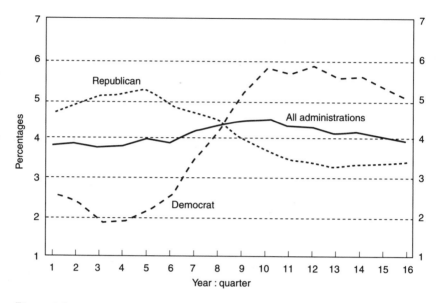

Figure 4.3
CPI growth

tant factors, however, such as the oil shocks of 1973 and 1979 or the
role of the exchange rate regime, that certainly contribute to inflation.

For the political business cycle hypothesis, the evidence is very
weak. First, table 4.1 shows that the average growth in the election
year (the fourth) is only slightly higher than the sample average (3.66
percent against 3.17 percent). This simple observation already excludes
large systematic opportunistic manipulations of the economy. Furthermore, figure 4.1 shows that the economy's growth rate tends to
accelerate beginning in the middle of the second year of an average
administration but decelerates during the election year. Although the
growth rate decelerates in the election year for both Democratic and
Republican administrations, there are some differences between the
two. Growth accelerates from the beginning of Democratic administrations (see table 4.1 and figure 4.1), until midterm and then decelerates
until election time. The reverse occurs for Republican administrations,
in which growth tends to fall until midterm, accelerate until the begin-

Table 4.3
Inflation rate, 1949–1994

	All	Republican	Democrat	Challenging		Incumbent	
				Republican	Democrat	Republican	Democrat
Average	4.03%	4.16%	3.83%	3.76%	4.56%	4.46%	2.75%
Years 1 & 2	3.94	4.85	2.66	4.83	3.64	4.87	1.20
Years 3 & 4	4.23	3.47	5.56	2.70	6.82	4.05	4.30
Year 1	3.80	4.94	2.21	5.52	3.46	4.50	0.32
Year 2	4.08	4.77	3.12	4.14	3.81	5.25	2.08
Year 3	4.40	3.60	5.78	2.39	6.24	4.51	6.32
Year 4	4.07	3.34	5.34	3.01	3.91	3.60	3.27

ning of the election year, and then decelerate again in the election year. Similarly, the unemployment rate appears to be on average lower in election years; this entire effect, however, is due to the falling unemployment rate in the last year of Republican administrations, which is likely to be the result of some mean reversion of unemployment rate after the partisan increases of the first half of Republican administrations; in Democratic ones, the unemployment rate tends to increase slightly between the third and the fourth year.

The evidence of political business cycle effects on inflation rates is also weak. There is no evidence that the inflation rate accelerates after elections (at least for six quarters after an election): The slight rise of inflation in the first year of Republican administrations is compensated by its fall during the first year of Democratic ones. The inflation rate falls very marginally on average in the last year of an administration, but the effect is likely to be driven entirely by the policy tightening and subsequent growth reduction during previously inflation-biased Democratic administrations.

These basic data suggest that, if there is any evidence of political business cycle effects, it is of a very different nature than previously thought: Democratic administrations, which are expansionary in the first half, observe by midterm a significant increase in the inflation rate. Because a high inflation rate may become a significant electoral liability, Democratic administrations contract the economy so that by the election year one observes a growth slowdown and a reduction in the inflation rate.[10] Conversely, Republican administrations that had anti-inflationary recessions in their first half pursue low inflation and accelerating growth in the second half, a combination that may give them an electoral benefit.[11]

4.4 Specification of the Empirical Tests

A natural and direct way of testing the various theories is to run a regression including a political variable among the regressors. For instance, for output growth, we run:

$$y_t = \alpha_0 + \alpha_1 y_{t-1} + \alpha_2 y_{t-2} \ldots + \alpha_n y_{t-n} + \alpha_{n+1}\mathrm{PDUM}_t + \varepsilon_t \qquad (4.1)$$

where y_t is GDP growth, defined as $y = ((x_t - x_{t-4})/x_{t-4})100$, where x_t = level of real GDP in quarter t, and PDUM is a political dummy variable that captures the implications of different theories. The auto-regressive specification for the dependent variable is chosen as the best using standard techniques.[12] We therefore do not take a structural stance on the determinants of the variables under consideration; we want to test whether, after having controlled for the (auto-regressive) history of these variables, we find a significant effect of the political dummies.[13] As shown by Alesina (1988b), at least for the case of the rational partisan theory, this specification can also be seen as the reduced form of a structural model. Table 4.4 reports and defines all the political dummy variables used in the empirical sections of the book.

4.5   Evidence on the Partisan Theories

4.5.1   The Rational Partisan Theory

We construct the following political dummy variable:

$$\mathrm{DRPTXN} = \begin{cases} +1 \text{ in the } N \text{ quarters starting with a Republican administration} \\ -1 \text{ in the } N \text{ quarters starting with a Democratic administration} \\ 0 \text{ otherwise} \end{cases}$$

We chose $N = 4, 6, 8$, because it is not certain a priori how long these temporary effects are likely to last; using the contract model interpretation, the persistence of the output effects will depend on the average length of wage contracts. The choice of number of quarters is

Table 4.4
Political dummy variables used in the text

DRPTXN =	+1	in the N quarters starting with a Republican (right-wing) administration
	−1	in the N quarters starting with a Democratic (left-wing) administration
	0	otherwise
DRPTN =	+1	in the N quarters starting with that of a change to a Republican (right-wing) administration
	−1	in the N quarters starting with that of a change to a Democratic (left-wing) administration
	0	otherwise
RADM =	1	if a Republican (right-wing) administration is in office, including the quarter of the change in administration
	−1	if a Democratic (left-wing) administration is in office, including the quarter of the change in administration
NRDN =	1	in the (N−1) quarters preceding an election and in the election quarter
	0	otherwise
NPOSTN =	1	in the N−1 quarters following an election and in the election quarter
	0	otherwise
ADM =	1	if a right-wing government is in office, including the quarter of the change in government
	1/2	if a center-right government is in office, including the quarter of the change in government
	1/2	if a center-left government is in office, including the quarter of the change in government
	−1	if a left-wing government is in office, including the quarter of the change in government

consistent with a wage contract model in which contracts have an average length of one or two years.[14]

Equation (4.2) reports the result using DRPTX6 (*t*-statistics in parentheses). The sample is 1947:1 to 1993:4.

$$y_t = 0.91 \quad +1.10\, y_{t-1} \quad -0.21\, y_{t-2} \quad -0.16\, y_{t-3} \quad -0.64\, \text{DRPTX6}_{t-1}$$
$$\quad (6.1) \quad (15.4) \qquad (2.02) \qquad (2.36) \qquad (4.27)$$

$$R^2 = 0.81 \tag{4.2}$$

The political dummy DRPTX6 has the correct sign and is statistically significant at the 1 percent confidence level: A change in government to a Republican (Democratic) administration leads to a transitory fall (increase) in output growth. The lag of one quarter in the political dummy is consistent with a reasonable interval between a change in regime (in quarter t) and change in policy (in period $t + 1$). The regressions with DRPTX4 and DRPTX8 (available upon request) yield analogous results: The pattern of the coefficient suggests that partisan effects are observable from about the second to the eighth or ninth quarters after a change in government.[15] The values of the coefficients in (4.2) imply that about eighteen months after a change of regime to a Republican (Democratic) administration, the rate of growth of GDP is about 1.2 percent below (above) its steady-state value.[16] Thus the difference in the rate of growth between the beginning of a left-wing government and that of a right-wing government reaches a peak of about 2.4 percent. This estimate is consistent with the results in chapter 7 of Alesina and Rosenthal 1995.[17]

In testing the rational partisan theory on unemployment, one has to be cautious because of the unemployment rate's high empirical persistence.[18] After experimentation, three lags of the dependent variable appeared to be sufficient to capture the auto-regressive components of the U.S. unemployment rate. Equation (4.3) shows results for the unemployment rate that are very consistent with those for GDP growth.

$$U_t = 0.25 \quad +1.66\,U_{t-1} \quad -0.89\,U_{t-2} \quad +0.19\,U_{t-3} \quad -0.13\,\text{DRPTX6}_{t-2}$$
$$\quad (2.9) \quad (22.7) \qquad (7.08) \qquad (2.68) \qquad (3.39)$$

$$R^2 = 0.96 \tag{4.3}$$

The political dummy DRPTX6 is significant at the 1 percent level. This variable is lagged two quarters to capture the slower response of unemployment to policy changes relative to output.[19] Similar results are obtained using DRPTX4 and DRPTX8. The values of the coefficients in (4.3) imply that about six quarters after the election of a Republican (Democratic) administration, the unemployment rate is about 1.6 percentage points above (below) normal.[20]

4.5.2   Robustness and Sensitivity Analysis

First, as discussed above, the degree of electoral surprise may be greater when the administration actually changes. We redefine the DRPTX variable to include only actual changes of U.S. administrations. The idea is that the reelection of an incumbent may be less surprising than a change of party control. Thus we define a new dummy variable DRPT as follows:

$$\text{DRPT}N = \begin{cases} +1 \text{ in the } N \text{ quarters starting with that of a change to} \\ \quad \text{a Republican administration} \\ -1 \text{ in the } N \text{ quarters starting with that of a change to} \\ \quad \text{a Democratic administration} \\ 0 \text{ otherwise} \end{cases}$$

The political dummy DRPT has the correct sign and is statistically significant at the 1 percent confidence level with $N = 4, 6, 8$: An actual change in government to a Republican (Democratic) administration leads to a transitory fall (increase) in output growth.[21] The t-statistics on the DRPT variable are uniformly lower than those obtained using DRPTX, but they are still statistically highly significant. Similar results are obtained when we use DRPT instead of DRPTX in the unemployment regression and all the other regressions in this chapter. In the following, we therefore continue showing only the results for DRPTX, and we postpone to chapter 5 a more detailed analysis of the exact degree of electoral uncertainty and its effects on the size of partisan growth cycles.

A second robustness issue is the stability of the above results over time. Political cycles may be stronger under flexible exchange regimes (*i.e.*, after the move to float in 1973) than under fixed exchange rates. In a fixed exchange rate regime with perfect capital mobility, the monetary authority loses all monetary authority, and manipulation of monetary policy for macro-stabilization purposes becomes impossible. The Bretton Woods system that ended in 1973 represents a period of fixed rates, although with a far from perfect degree of capital mobility. Equations (4.4) and (4.5) test for a structural change in 1973.

1947–72 sample:

$$y_t = 1.19 \quad +1.07\,y_{t-1} \quad -0.19\,y_{t-2} \quad -0.20\,y_{t-3} \quad -0.81\,\text{DRPTX6}_{t-1}$$
$$(5.1) \quad (10.8) \qquad (1.29) \qquad (2.12) \qquad (3.59)$$

$$R^2 = 0.81 \tag{4.4}$$

1973–93 sample:

$$y_t = 0.68 \quad +1.11\,y_{t-1} \quad -0.22\,y_{t-2} \quad -0.14\,y_{t-3} \quad -0.44\,\text{DRPTX6}_{t-1}$$
$$(3.6) \quad (10.4) \qquad (1.41) \qquad (1.33) \qquad (2.24)$$

$$R^2 = 0.79 \tag{4.5}$$

These regressions show that partisan cycles are not only a post-1973 phenomenon; the coefficient value on DRPTX and its statistical significance is actually higher in the 1947–1972 period. Similar tests on unemployment suggest similar conclusions. To interpret these results, one should observe three factors. First, capital controls in the United States were widespread in the Bretton Woods period, so that the Fed maintained a certain degree of monetary autonomy despite the fixed exchange rates. Second, the United States was a large and not very open economy, so that it could affect world interest rates despite fixed parities. Third, the United States was the leader of the Bretton Woods system and was therefore able to influence the monetary policy of the entire system heavily. All three factors imply that the United States could set its monetary policy almost independently and had much more monetary autonomy than the rest of the industrialized countries.

A third issue of robustness concerns the effects of economic shocks from the rest of the world to the U.S. economy. One major source of external shock is the fluctuation of oil prices, which jumped upward in 1973–74 and 1979–80. A second source of external influence is trade, affected by the world business cycle. Note that although this second issue is critical for small open economies (see chapter 6), it is much less so for the U.S. economy, where the size of the import-export sector is smaller relative to GNP. In equation (4.6), we add to our basic regression (with DRPTX6) a variable OIL representing the yearly percentage change in the international price of oil.

$$y_t = 0.96 \quad +1.10\,y_{t-1} - 0.21\,y_{t-2} \quad -0.16\,y_{t-3} \quad -0.61\,DRPTX6_{t-1}$$
$$ (6.4) \quad (15.4) \qquad (2.01) \qquad (2.33) \qquad (4.10)$$

$$-0.009\,OIL_t$$
$$(1.89) \tag{4.6}$$

$$R^2 = 0.81$$

The OIL variable is significant at the 10 percent confidence level with the expected sign: Increases in the rate of oil inflation are associated with a slowdown in economic growth. In any case, the results on the partisan dummy are unchanged after controlling for oil price inflation. Similar results on DRPTX are obtained when we also control for the world business cycle by adding proxies of world growth (with and without the oil price variable).[22]

Controlling for the world business cycle in the unemployment equation gives similar results. The oil variable is significant and controlling for this variable tends to improve the significance of the partisan dummies: The t-statistics on the DRPT dummies uniformly improve when we control for oil shocks.[23]

4.5.3   Partisan Tests on the Inflation Rate

Next, we consider the evidence on the inflation rate. The partisan theory implies that one should observe permanent differences across administrations in the inflation rate. Thus, we define a political dummy RADM that classifies administrations as Democratic or Republican:

$$\text{RADM} = \begin{cases} 1 \text{ if a Republican administration is in office, including} \\ \text{the quarter of the change in administration} \\ -1 \text{ if a Democratic administration is in office, including} \\ \text{the quarter of the change in administration} \end{cases}$$

As discussed in section 4.3, in studying the determinants of inflation rate we must control for two important factors: First, global inflationary shocks such as the 1973 and 1979 oil shocks have affected U.S. inflation rates; second, inflation rates were lower in the Bretton Woods period of fixed exchange rates when monetary policy autonomy was more limited. To control for these factors, we run the following regression for the inflation rate:

$$\pi_t = \alpha_0 + \alpha_1 \pi_{t-1} + \alpha_2 \pi_{t-2} \ldots + \alpha_3 \text{POIL}_t + \alpha_4 \text{D73} + \alpha_5 \text{RADM}_t$$

$$+ \alpha_6 \text{INTADM}_t + \varepsilon_t \tag{4.7}$$

The dependent variable is domestic inflation (π), defined as the yearly rate of change of the consumer price index (CPI), that is, $\pi = ((\text{CPI}_t - \text{CPI}_{t-4})/\text{CPI}_{t-4})100$. To control for world inflation shocks, we add to the regression the rate of change of the dollar price of oil (POIL). To control for flexible exchange rate regimes, we add a time dummy variable D73 for the post–1972 period; RADM is the partisan

Table 4.5
Partisan theory
Dependent variable: inflation rate (π)

Independent variables	(1) Coefficient (t-statistics)	(2) Coefficient (t-statistics)	(3) Coefficient (t-statistics)
Constant	0.46	0.46	0.62
	(4.87)	(4.89)	(6.51)
$\pi(-1)$	1.13	1.13	1.14
	(14.8)	(14.8)	(14.7)
$\pi(-2)$	−0.21	−0.21	−0.21
	(1.89)	(1.91)	(1.88)
$\pi(-3)$	−0.13	−0.13	−0.13
	(1.93)	(1.93)	(1.89)
POIL	0.02	0.02	0.02
	(5.16)	(5.17)	(5.32)
D73	0.75	0.75	0.62
	(5.03)	(5.05)	(4.38)
INTADM(-3)	−0.29	−0.31	—
	(2.67)	(3.18)	
RADM(-3)	−0.01	—	−0.11
	(0.19)		(1.97)
R^2	0.95	0.95	0.95

dummy and INTADM is an interaction term between RADM and D73, which tests for a structural change in the influence of political factors on inflation in the U.S. economy after the move to flexible exchange rates.

Columns (1) through (3) of table 4.5 present the results of these regressions: Column (1) presents all the variables in regression (4.7), whereas column (2) drops the insignificant RADM and tests for partisan effects only through the interaction term INTADM; column (3) presents the results when we include RADM but not the interaction dummy. We take three lags of the political dummies to capture the delay between administration change, change in policy, and effect of policy on the inflation rate. The three lags of inflation, the oil dummy, and the flexible exchange rate dummy are statistically significant in all regressions. In column (1), the RADM partisan dummy, is not statistically significant, but the post–1972 partisan interaction dummy has the right sign and is statistically significant at the 5 percent significance level: that is, after the move to flexible exchange rates in 1973, inflation rates are higher under Democratic administrations than under Republican ones. Because the RADM variable is not significant in column (1), we drop it in column (2): The partisan interaction dummy is again of the right sign and now statistically significant at the 1 percent confidence level. Column (3) shows that, in the absence of a post–1972 interaction dummy, the partisan dummy RADM is significant, that is, although inflation rates are overall higher after the collapse of the Bretton Woods system, partisan differences in inflation rates are evident both before and after the move to flexible exchange rates. The value of the coefficient on INTADM in the regression in column (2) implies that, after 1972, the difference in the steady state inflation rate between a Democratic and a Republican regime is about 1.8 percent per year.[24]

4.5.4 *The Traditional Partisan Theory*

We move now to tests of the traditional partisan theory, which implies permanent effects of partisan policies. One way of comparing Hibbs's traditional partisan theory with the rational partisan theory is to run the same regressions (4.2) and (4.3) using the permanent partisan dummy RADM rather than the transitory political dummy DRPTX. Table 4.6 shows the results. In both the growth and the unemployment regressions (columns (1) and (2)), the coefficient on the political dummy RADM has the right sign and is statistically significant at the 5 percent confidence level. Although these results would suggest permanent differences in economic activity, they are indeed spurious because of the strong evidence of a transitory rational partisan theory effect in the data. In fact, in columns (3) and (4), we define a new

Table 4.6
Traditional partisan theory
Dependent variable: rate of growth of output (y) (columns (1), (3)), unemployment rate (U) (columns (2), (4)).

Independent variables	(1) Coefficient (t-statistics)	(2) Coefficient (t-statistics)	(3) Coefficient (t-statistics)	(4) Coefficient (t-statistics)
Constant	1.03 (6.23)	0.32 (3.58)	0.97 (5.93)	0.27 (2.85)
$y(-1)$	1.13 (15.6)	—	1.10 (15.3)	—
$y(-2)$	−0.21 (1.94)	—	−0.21 (1.95)	—
$y(-3)$	−0.22 (3.03)	—	−0.18 (2.50)	—
$U(-1)$	—	1.68 (22.8)	—	1.66 (22.6)
$U(-2)$	—	−0.91 (7.06)	—	−0.89 (7.06)
$U(-3)$	—	0.16 (2.33)	—	0.19 (2.64)
RADM(−1)	−0.34 (3.33)	0.05 (2.20)	—	—
DRPTX6(−1)	—	—	−0.64 (4.30)	0.13 (3.37)
SEC6(−1)	—	—	−0.11 (0.86)	0.01 (0.36)
R^2	0.80	0.96	0.81	0.96

dummy variable SECN, which is the complement of the DRPTX variable: that is, it takes the value of 1 during Republican administrations after the first N quarters and −1 after the first N quarters of Democratic administrations. If Hibbs's traditional partisan theory view is correct, both DRPTX and SECN should be significant; if instead the rational partisan theory view is the right one, SECN should not be significant. The coefficients on all SECN dummies are statistically insignificant: There is no second-half partisan difference in growth or unemployment rates. On the contrary, the coefficients on the DRPTX dummies remain of the expected sign and are statistically highly significant. This test confirms that the effects of changes in governments on growth and unemployment are transitory rather than permanent.[25] It also suggests that previous results (as in Hibbs 1987a) presenting evidence consistent with the traditional partisan theory were biased by the fact that in the first part of an administration, the traditional partisan theory variable overlaps with the rational partisan theory variable.

4.6   Evidence on Political Business Cycles

Nordhaus's (1975) political business cycle model can be tested on growth and unemployment by constructing a political dummy of the following form:

$$
\text{NRD}N = \begin{cases} 1 \text{ in the } (N-1) \text{ quarters preceding an election and in} \\ \text{the election quarter} \\ 0 \text{ otherwise} \end{cases}
$$

We have chosen $N = 4$, 6, and 8. A relatively short preelectoral output expansion is consistent with this theory, which views the electorate as short-sighted (Nordhaus 1975, 1989). Table 4.7 reports the results on output and unemployment for $N = 4$. The coefficients of the NRD dummies are insignificant even if most of the coefficient signs are as expected.[26] Several alternative specifications, controlling for the world business cycle, oil shock effects and alternative lag structures, yield no support for the theory. We also tested whether the NRD dummy approaches statistical significance when partisan effects are held constant. Other regressions, including both the DRPTX and the NRD dummies were run, with no support for the political business cycle, although the DRPTX dummy remained statistically significant.

Our results were also confirmed when we ran a general nesting model. Specifically, we estimated regressions on growth and unemployment in which all three dummy variables—DPRTX, SECN, and

Table 4.7
Political business cycle theory
Dependent variable: rate of growth and output (y) (column (1)), unemployment rate (U)
(column (2))

Independent variables	(1) Coefficient (t-statistics)	(2) Coefficient (t-statistics)
Constant	0.81 (5.15)	0.30 (3.33)
$y(-1)$	1.17 (16.0)	—
$y(-2)$	−0.25 (2.25)	—
$y(-3)$	−0.17 (2.30)	—
$U(-1)$	—	1.71 (23.4)
$U(-2)$	—	−0.95 (7.32)
$U(-3)$	—	0.18 (2.53)
NRD4(−1)	−0.13 (0.58)	−0.06 (1.15)
R^2	0.79	0.96

NRD—were included. Only the DRPTX variable was found to be significant. We also calculated an F-test comparing the unrestricted model with all three political variables and the restricted model with only the DRPTX: We could not reject the restricted model, at very high levels of significance.[27]

The opportunistic political business cycle theory, not only in the traditional formulation by Nordhaus (1975) but also in the rational models by Rogoff and Sibert (1988) and Persson and Tabellini (1990), implies an increase in the inflation rate around elections. Specifically, if there is lag between the output and the price effects of the preelectoral expansion, inflation should tend to increase immediately after an election. Furthermore, governments may prefer to raise prices under their direct control after, rather than before, elections, thus directly contributing to a postelectoral upward jump in inflation. We have tested this implication in equation (4.8), where the dummy NPOST is defined as follows:

$$\text{NPOST}N = \begin{cases} 1 \text{ in the } N - 1 \text{ quarters following an election and in} \\ \quad \text{the election quarter} \\ 0 \text{ otherwise} \end{cases}$$

The result of (4.8) shows that the dummy NPOST is not statistically significant for $N = 5$; there is no postelectoral increase in the inflation rate.

$$\pi_t = 0.25 \quad +1.46\,\pi_{t-1} \quad -0.52\,\pi_{t-2} \quad +0.04\,\text{NPOST5}_{t-1}$$
$$\quad (2.4) \quad (23.0) \qquad (8.39) \qquad (0.31)$$

$$R^2 = 0.93 \tag{4.8}$$

Various robustness tests, including using $N = 3, 4, 6, 7$, fail to show any evidence of an increase in inflation after elections.

4.7 Political Cycles in Monetary Policy

We move now to tests on policy instruments and in particular on monetary policy. We consider quarterly observations on money supply growth rates and on short- and long-term interest rates.

The first issue in specifying the empirical tests for monetary policy is identifying the correct monetary policy instrument. A priori, it is neither theoretically nor empirically obvious whether we should use monetary aggregates or interest rates. Over different periods, the Fed has used both monetary aggregates and short-term interest rates as instruments of monetary policy. The use of monetary aggregates as proxies for monetary policy is common in the literature[28] but is not without problems. First, it is unclear which monetary aggregate should be used. Second, the evidence on the last two decades shows that money velocity has been very unstable in the United States, both cyclically and over the long run. Third, financial innovations and deregulation have structurally changed the money demand, particularly since the beginning of the 1980s. A cursory look at the yearly rates of growth of two different monetary aggregates in the United States (M0 and M1) reveals that they are very volatile over time and show no systematic pattern. In addition, except for a short period in the late 1970s when monetary growth targets became the intermediate instrument of U.S. monetary policy, a short-term interest rate (such as the federal funds rate) has been, and is, the main instrument of monetary policy in the United States. Therefore, in this section we take the approach of deriving the implications of various political theories for both monetary aggregates and interest rates and use both measures in our empirical tests. Moreover, given the observed instability in the demand for money, we also test the stability of our results on subsamples.

To test for the existence of political cycles in monetary policy instruments, we must first identify the Fed's monetary policy reaction function. We do so by estimating a reaction function, originally derived in Alesina 1988b, that is the semireduced form solution of a partisan model where there is persistency in the output growth process:

$$m_t = \alpha_0 + \alpha_1 m_{t-1} + \alpha_2 m_{t-2} \ldots + \alpha_n U_{t-1} + +\alpha_{n+1}\text{PDUM}_t + e_t \qquad (4.9)$$

In (4.9), m_t is the vector of time-series data on money growth; this rate of the money supply is defined as $m = ((M_t - M_{t-4})/M_{t-4})100$, where M_t is the level of the monetary aggregate in the regression. The reaction function implies that monetary growth has an autoregressive component and also depends on business cycle conditions (U representing the unemployment rate): When the unemployment rate is falling, monetary policy becomes tighter than otherwise, because the Fed tries to avoid the inflationary consequences of excessive growth. We obtain similar results if we use the lagged growth rate rather than the lagged unemployment rate as the measure of business cycle conditions. The sample period for the quarterly data on monetary aggregates is 1949:1 to 1994:3; we use two different monetary aggregates, the monetary base more closely controllable by the Fed (M0) and a wider monetary aggregate (M1); PDUM is a dummy variable that captures the dynamic implication of different theories (RADM for tests of the partisan theory).[29] With the exception of the PDUM variable, this specification is identical to that of Barro (1979).

The regressions for the interest rates are similar to those for the monetary growth rates. Instead of the growth rate of a monetary aggregate, we use the level of the relevant interest rate. We use four different interest rate measures: Two are effectively under the Fed's direct control (the federal funds rate and the discount rate) and two are market determined (the three-month Treasury bill rate and the rate on ten-year Treasury notes).

We start with tests of the partisan theory. Both the rational and the traditional versions of the partisan theory imply that money growth should be larger during Democratic administrations and, because inflation is also higher, nominal interest rates should be higher as well. Table 4.8 presents the results of the regression for the two monetary growth rates (M0 and M1). We consider two different samples—the full sample from 1949 until 1994 and a shorter sample from 1949 until the end of 1982—to capture the effects of a break in the stability of the money process. The date of 1982 is chosen to capture changes both in the money supply and in the money demand process; on one side, 1982 dates the end of the monetarist experiment of controlling monetary aggregate tightly; on the other, it also captures the period when changes in financial regulation and innovation made the money demand structurally more unstable.

The 1949–1994 regressions show that the monetary growth process is highly persistent and that the cyclical variable has the expected sign and is statistically significant: Monetary policy is tighter when the unemployment rate falls. The coefficient on the partisan variable

Table 4.8
Partisan theory
Dependent variable: rate of growth of money (m)

Independent variables	(1) Coefficient (t-statistics)	(2) Coefficient (t-statistics)	(3) Coefficient (t-statistics)	(4) Coefficient (t-statistics)
	1949–94 sample		1949–82 sample	
Constant	−0.18 (0.95)	−0.58 (1.84)	−0.21 (1.04)	−0.63 (2.0)
$U(-1)$	0.10 (2.87)	0.22 (3.88)	0.10 (2.53)	0.22 (4.09)
M0(-1)	1.25 (17.2)	—	1.07 (11.9)	—
M0(-2)	−0.32 (4.52)	—	−0.13 (1.49)	—
M1(-1)	—	1.23 (17.9)	—	1.03 (12.7)
M1(-2)	—	−0.36 (5.50)	—	−0.15 (1.84)
RADM(-2)	−0.07 (1.20)	−0.09 (1.12)	−0.11 (1.83)	−0.20 (2.41)
R^2	0.94	0.90	0.94	0.87

RADM is negative (*i.e.*, money growth rates are lower under Republican administrations) but is statistically not significant at standard confidence levels.[30] When the sample is restricted to 1949–1982, however, the results are different: The RADM variable has the expected sign and is now statistically significant at the 10 percent level in the M0 equation and at the 5 percent level in the M1 equation. Economically, these estimates imply that the steady-state yearly difference in monetary growth rates between the two administrations is 3.8 percent for M0 and 3.3 percent for M1. The high instability in money velocity is very likely the reason for the inconclusive results the 1949–94 sample period.[31]

In table 4.9, we show the results of the tests on interest rates, where we used four different short- and long-term interest rate measures (the

Table 4.9
Partisan theory
Dependent variable: interest rate (i)

Independent variables	(1) Coefficient (t-statistics)	(2) Coefficient (t-statistics)	(3) Coefficient (t-statistics)	(4) Coefficient (t-statistics)
	Federal funds rate	Discount rate	3-month T-bill	10-year Treasury note
Constant	0.25 (1.25)	0.10 (1.07)	0.17 (1.02)	0.12 (0.86)
$i(-1)$	1.17 (14.5)	1.40 (16.5)	1.15 (14.2)	1.21 (14.1)
$i(-2)$	−0.44 (3.60)	−0.55 (3.95)	−0.50 (4.16)	−0.30 (2.24)
$i(-3)$	0.24 (2.94)	0.13 (1.56)	0.32 (4.00)	0.07 (0.85)
RADM(-2)	−0.29 (2.96)	−0.13 (2.96)	−0.24 (3.25)	−0.11 (2.17)
R^2	0.90	0.97	0.91	0.96

federal funds rate, the discount rate, the three-month Treasury bill rate, and the rate on ten-year Treasury notes).[32] If monetary policy is systematically more expansionary during Democratic administrations, we expect higher inflation rates and higher short- and long-term nominal interest rates during these administrations than during Republican ones.[33] The results in table 4.8 are consistent with this view: The coefficient on the partisan dummy is negative (*i.e.*, interest rates are lower under Republican administrations) and statistically significant at the 5 percent level or better for all the four interest rate measures used.[34] The values of the coefficients on RADM in the regressions in table 4.8 imply that the difference in the steady-state federal funds rate between a Democratic and a Republican administration is about 4.5 percent (3.6 percent for the three-month T-bill rate). These differentials are larger than the inflation rate differentials found above for Democratic and

Republican administrations. Most likely, since interest rates are pro-cyclical and the average growth rate is higher under Democratic administrations, the interest rate differential will tend to be higher than the inflation differential.

One additional observation: In addition to the real wage effects of unexpected inflation that the basic partisan model stresses, partisan output effects might also derive from a transitory reduction in real interest rates generated by an expansionary monetary policy (the so-called liquidity effect of monetary policy). In fact, although money growth rates, inflation rates and nominal interest rates should on average be higher during left-wing administrations (a Fisherian effect), the partisan hypotheses are also consistent with a view that a looser monetary policy will lead to an increase in economic activity (transitory according to the rational partisan theory, permanent in the Hibbs version of the model) via a (transitory or permanent) real interest rate effect (a liquidity effect). In this case, in a partisan cycle, real interest rates may be relatively low and contribute to the positive output effect. Such a liquidity effect is likely to be stronger for short-term interest rates, whereas the Fisherian effect may be more pronounced for long-term interest rates. We tested for real interest rate effects in the data but found no evidence of permanent or temporary partisan differences in real interest rates in the United States at either the short or long end of the maturity structure. In chapter 7, we discuss such evidence and the possible reasons for the lack of partisan effects on real interest rates.

We move next to tests of political business cycle effects in monetary policy before elections. Table 4.10 reports the results of political business cycle tests on money growth and interest rates using the preelectoral dummy NRD4. For both money growth measures the coefficient on NRD4 is statistically insignificant. Several alternative specifications with NRD6 and NRD8, controlling for post-1973 dummies, including and excluding business cycle measures, oil-driven inflation, and alternative lag structures, yield no support for the hypothesis of more

Table 4.10
Political business cycle theory
Dependent variables: rate of growth of money (m), interest rates (i)

Independent variables	(1) Coefficient (t-statistics) $m0$	(2) Coefficient (t-statistics) $m1$	(3) Coefficient (t-statistics) Federal funds rate	(4) Coefficient (t-statistics) Discount rate	(5) Coefficient (t-statistics) 3-month T-bill	(6) Coefficient (t-statistics) 10-year Treasury note
Constant	-0.14 (0.76)	-0.53 (1.71)	0.33 (1.54)	0.17 (1.58)	0.25 (1.36)	0.22 (1.64)
$U(-1)$	0.09 (2.60)	0.20 (3.72)	—	—	—	—
$m(-1)$	1.26 (17.4)	1.25 (18.0)	—	—	—	—
$m(-2)$	-0.32 (4.60)	-0.38 (5.67)	—	—	—	—
$i(-1)$	—	—	1.21 (14.2)	1.45 (16.7)	1.19 (14.3)	1.24 (14.3)
$i(-2)$	—	—	-0.45 (3.54)	-0.55 (3.83)	-0.51 (4.07)	-0.30 (2.25)
$i(-3)$	—	—	0.19 (2.27)	0.08 (0.92)	0.26 (3.27)	0.04 (0.45)
NRD4	0.02 (0.17)	0.16 (0.85)	0.07 (0.36)	-0.04 (0.46)	0.05 (0.36)	-0.01 (0.10)
R^2	0.94	0.90	0.90	0.96	0.91	0.96

expansionary monetary policies before elections.[35] We also created dummy variables for each of the four years of an administration (YEAR4, YEAR3, YEAR2, YEAR1) and tested whether any was significant: The fourth-year dummy (the election year in the United States) was never significant, and similar results were found for the others.[36] Similar results apply to interest rates: The coefficient on NRD4 is statistically insignificant for all four measures of interest rates. Robustness tests similar to those performed for money growth give similar results with one exception. When we use year-of-administration dummies (YEAR4, YEAR3 and YEAR2) instead of the NRD dummies, we find systematic evidence that the three measures of short-term interest rates are significantly higher in election years than in the other administration years.[37]

In summary, the results found in this section for monetary policy match those found in the previous sections for economic outcomes. The evidence on monetary policy is consistent overall with the view that Democratic administrations follow more expansionary and inflationary monetary policies than Republican administrations: Although the poor performance of monetary growth aggregates as proxies for monetary policy after 1982 implies that partisan differences are hard to detect when money is unstable, both short- and long-term interest rates are systematically higher during Democratic administrations. Conversely, and consistently with the results in section 4.6 of tests of the political business cycle hypothesis on economic outcomes, we find no evidence of a loosening of monetary policy before elections.

4.8   Political Cycles in Fiscal Policy

We now turn to fiscal policy. First, the idea that budget deficits are higher before elections is grounded in the view that lower taxes and higher spending and transfers might increase votes for the incumbent administration. Second, different components of the budget may also be affected differently by the electoral cycle. Certain more visible and politically sensitive programs, such as transfers, may be more easily and productively manipulated than others.[38] Concerning partisan effects, according to a conventional (but not necessarily correct) view, Democratic administrations should be more eager than Republican ones to use deficit spending. However, although there may be some evidence for the idea that Democratic administrations are more willing to increase government spending to achieve policy objectives, these administrations may also be more willing to increase taxes. Therefore, the question of whether fiscal deficits will be higher under Democratic administrations has no obvious answer.

We begin with political effects in fiscal deficits. We use a structural model of fiscal deficits to control for the economic determinants. In particular, we follow the tax-smoothing model of Barro (1979, 1986) according to which fiscal deficits emerge from the decisions of policy-makers trying to minimize over time the costs of distortionary taxation in the face of transitory output and government spending shocks. According to this model, when there is a negative transitory output shock (such as a recession) or a positive transitory spending shock (as in the case of a war), it is optimal to maintain tax rates approximately constant, run a fiscal deficit, and build up the stock of public debt. These deficits and debt accumulation are reversed in periods of economic boom or when the temporary spending disturbance has disappeared.[39] Although the deficit model estimated is formally derived from Barro's tax-smoothing model, the view that fiscal deficits emerge during recessions and are higher when spending is temporarily high is common to a broader set of Keynesian and other models of deficit determination. Therefore, one can think of the estimated regression as a test of partisan and electoral effects in budget deficits after controlling for standard economic determinants of these deficits.[40]

Given the available data on budget deficits, the model is estimated, as in Barro, on yearly data; the sample period runs from 1946 to 1994. The estimated regression is

$$db_t = \alpha_0 + \alpha_1 \, db_{t-1} + \alpha_2(b_{t-1}\pi_t^e) + \alpha_3 \text{YVAR}_t + \alpha_4 \text{GVAR}_t$$

$$+ \alpha_5 \text{PDUM}_t + \varepsilon_t \tag{4.10}$$

Table 4.11
Political effects on budget deficits
Dependent variable: Budget deficit (% of GDP) (db)

Independent variables	(1) Coefficient (t-statistics)	(2) Coefficient (t-statistics)	(3) Coefficient (t-statistics)	(4) Coefficient (t-statistics)	(5) Coefficient (t-statistics)
Constant	0.009	0.006	0.004	0.004	0.007
	(1.94)	(1.03)	(0.83)	(0.79)	(1.39)
$db(-1)$	0.003	−0.002	−0.007	−0.007	−0.023
	(0.16)	(0.11)	(0.32)	(0.32)	(0.93)
$b(-1)\pi^e$	0.01	0.01	0.01	0.01	0.01
	(3.27)	(3.06)	(3.33)	(3.30)	(2.82)
YVAR	0.03	0.03	0.02	0.02	0.02
	(4.90)	(5.07)	(3.67)	(3.69)	(3.23)
GVAR	−0.38	−0.12	−0.12	−0.12	−0.07
	(2.89)	(1.28)	(1.35)	(1.35)	(0.83)
NRD4	—	0.001	—	0.001	—
		(0.35)		(0.27)	
RADM(−1)	—	—	0.004	0.003	0.000
			(2.12)	(2.10)	(0.04)
R^2	0.34	0.31	0.29	0.29	0.22

where db is the change in the stock of public debt held by the public as a share of GDP; YVAR is the deviation of the unemployment rate from its trend value; GVAR is the deviation of government spending (as a share of GDP) from its trend value; ($b\pi^e$) is a term representing the effects of expected inflation (π^e) on the public debt to GDP ratio (b) and PDUM is a political dummy capturing the effects of partisan or electoral effects. Because we need a measure of expected inflation, as in Barro, we effectively estimate a system of two equations, one for deficits and one for inflation. Expected inflation is generated as a forecast via a regression of inflation on two lags of inflation and lagged monetary growth. Formally, the system is estimated through iterative weighted least squares.

Table 4.11 presents the results of this regression estimated with annual data for 1948–1994. Column (1) shows the results when we do not introduce political variables (the Barro regression): Deficits are persistent over time, inflation seems to affect the real value of debt, and deficits are countercyclical (the coefficient on YVAR); surprisingly, over this sample, transitory shocks to government spending tend to reduce real deficits. When we introduce in column (2) a preelectoral dummy (NRD4), the sign of the estimated coefficient suggests that deficits are higher in election years, but the effect is not statistically significant. In columns (3) and (4), we add a partisan dummy either in conjunction with NRD or without it. In both cases, the coefficient is positive and statistically significant at the 5 percent level, implying that fiscal deficits are higher during Republican administrations. A simple test shows that this result is entirely driven by the deficits during the Republican administrations of Reagan and Bush; if, as in column (5), we estimate the model up to 1981, we find that the partisan dummy is not statistically significant, namely, deficits are not different during either type of administration. These results suggest that preelectoral increases in the overall fiscal deficits might be not feasible and that one should try to find possible electoral effects in subcomponents of government spending that can be more easily manipulated before elections. Moreover, it suggests that fiscal deficits are not higher during Democratic administrations, a result consistent with the view that Democrats might be more eager to spend more but are also more willing to increase revenues.

Next, we consider transfer payments that might be more easily controlled in election years; we take the ratio of personal transfers (total federal transfers to U.S. citizens minus personal contributions to social insurance) over seasonally adjusted GNP as our measure of net personal transfers. In the regressions, we add two autoregressive terms capturing the persistence of this variable; a trend variable to capture the long-run upward trend in this variable;[41] seasonal dummies to control for possible seasonal components of transfers; and a political dummy capturing either electoral or partisan effects. To capture parti-

Table 4.12
Political effects on government transfers
Dependent variable: Personal transfers (% of GNP) (TR)

Independent variables	(1) Coefficient (t-statistics)	(2) Coefficient (t-statistics)	(3) Coefficient (t-statistics)
Constant	−0.67	−0.66	−0.62
	(5.80)	(5.75)	(5.51)
TR(−1)	0.52	0.53	0.54
	(7.06)	(7.09)	(7.25)
TR(−2)	0.01	0.01	0.02
	(0.25)	(0.26)	(0.30)
Trend	−0.0003	−0.0003	−0.0001
	(0.52)	(0.62)	(0.23)
LR	0.20	0.20	0.19
	(7.16)	(7.17)	(6.97)
RADM	−0.01	—	—
	(0.66)		
NRD4	—	0.02	—
		(0.38)	
EV	—	—	0.03
			(0.68)
R^2	0.82	0.82	0.82

san differences, we use the RADM variable. Remember that it has been argued that transfers may affect voting behavior if very close to election time. Therefore, in addition to our NRD4 variable, we use in the regressions another electoral variable used by Alesina (1988b), EV, taking the value of 1 in the quarter before and the quarter of the presidential elections and of −1 in the following two quarters.[42] Table 4.12 shows that none of the electoral and partisan dummies are significant in the regressions for the sample 1947–1994. The results are consistent with those of Alesina (1988b), who found significant electoral effects in a 1961–1985 sample but not when including the pre-1961 period. Note, however, that if we start the sample in 1961 but also include the last decade of data (1986–1994), we still find no significant electoral effects. The lack of effects in the sample including the most recent decade suggests, perhaps, that most transfer programs have become long-term mandatory spending programs (such as Social Security and welfare programs) that cannot be easily manipulated for short-run purposes. This latter observation may also explain the failure to find any significant partisan effects in transfer payments. Although it is likely that many of these transfer programs were originally introduced during Democratic administrations and initially opposed by Republicans, most have become over time permanent programs of mandatory spending hardly affected by the party of the administration in power.

4.9 Discussion: Alternative Hypotheses

A recent study by Hibbs (1994) presents a model in which expected macropolicy might lead to transitory rather than permanent partisan effects. Two factors drive the results in the Hibbs model: first, time-varying weights that Democrats and Republicans attach to the growth and inflation targets; second, a time-varying Phillips curve trade-off between growth and inflation implying that partisan effects might be temporary even when expected (as well as unexpected) policies affect economic activity. Hibbs's results depend crucially on the assumed hypothesis that the inflation-growth trade-off becomes less (more) favorable after the initial Democratic (Republican) expansion (contraction). Although Hibbs is vague on this point, it is very likely that the Phillips curve becomes steeper in the second half of a Democratic (Republican) administration because wages adjust to the higher (lower) inflation engineered by Democrats (Republicans) in the first half of their administration. In this respect, Hibbs's model is effectively just a variant of the rational partisan theory rather than a hypothesis alternative to it.

Moreover, although Hibbs's model provides results that may be consistent with transitory partisan growth effects, it is possible to provide further evidence in favor of the rational partisan theory by considering directly one of the crucial implications of this hypothesis, that is, that the size of the transitory output shocks depends on the size of the electoral surprise. We formally address this implication and provide evidence in its favor in the next chapter.

4.10 Conclusions

Data on the postwar United States generally supports the rational partisan theory. Results are somewhat stronger on growth and unemployment than on inflation because several other factors specifically influence the latter, such as oil shocks and the exchange rate regime. Subsample instability of the relationship between instruments and outcomes and the fact that different administrations of the same party may use different instruments to achieve the same goal complicate tests of partisan effects in monetary and fiscal policy instruments.

We found, on the other hand, hardly any evidence in favor of Nordhaus's opportunistic political business cycle model. We found no evidence that the economy grows faster or that the unemployment rate is lower during election years; similarly, monetary policy does not appear to be more expansionary in election years, and there is no evidence of a postelectoral increase in the inflation rate. Concerning preelectoral manipulation of fiscal policy, we found no evidence that government transfers are greater close to election quarters nor that fiscal deficits are higher in election years, when the full 1947–1994 sample is considered.

Appendix

Table 4.A.1
Economic data for the United States

Quarterly data:

Real GDP, seasonally unadjusted. Sample: 1947:1–1994:4. Source: U.S. Econ Database at the Federal Reserve Bank of New York (FED).

Unemployment rate, total, seasonally adjusted. Sample: 1947:1–1994:4. Source: OECD Main Economic Indicators.

Consumer Price Index. Sample: 1947:1–1994:4. Source: International Monetary Fund, International Financial Statistics.

Monetary base (M0). Sample: 1949:1–1994:3. Source: FED.

Money supply (M1). Sample: 1949:1–1994:3. Source: FED.

Federal funds rate. Sample: 1960:1–1994:3. Source: FED.

Discount rate. Sample: 1960:1–1994:3. Source: FED.

Three-month Treasury bill rate. Sample: 1960:1–1994:3. Source: FED.

Ten-year Treasury note rate. Sample: 1960:1–1994:3. Source: FED.

Dollar price of oil. Sample: 1947:1–1994:4. Source: FED.

Personal transfers. Sample: 1947:1–1994:3. Source: FED

Annual data for deficit regressions:

For the period 1946–82, the data are the same as those used in Barro 1986; after 1982, the variables are updated with data from the FED data set.

Table 4.A.2
Political data for the United States

E	= Election	
CH L	= Change to a Democratic administration	
CH R	= Change to a Republican administration	

Exogenous timing of presidential elections: 4 years

1944:4	E	Democratic administration
1948:4	E	
1952:4	E	CH R
1956:4	E	
1960:4	E	CH L
1964:4	E	
1968:4	E	CH R
1972:4	E	
1976:4	E	CH L
1980:4	E	CH R
1984:4	E	
1988:4	E	
1992:4	E	CH L

5

Polls, Electoral Uncertainty, and the Economy

5.1 Introduction

In September 1948, Harry Truman trailed far behind in the polls, commanding about 43 percent of the two-party vote. The popular press prepared the public for their new President, Thomas Dewey. As the election drew closer, Truman's reelection chances plummeted, and Dewey began making preparations to move to Washington, DC. Then, on November 2, the unthinkable occurred: Truman handily defeated Dewey! The *Chicago Daily Tribune*'s infamous premature headline "Dewey Defeats Truman" expressed the extent of the electoral surprise.

What were the economic consequences of this electoral surprise? The stock market plummeted by 4.6 percent the day after the election, but by Truman's second year in office, real GDP was growing at an annual rate of 8.7 percent. Did the unexpected nature of Truman's victory give him more latitude for implementing his economic policies? Why did the stock market react so strongly? Was Dewey's victory already capitalized into stock prices? In this chapter we answer these questions by using the framework presented in the previous chapters and developing a rigorous empirical procedure to test them on U.S. data. More precisely, we ask: Does the extent of electoral surprise affect the postelectoral economy? Do financial markets incorporate electoral information prior to the election?[1]

Our analysis relies on a calculation of the probability of electoral outcomes based on information available to the public. This calculation, which we call the electoral option model, employs the techniques used to price an option. Given these probabilities, we estimate the impact of electoral information on both pre- and postelectoral economic outcomes.

As we have discussed, one of the rational partisan theory's critical and less obvious implications is that the size of the postelectoral real effect of monetary and fiscal policies depends on the degree of electoral surprise: The more unexpected the electoral outcome, the less anticipated the postelectoral policies, and thus the larger the economic impact. Using our constructed ex ante probabilities of electoral outcomes, our results lend strong support to this implication of the rational partisan theory.

Another outcome of the rational partisan theory is that inflation rates across Republican and Democratic administrations systematically differ, and the public expects these differences. If this is the case, given the existence of distinct partisan postelectoral economic policies and outcomes, forward-looking market participants should react to changes in electoral probabilities. Specifically, we explore how preelectoral information is capitalized into the U.S. Treasury bond market. Our empirical analysis indicates that as the probability of an inflation-averse Republican administration increases, expected future nominal interest rates decline. This results in a concomitant decline in current bond yields.

This chapter is organized as follows. Section 5.2 describes the methodology (based on option models) to construct a measure of electoral surprise and applies this measure to the growth and unemployment equation. Section 5.3 discusses the effect of polls and electoral information on financial markets. The last section concludes.

5.2 The Electoral Option and Its Application to Models of Partisan Politics

5.2.1 Overview and Summary of Previous Empirical Results

The rational partisan theory has straightforward testable implications about the effect of electoral surprise on postelectoral macroeconomic outcomes. Here we extend chapter 4's empirical analysis by testing a model of partisan differences that incorporates an explicit measure of electoral surprise. To calculate the electoral surprise, we update the electoral option technique developed in Cohen 1993.

Very few economists have related electoral forecasts to macro-economic variables using rational, forward-looking models. Chappell and Keech (1988) are an exception. They connect movements of the unemployment rate to money growth forecast errors. Because they use a partisan model, their money growth forecasts depend upon forecasts of electoral outcomes. Their estimates of electoral probabilities, how-ever, lack sufficient degrees of freedom and suffer from generated regressor problems.[2]

Roberts (1989) also converts preelectoral polls into probabilities to study the explanatory power of electoral information on politically sensitive assets in the 1980 election. His methodology is based solely on the polls' statistical properties and does not consider how far in advance of the election the poll is published. Therefore, all polls with the same outcome, irrespective of the time remaining to the election, yield the same electoral probability. Finally, Hibbs (1992) notes that electoral preference polls "are natural vehicles to calibrate public per-ceptions of the probability of partisan change at any period." Hibbs does not suggest a calibration methodology, however, and feels that, contrary to the results we present below, "the rational partisan theory, once subjected to proper tests, will not fare well in the data....(370)"

It should be stressed that our electoral option model is not geared toward predicting electoral results. Rather, it is an attempt to back out an estimate of the market's assessment of electoral probabilities. Therefore, as the results presented in section 5.2.3 indicate, the elec-toral option model incorrectly predicts a Dewey victory in the 1948 election. In our view, this is a success for the methodology: Our goal is not to accurately predict the election, but to reflect public sentiment before each election.

More generally, we show below that our estimate of preelectoral probabilities reflects public opinion before elections: for instance, the uncertainty of the 1960 election and near certainty of the 1964, 1972, and 1984 elections. When we then use these probabilities in growth and unemployment regressions, we broadly confirm the implications of the rational partisan theory. The more unexpected is the presidential election result, the farther growth and unemployment deviate from their natural (or average) levels.

5.2.2 Converting Preelectoral Polling into Probabilities—A Nontechnical Discussion

The methodology used for transforming preelectoral polls into probabilities employs techniques similar to those implemented when an option is priced. In option pricing, the market knows the current price of the asset, the strike price, the time to maturity of the option, are the risk-free rate of return, and can measure the variance of changes in the asset's price. Given only this information, the market calculates the probability that the asset will reach the strike price and therefore, the value of the option.

The conversion of polls into electoral probabilities can be thought of in a similar fashion. When a poll is announced, the public knows the time to the election and can estimate the mean and variance of changes in the polls. With this information, one can compute the probability of a candidate's receiving a majority of the two-party vote or exceeding the "strike price" of 50 percent of the two-party vote, thus winning the election. The assumption of a strike price of 50 percent of the two-party vote is made to avoid complications involving the electoral college system and elections that may include more than two candidates.[3] Mathematically, the probability that the Democratic candidate will garner more than 50 percent of the two-party vote and thus win the election (P_t^D), can be represented as

$$P_t^D = \text{Prob}[V_{t+\tau}^D > 50\% \,|\, V_t^D; \tau; \mu; \sigma] \tag{5.1}$$

where V_t^D is the Democratic share of two-party preelectoral polling; τ is the number of months remaining until the election; μ equals the sample mean monthly change in polls; and σ equals the sample standard deviation of month-to-month changes in the polls.

To implement the electoral option model, we must make the following three assumptions about the movement of polls across time: Changes in polls are (a) independent, (b) identically distributed, and (c) distributed normally. Intuitively, assumption (a) states that in a manner similar to that of stock price movements, individuals change their response to a poll based only on new information. Thus current changes in a candidate's polled vote share yield no information about future changes. Assumption (b) asserts that changes in the polls fluctuate in the same manner regardless of the amount of time preceding the election. Finally, assumption (c) provides the distribution from which we can convert the polls into probabilities. Appendix A discusses each of these assumptions and describes the empirical analysis that confirms their validity.

Given that polls follow these three assumptions, the following expression solves equation (5.1):

$$P_t^D = \Phi\left(\frac{V_t^D + \mu\tau - 50}{\sigma\sqrt{\tau}}\right) \tag{5.2}$$

where Φ is the cumulative standard normal distribution. Intuitively, this model states that the expected value of a Democratic candidate's two-party vote share τ months from now is the current polled vote share (V_t^D) plus the expected change in the polls, which equals the mean monthly change multiplied by the number of months to the election $(\mu\tau)$. This estimate is then translated into an electoral probability by calculating the statistical significance of the difference between the expected vote share and the strike price of 50 percent. Statistically, this implies subtracting the strike price of 50 and then, to standardize to a normal distribution, dividing by the standard deviation of the sum of the τ changes in the polls that will occur before the election. Under assumptions (a) and (b), the denominator is the sample standard deviation of changes multiplied by the square root of the time to the election $(\sigma\sqrt{\tau})$. Following assumption (c), the probability estimate is calculated by finding where this estimate lies under a normal distribution.

As we discussed above, analysis of preelectoral polling data indicates that equation (5.2) conforms nicely to the underlying theory; nevertheless, two characteristics of the model should be addressed. One concern may be that the model does not explicitly account for incumbency advantage. Although this is true, any incumbency advantage is already incorporated into the polling results. That is, a popular president should do well in the polls, and therefore the electoral option model will reflect that popularity.

Second, the electoral option model is formulated so that, depending on the value of the mean expected change in the polls (μ), for large τ, the probability of being elected approaches zero, one-half, or one. If $\mu = 0$, the model yields the result that long before an election, irrespective of the poll, the probability of a Democrat's election approaches 50 percent. Furthermore, positive (negative) values of μ imply a bias for (against) Democrats, thus for large τ, the probability approaches one (zero). This issue is somewhat mitigated because elections occur every four years, consequently the electoral option will be priced for a maximum of forty-eight months.

Fortunately, a bias that drives the probability to the extremes (0, 1) may be beneficial in further capturing any incumbency advantage not already incorporated into the polls themselves. Because the current administration should have had favorable polling as a sign of their electoral victory (with the possible exception of Truman's 1948 victory), the current value of μ should reflect the incumbent party's gains. Because the option is priced only for a maximum of 48 months, however, the added incumbency bias from μ is small. Nevertheless, the results of this model may depend on the values of μ and σ. Therefore, we implement different methodologies for calculating the mean and standard deviation of changes in the polls in the following section.

5.2.3 Implementation of the Electoral Option Model

Since 1936, and for every subsequent election, the Gallup Organization has been polling voters' presidential preferences. Gallup's tests presidential preferences by conducting presidential candidate trial heats in which the candidates are run against each other. The results of these trial heats are then converted into the Democratic share of the two-party vote to produce the preelectoral polling variable V_t^D.[4]

Bringing together the electoral option model presented in section 5.2.2 and the poll data described in the previous paragraph, the probability that a Democratic candidate will be elected (P_t^D) can be calculated. As we discussed earlier, the value of the current Democratic vote share (V_t^D) and the number of periods remaining until the election (τ) are known with certainty. The mean monthly change in the polls (μ) and standard deviation of month-to-month changes (σ) must be calculated from data available to the market. Therefore, to incorporate new information gained by the publication of each poll and to capture changes in partisan support throughout history, we employ various techniques to estimate μ and σ.[5]

The two procedures used to calculate μ and σ utilize only information available at the time the poll is announced (including the new poll itself, to update the information set).[6] Consequently, the September 1948 probability estimate uses only information from 1936 (when polling began) through September 1948 to calculate μ and σ. This cumulative moving average technique is so named because the information window becomes larger as time passes. Because of this, the cumulative moving average methodology also incorporates changes in partisan support over time. Thus, in addition to any incumbency advantage that the polls should reflect, the constant incorporation of new information generally leads to small changes in μ favorable to the incumbent party.[7] Figure 5.1 illustrates the electoral probabilities from 1948 through 1992 that result from the cumulative average technique.

One further improvement on the cumulative moving average methodology is to give recent changes in the polls more weight in the calculation of μ and σ. Figure 5.2 depicts the results from this weighted cumulative moving average technique using linear weights. As figures 5.1 and 5.2 indicate, the difference between these two procedures is small. The major distinction between them is that the weighted means

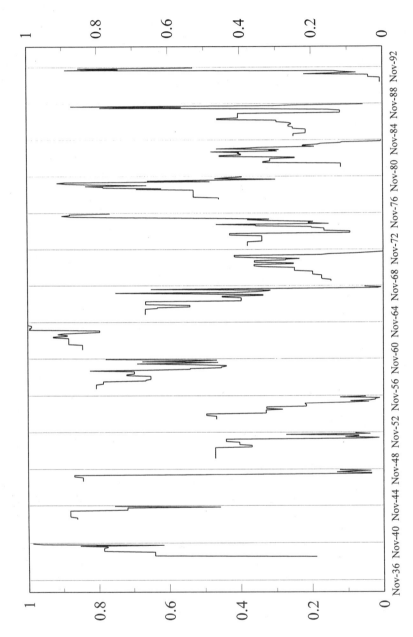

Figure 5.1

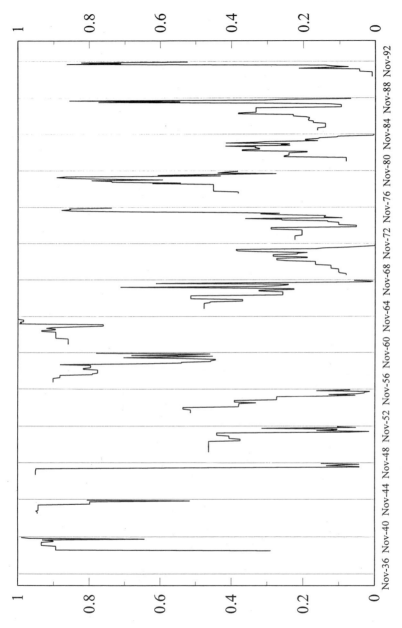

Figure 5.2

and variance may lead to a larger incumbency advantage due to the added weight given to the most recent polling observations.

Most significantly, all of the techniques produce realistic probabilities around the election (when the probabilities are most relevant). That is, the probabilities approach nearly certain Republican victories in 1972 and 1984, a certain Democratic victory in 1964, and uncertainty about the 1960 election. In addition, the models yield a high probability of a Republican victory in 1948, reflective of the public sentiment at that time.

5.2.4 Electoral Surprise, Growth, and Unemployment

According to the rational partisan theory, if at the end of period $t - 1$ the Democratic party wins the presidential election, growth in period t (y_t^D) can be modeled as follows:

$$y_t^D = \gamma(1 - P_t^D)(\pi^D - \pi^R) + \text{other predetermined variables} \qquad (5.3)$$

where $(1 - P_t^D)$ is the electoral surprise that occurs when a Democrat is elected President.

If, instead, the Republican party wins, we have

$$y_t^R = \gamma(0 - P_t^D)(\pi^D - \pi^R) + \text{other predetermined variables} \qquad (5.4)$$

with the electoral surprise defined as $(0 - P_t^D)$. Thus we can combine (5.3) and (5.4) to yield the following testable equation:

$$y_t = \beta_0 + \beta_1 y_{t-1} + \beta_2 y_{t-2} + \beta_3 \, \text{OIL}_{t-1} + \beta_4 \, \text{SURPRISE} \#_t + \varepsilon_t \qquad (5.5)$$

with y_t representing the annualized quarterly growth rate of GDP, SURPRISE $\#_t$ defined as $(1 - P_t^D)$ for Democrats and $(0 - P_t^D)$ for Republicans, and $\#$ indicating the length of the contract that yields the electoral surprise variable. Thus, electoral surprise is defined as the true electoral outcome minus the probability of this outcome occurring. Theory indicates that estimations should yield a larger postelectoral boom (recession) to the degree that the Democratic (Republican) surprise is greater, or mathematically $\beta_4 > 0$. For reasons extensively discussed in chapter 4, we add autoregressive terms in the regression and a lagged measure of the price of oil as a proxy for supply shocks.

When calculating the surprise variable, three important factors must be considered. The first is the lag between election and policy effect. To ensure consistency with the analytical framework outlined in chapter 4, we assume either a one- or two-quarter lag between the start of an administration and the impact of its economic policies.[8] The second issue is the length of the rigidities in the economy. Following the nominal wage contract literature, the surprise variable is calculated assuming that new wage contracts are signed uniformly across time. Thus, every quarter $100/\#$ percent of all workers sign a new fixed-term contract $\#$ quarters long (with $\# = 4, 6, 8, 10,$ or 12).

The third factor is the measure of the effective electoral probability. The probabilities calculated in section 5.2.3 using the electoral option model reflect, at each period in time, the current best estimate of the probability of Democratic victory. Given multiperiod contracts, however, the relevant electoral probability, as reflected in the economy through those contracts, is not just the current best estimate of the electoral probability but a combination of the current and past probabilities. This implies that, given the existence of two-year overlapping contracts and assuming that these contracts are signed uniformly across time, the electoral surprise after the election should be defined as the realized ex post probability minus the average of the current and past seven probabilities, or:

$$\text{SURPRISE8}_t = \text{REALIZED}_t - \frac{1}{8} \sum_{i=0}^{7} P_{t-i}^{D} \tag{5.6}$$

where REALIZED_t is the electoral outcome (0 after a Republican victory, 1 after a Democratic victory). Before the election, P_t^{D} is the measure of electoral probability calculated in section 5.2.3 using the electoral option model.[9] After the election, P_t^{D} takes on a value of 0 or 1 (depending on the victor), so that the electoral surprise variable

Table 5.1
Effect of electoral surprise on GDP growth
Dependent variable: GDP growth (y_t)

	(1) Coefficient (t-statistics)	(2) Coefficient (t-statistics)	(3) Coefficient (t-statistics)	(4) Coefficient (t-statistics)	(5) Coefficient (t-statistics)
Constant	1.79 (4.81)	1.80 (4.90)	1.93 (5.33)	2.07 (5.64)	2.11 (5.69)
y_{t-1}	0.33 (4.46)	0.31 (4.25)	0.27 (3.77)	0.26 (3.52)	0.26 (3.53)
y_{t-2}	0.11 (1.49)	0.12 (1.61)	0.11 (1.49)	0.08 (1.16)	0.07 (0.97)
OIL_{t-1}	−0.01 (−1.16)	−0.01 (−1.11)	−0.01 (−1.08)	−0.01 (−1.12)	−0.01 (−1.25)
$SURPRISE4_t$	7.32 (0.77)	—	—	—	—
$SURPRISE6_t$	—	8.20 (2.03)	—	—	—
$SURPRISE8_t$	—	—	8.93 (3.30)	—	—
$SURPRISE10_t$	—	—	—	7.58 (3.51)	—
$SURPRISE12_t$	—	—	—	—	6.04 (3.31)
R^2	0.16	0.17	0.20	0.21	0.20

diminishes over time as new contracts, which incorporate the election result, are written. Finally, when all contracts written before the election expire, $SURPRISE\#_t$ becomes zero.

Table 5.1 illustrates the results of estimating equation (5.5) using the weighted cumulative moving average probabilities.[10] The positive and strongly significant coefficients on the SURPRISE# variables concur with the rational partisan theory.[11] By noting that the SURPRISE# variable is by definition negative (positive) for Republicans (Democrats), the estimates indicate that the postelectoral path of output growth is different under Republican than Democratic regimes. Furthermore, as our theory suggests, the greater the electoral surprise, the larger the effect on output growth. A simulation using the coefficients on the two-year contract (the SURPRISE8 variable in table 5.1) implies that six quarters after an election, a 20 percent Democratic surprise yields growth 1.2 percent above normal.[12]

The table also shows that the two- to three-year contracts (columns (3) through (5)) have the greatest explanatory power, suggesting that the impact of the electoral surprise is relatively long lived. These results are consistent with those presented in chapter 4 for the DRPTX dummy variables. Finally, our conclusions are robust to different autoregressive specifications, exclusion of the OIL variable (which has the expected sign), and changes in various assumptions concerning the construction of the SURPRISE# variable.

We now turn to unemployment. We estimate the following model using monthly data from January 1948 through March 1995:

$$U_t = \beta_0 + \sum_{i=1}^{5} \beta_i U_{t-i} + \beta_6 \, OIL_{t-3} + \beta_7 \, SURPRISE\#_t + \varepsilon_t \qquad (5.7)$$

with SURPRISE#$_t$ defined on a monthly basis corresponding to the quarterly definition described above. In contrast to the quarterly averaging in the output estimations, the use of higher frequency unemployment data enables us to fully utilize our monthly polling data and calculated probabilities. Thus the two-year contract monthly electoral surprise variable is defined as follows:

$$SURPRISE24_t = REALIZED_t - \frac{1}{24} \sum_{i=0}^{23} P_{t-i}^D. \qquad (5.8)$$

Because the data are monthly, the OIL variable is lagged three months, or one quarter, while the SURPRISE# variable is calculated assuming six months (two quarters) between the inauguration and policy implementation. Theory implies that the coefficient on OIL should be positive, but the coefficient on SURPRISE# should be negative. Thus, the larger the Democratic electoral surprise, the lower the resulting unemployment rate.

The results of the estimation of equation (5.7) presented in table 5.2 provide additional support for the rational partisan theory. The negative and statistically significant coefficients on the SURPRISE# variables indicates postelectoral partisan differences in unemployment and that the greater the electoral surprise, the larger the partisan impact.[13] In addition, as we discussed earlier, the two- to three-year contracts (columns (3) through (5)) have more explanatory power. Finally, the coefficient estimate on two-year contracts, SURPRISE24 variable in table 5.2, suggests 0.5 percent lower unemployment eighteen months after a 20 percent Democratic surprise. Therefore, on average, within two years of taking office the policies of Democratic Presidents will lead to 1 percent lower unemployment than those of their Republican counterparts. The impact of these policies are, however, temporary and dependent on the level of electoral surprise.

To summarize this section's results of this section, the electoral option model produces what seem to be realistic electoral probabilities. That is, the probabilities generated appear to reflect public sentiment prior to the election. With these electoral probabilities computed, we estimate the impact of electoral surprise on postelectoral macroeconomic outcomes. Empirical analysis of output growth and unemployment indicates that the more surprised is the public, the larger is the postelectoral economic impact. This result supports the rational partisan theory.

5.3   Political Information and Financial Markets: An Overview

Governor Clinton—he talks about the reaction to the markets. There was a momentary fear that he might win and the markets went phwwt, down like that.
—President George Bush, Presidential Debate, October 11, 1992

In the previous section we discussed how preelectoral polling data can be used to gauge the extent of postelectoral surprise. What follows examines this issue from a different perspective by studying whether forward-looking financial markets use preelectoral information to dis-

Table 5.2
Effect of electoral surprise on unemployment
Dependent variable: unemployment (U_t)

	(1) Coefficient (t-statistics)	(2) Coefficient (t-statistics)	(3) Coefficient (t-statistics)	(4) Coefficient (t-statistics)	(5) Coefficient (t-statistics)
Constant	0.12 (3.38)	0.11 (3.20)	0.11 (3.13)	0.11 (3.26)	0.12 (3.45)
U_{t-1}	0.99 (23.57)	0.98 (23.51)	0.97 (23.27)	0.97 (23.07)	0.97 (23.03)
U_{t-2}	0.25 (4.22)	0.25 (4.27)	0.25 (4.30)	0.25 (4.27)	0.25 (4.24)
U_{t-3}	−0.07 (−1.10)	−0.06 (−1.02)	−0.06 (−1.03)	−0.06 (−1.07)	−0.07 (−1.12)
U_{t-4}	−0.10 (−1.63)	−0.09 (−1.58)	−0.09 (−1.55)	−0.09 (−1.55)	−0.09 (−1.56)
U_{t-5}	−0.10 (−2.29)	−0.10 (−2.37)	−0.09 (−2.17)	−0.08 (−1.95)	−0.08 (−1.85)
OIL_{t-3}	0.0001 (0.58)	0.0001 (0.58)	0.0001 (0.54)	0.0001 (0.52)	0.0001 (0.59)
SURPRISE12$_t$	−0.58 (−0.97)	—	—	—	—
SURPRISE18$_t$	—	−0.50 (−2.75)	—	—	—
SURPRISE24$_t$	—	—	−0.39 (−3.50)	—	—
SURPRISE30$_t$	—	—	—	−0.32 (−3.79)	—
SURPRISE36$_t$	—	—	—	—	−0.25 (−3.62)
R^2	0.98	0.98	0.98	0.98	0.98

count the election results prior to election day. Our interest in this analysis is twofold. First, we wish to examine whether financial markets perceive partisan differences in economic policy; if so, this finding would provide additional support for the rational partisan theory. Second, we study whether there is a smooth transition to the new electoral equilibrium as markets slowly update their subjective probabilities of a candidate's being elected based on information available to the market. If this is true, we would understand why, in most cases, markets do not react more strongly upon learning the outcome of an election.

We empirically test our hypothesis by examining the impact of our previously calculated electoral probabilities on the U.S. Treasury bond market. This analysis, which updates Cohen 1993, draws upon two strands of economic theory. The first is the rational partisan theory. The second concerns the extent to which financial markets assimilate political or economic information.

The efficient market hypothesis predicts that news about future earnings, output growth, or inflation will have an immediate impact on financial markets. Therefore, given the policies predicted under the rational partisan theory, the market's expectation of future policies should shift as each candidate's probability of election changes. For example, as the probability of a Democratic candidate's being elected increases, the market's expectation of future inflation should rise. This should result in a concomitant increase in current bond yields.

This section brings together these two strands of theory and explores how changes in a political party's electoral probability affect interest rates. We will refer to this theory as the "electoral information hypothesis," reflecting the effect of information about the outcome of the election on financial markets.

5.3.1   Electoral Politics and Financial Markets—The Press and the Academic Literature

The idea that financial markets react to political news is a familiar concept in the popular press. At many times throughout postwar presidential campaigns and after candidates' victories, the media has discussed how electoral information has influenced and will influence financial markets. For example, in 1948, after Truman's victory and the resulting stock price movement, Forrest (1948) wrote that, because the stock market had been "led on by the political polls—like everyone else—there was no indication in the preelection day market that a storm was imminent."

Twenty years later, in response to the bond market's lackluster response to the 1968 election outcome, Hershey (1968) explained that although "in general Wall Street believes that bond prices should rise [yields should decline] on the election of a Republican President because that party would normally be expected to fight harder against inflation than would the Democrats," there existed "the possibility that [Nixon's] election had been fully anticipated."

More recently, for many months prior to the 1992 U.S. presidential election, newspapers attributed stock and bond markets' movements to electoral information. In August 1992, Levingston (1992) noted that the "pivotal factor in the coming weeks will be the President's standing in the polls.... If it looks likely Clinton's going to win, the markets are going to sell off in a reaction to uncertainty and to the prospect of a Republican President being defeated." Throughout October 1992 readers encountered headlines such as: "Is Clinton Driving Bond Market?" and "Bonds Drop on Fears of Clinton's Economic Plan," in which Fuerbringer (1992) described how "the bond market fell sharply as investors and dealers were said to be positioning themselves for the likelihood that Gov. Bill Clinton of Arkansas would win the Presidential election and would try to stimulate the economy with increases in government spending." In addition, analysts such as Greenhouse (1992) even noted that "some experts say stocks and bonds might not react much to a Clinton victory, suggesting that financial markets have already discounted this possibility."

Although the electoral information hypothesis has received substantial media coverage, other than Cohen 1993, there are very few formal analyses of the specific effects of electoral probabilities on financial markets. Brander (1991) examines the reaction of the Toronto Stock Exchange (TSE) to poll results prior to the 1988 Canadian general election and finds that a one-point increase in Conservative party popularity led to a five-point increase in the TSE. Employing event study methodology, Roberts (1989, 1990b) concludes that, in the 1980 election, electoral news had some explanatory power regarding the rate of return on politically sensitive assets.

In addition to these studies, a number of authors such as Bachman (1992), Blomberg and Hess (1997), Cutler et al. (1989), Niederhoffer (1971), and Sheffrin (1989) have analyzed the impact of electoral outcomes on financial markets. Most of these analyses, however, are based on the hypothesis that the election result becomes certain only after the voting and is not anticipated prior to the election.[14]

The most interesting result arising from studies of "qualitative news" is the negligible effect of the realization of presidential electoral outcomes on the stock market. In only one election since 1948, the surprise Truman victory, could the post–election day 4.6 percent decline in the S&P500 stock index not be explained by chance at the 5 percent level. As we noted earlier in this chapter, prior to the 1948 election our measure of electoral probability clearly pointed toward a Truman loss. Thus, according to our theory, the market was reacting strongly to the unexpected Truman victory.[15]

Although the above evidence illustrates the implication of the electoral influence hypothesis on the stock market, here we choose to study the bond market rather than the equity market in hopes of avoiding a number of complicating factors. If equity markets are forward looking, as we assume financial markets are, then the stock market could react differently to the potential short-term as opposed to long-term implications of a given party's victory. For example, a Republican victory may lead to a recession in the short run, but in the long run, lower inflation and pro-business tax and regulatory policies could have the opposite effect on the stock market.[16] Furthermore. following Roberts (1990a,b), the combined impact of the presidential and congressional elections may have very different implications for individual stocks.[17] Therefore, this analysis will concentrate on the U.S. Treasury bond market, which has fixed maturities and no state- or region-specific components, yielding a more distinct reaction to expected presidential electoral outcomes than the stock market.

5.3.2 The Electoral Information Hypothesis

The electoral information hypothesis is based on two theories. The first is that different electoral outcomes will yield distinct economic policies. The second is that forward-looking financial markets react to information that portends future outcomes. Appendix B develops a formal model characterizing how electoral information is incorporated into the bond market. Here we provide a less technical discussion. The model of the effect of electoral information on the bond market results in the following testable equation:

$$\Delta F1_{v,t} = (r^e_{1,t+v-1|t} - r^e_{1,t+v-1|t-1}) + (P^D_{t+v-1|t} - P^D_{t+v-1|t-1})(\pi^D - \pi^R) + \Lambda_{k,t}$$
$$(5.9)$$

where $\Delta F1_{v,t}$ is the forward rate revision illustrated below; $r^e_{1,t+v-1|t}$ is the expected one-period real return on a bond beginning at time $t + v - 1$; $P^D_{t+v-1|t}$ the subjective probability the Democratic candidate will win the election and thus be in power at time $t + v - 1$; π^i is the inflation rate under party i (with $i = D$ or R); and $\Lambda_{k,t}$ is the change in the term premium. The forward interest rate at time t ($F1_{v,t}$) is the one-period spot rate for the period $t + v - 1$. The forward rate revision can be thought of as the change in expectations from time $t - 1$ to time t of the interest rate on the same one-period bond beginning in period $t + v - 1$. Therefore, the left-hand side of equation (5.9) represents a change in expectations and thus is affected only by the change in the term premium, which is assumed to be constant, and "news" concerning real interest rate and inflation expectations.

The model does not specify the mechanism generating real interest rate movements. However, economic and political factors such as expected growth, neutrality of the tax system with respect to inflation, and government deficit-spending policies must be considered and consequently are controlled for in the estimations.[18]

Concerning inflation expectations, if inflation is greater under a Democrat than a Republican ($\pi^D > \pi^R$), then equation (5.9) can be used to test whether new information pertaining to the probability of a specific party's being elected has an impact on the term structure of interest rates. That is, given new electoral information, the relative prices and yields of bonds of different maturities should change reflecting the market's adjustment of the subjective probabilities of electoral victory of the different political parties. More specifically, our framework indicates that as the probability of a Democratic candidate increases, the bond market expects higher inflation and long-term bond yields, and thus forward interest rates increase.[19]

The model of the electoral information hypothesis utilizes two principal variables. The first is a measure of the change in the probability that a Democratic or Republican will be elected. For the following analyses, we use the electoral probabilities calculated in section 5.2.3 via the electoral option model. Second, we employ the forward rate revision $\Delta Fn_{v,t}$ to gauge bond market responsiveness to political information. Forward rate revisions can be thought of as the change in expectations concerning the yield of a bond that matures in the future. They are computed by comparing the yield on the same bond over time. Figure 5.3 illustrates the calculation of $\Delta F24_{12,t}$, the forward rate revision, or revision in expectations, for the same twenty-four-month forward rate (which spans from time $t + 11$ to time $t + 35$) given information first at time $t - 1$ and then at time t.

Appendix C discusses in detail the derivation of the forward rate revisions. These revisions are calculated using interest rate data that consists of end-of-month, continuously compounded zero coupon yields of U.S. Treasury securities from December 1946 through February

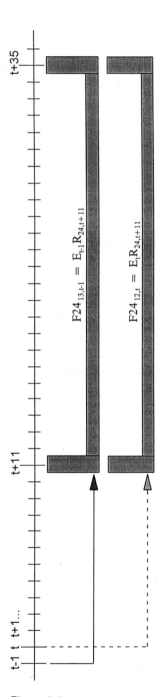

Figure 5.3

1991.[20] The important fact to remember throughout this analysis is
that in calculating the forward rate revision, we are following movements of the interest rate on the same one-, two-, three-, or four-year
bond throughout time.

To assess the impact of electoral information on forward-looking
financial markets, there must be evidence of the differing impact of
partisan politics on postelectoral macroeconomic outcomes. Because
we found evidence of partisan policies, and take as given that financial
markets should expect them, we can now conduct a more formal test
of the electoral information hypothesis.

Employing methodology similar to that of Fama (1984a), Baxter
(1989), and Plosser (1982, 1987), we study whether changes in electoral probabilities have an impact on the bond market. The estimation of an equation of factors that influence the forward rate revision
must consider only variables available to the market. Thus, much care
is taken to include the appropriate lag structure of the explanatory
variables in the regression.

We estimate the impact of economic and political variables on forward rate revisions of one-, two-, three-, or four-year spot rates with
the following specification:

$$\Delta Fn_{v,t} = \beta_0 + \beta_1 \Delta Fn_{v,t-1} + \beta_2 \Delta Fn_{v,t-2} + \beta_3 \Delta \pi_{t-1}$$

$$+ \beta_4 \Delta U_{t-1} + \beta_5 \Delta M1_{t-1} + \beta_6 \Delta P_t^D + \varepsilon_t \qquad (5.10)$$

$\Delta Fn_{v,t}$ represents the forward rate revision for various n-month bonds
over time; $\Delta \pi_{t-1}$ is the one-month change in the inflation rate at time
$t-1$; ΔU_{t-1} is the one-month change in the unemployment rate for
time $t-1$; and $\Delta M1_{t-1}$ is the one-month log change in M1 at time
$t-1$. Finally, ΔP_t^D is the time t, one-month change in the probability
of a Democratic President's being elected. This probability is calculated using our electoral option model and is based on information
announced before to the end of month t.

Two factors govern the particular lag structure of equation (5.10).
The lags of the dependent variable attempt to correct for the serially

correlated errors manifested by the autocorrelation in the forward rate revision data and the low Durbin-Watson statistic calculated during estimations without the lags of the dependent variable. The use of lagged changes in inflation, unemployment, and money growth are explained by the fact that, at time t, only information about last month's inflation, unemployment and money growth are available.[21]

The choice of the specific economic variables utilized in estimating equation (5.10) follows the work of Plosser (1982, 1987) and Baxter (1989). In addition to those variables depicted in equation (5.10), variables such as the one-month innovation in the index of leading indicators, industrial production, public debt, and the S&P500 were included; we could not reject an F-test of the joint hypothesis of zero coefficients for these extra variables and we therefore excluded them from the estimation.[22]

Table 5.3 displays the results of the estimation of equation (5.10) for the various forward rate revisions, over the sample period May 1948 through October 1988. This sample contains data only for the 12 months prior to each election because we hypothesize that the markets become concerned with the post-electoral impact only a year or so before the election.[23] As table 5.3 indicates, the coefficients on ΔP_t^D (the change in the probability of a Democrat's being elected President) are significant and have the expected positive sign. Thus, as the probability of a Democratic President increases, the market expects higher future nominal interest rates because it expects higher inflation, real interest rates, or both. An increase in the probability of a Democrat's being elected President causes an upward shift or a steepening of the yield curve, or both. That is, either the overall level of interest rates rises or the spread between short- and long-term interest rates widens, or both.[24]

Summarizing table 5.3, the magnitude of the coefficients on ΔP_t^D indicates that a 10 percentage point change in the calculated probabilities (the mean absolute monthly change) leads to between a five- and eight-basis-point move in the implied rate of a one-, two-, three-, or

Table 5.3
Effect of electoral information on the bond market
Dependent variable: forward rate revision $(\Delta Fn_{v,t})^*$

	$\Delta F12_{12,t}$ Coefficient (t-statistics)	$\Delta F24_{12,t}$ Coefficient (t-statistics)	$\Delta F36_{12,t}$ Coefficient (t-statistics)	$\Delta F48_{12,t}$ Coefficient (t-statistics)
Constant	0.02 (0.27)	0.01 (0.10)	0.01 (0.11)	0.01 (0.19)
$\Delta Fn_{v,t-1}$	0.20 (1.11)	0.15 (0.93)	0.14 (0.84)	0.13 (0.83)
$\Delta Fn_{v,t-2}$	−0.22 (−1.22)	−0.13 (−0.83)	−0.17 (−1.22)	−0.18 (−1.36)
$\Delta \pi_{t-1}$	0.13 (1.00)	0.10 (0.85)	0.08 (0.72)	0.07 (0.72)
ΔU_{t-1}	0.33 (0.73)	0.32 (0.81)	0.24 (0.71)	0.20 (0.66)
$\Delta M1D_{t-1}$	0.23 (1.43)	0.23 (1.63)	0.14 (1.12)	0.10 (0.88)
ΔP_t^D	0.83 (2.43)	0.65 (2.19)	0.57 (2.36)	0.51 (2.49)
R^2	0.24	0.17	0.15	0.13

*Standard errors are corrected for heteroskedasticity using White 1980. A sample calculation of a forward rate revision can be found in Appendix C.

four-year bond that begins eleven months in the future. A simulation using these coefficients suggests that an increase in the probability of a Democratic victory from 10 to 80 percent, something similar to that which occurred during the 1992 election, implies that forward rates will rise by between thirty-five and sixty basis points. Therefore, over the course of an election cycle, fluctuations in electoral probabilities can lead to relatively large swings in interest rates.

5.4   Conclusion

The empirical analysis conducted in chapter 4 produced a series of results that support the existence of rational partisan political cycles.

One serious limitation evident in both the estimations in chapter 4 and in the literature as a whole is the inability to measure explicitly variables such as political uncertainty and electoral probabilities. This chapter has proposed a solution by measuring the probability that a candidate will win an election using a calculation of the electoral probability based on information available to the market prior to the election. This technique, which we call the electoral option, produces what seem to be realistic electoral probabilities. That is, the probabilities generated reflect public sentiment prior to the election.[25]

This chapter presents two applications that test models of partisan political cycles using our calculated electoral probability data. The first improves the estimations presented in chapter 4 by including an explicit measure of postelectoral surprise, rather than dummy variables. The second measures the response of preelectoral financial markets to electoral information. Bringing together the rational partisan theory and rational expectations models of financial markets yields well-defined and testable reactions to preelectoral probabilities. The results presented in this chapter provide strong support for the rational partisan theory.

Appendix A

Converting Preelectoral Polling into Probabilities

The conversion of preelectoral polls into probabilities is based on the following equation:

$$P_t^D = \text{Prob}[V_{t+\tau}^D > 50\%] = \Phi\left(\frac{V_t^D + \mu\tau - 50}{\sigma\sqrt{\tau}}\right). \qquad \text{(A.5A.1)}$$

As noted in the text and discussed in greater detail below, to produce equation (A.5A.1) the polling data must exhibit the following three characteristics:

a. Changes in polls are independent. Therefore, $\text{cov}(\Delta V_{t+1}^D, \Delta V_t^D) = 0$. This property allows the model to equate the variance of the sum of the changes in the polls to the sum of the individual variances, or mathematically, $\text{var}(\Delta V_{t+1}^D + \Delta V_t^D) = \text{var}(\Delta V_{t+1}^D) + \text{var}(\Delta V_t^D)$. Intuitively, this assumption asserts that in a manner similar to that of stock price movements, individuals change their response to a poll based only upon new information. Thus, current changes in a candidate's polled vote share yield no information about future changes. This assumption may contradict theories stating that a candidate who makes a strong showing in the polls can expect further gains as undecided voters switch to the popular candidate. Because we are using only the share of the two-party vote, however, these so-called momentum effects may already be incorporated into the data.[26] Finally, because momentum may be short-lived, our use of monthly data may further mitigate any momentum effects.[27] Empirical analysis indicates that changes in the polls are not serially correlated and thus supports our independence hypothesis.

b. Changes in polls are identically distributed. An additional complication that may occur with polling data is that the variance of the change in polls may deviate over the course of an electoral cycle. That is, the variance may be larger long before the election as voters have not yet decided, are less informed, or are not yet concerned about the future election. Assuming identically distributed changes implies that polls do not fluctuate any more two years before the election than they do three months before the election. Empirical analysis fails to reject the hypothesis of a uniform variance under an LM test for Autoregressive Conditional Heteroscedasticity (ARCH) and thus supports our claim.[28]

c. Changes in polls are distributed normally. To calculate the probability that the expected vote share is greater than the strike price, we must make some distributional assumptions about the movement of the polls. In option pricing theory, normality is assumed by invoking the central limit theorem under the supposition of continuous trading and a log-normal distribution of stock prices (thus insuring nonnegative stock prices and a finite variance). In the electoral option model, the normality assumption leads to a positive probability of negative polls. The symmetric properties of the normal distribution of the polling data are more realistic than a log-normal distribution, however. In addition, the normality assumption appears empirically valid. The hypothesis that both the polls and their changes are distributed normally cannot be rejected using both Pearson χ^2 and Kolmogorov-Smirnov goodness-of-fit tests.

The acceptance of all three assumptions allows us to implement the electoral option model described by equation (A.5A.1).

Appendix B

The Effect of Electoral Information on the Bond Market

The key assumption throughout this model is that capital markets are efficient. The standard rational expectations model of the term structure of interest rates follows that of Roll (1970), Fama (1984a), and Shiller and McCulloch (1990). More specifically, the model used is similar to those employed by Baxter (1989) and Plosser (1982, 1987).

We define $Q_{k,t}$ as the price at time t of a zero-coupon, pure discount bond with k periods to maturity and maturity value of \$1. Thus

$$Q_{k,t} = e^{(-kR_{k,t})} \tag{A.5B.1}$$

with $R_{k,t}$ the continuously compounded k-period yield to maturity (the k-period interest rate). The expectations theory of the term structure gives the following relationship:

$$R_{k,t} = \frac{1}{k}(R_{1,t} + E_t R_{1,t+1} + E_t R_{1,t+2} + \cdots + E_t R_{1,t+k-1}) + \Psi_{k,t} \tag{A.5B.2}$$

where $\Psi_{k,t}$ is interpreted as a liquidity or term premium with unspecified time series properties, and $E_t R_{1,t+k-1}$ is the expectation taken at time t of the one-period spot rate for the period $t + k - 1$. The price can also be expressed as the combination of the current one-period spot rate and a sequence of one-period forward interest rates:

$$Q_{k,t} = e^{(-R_{1,t} - F1_{2,t} - F1_{3,t} - \cdots - F1_{k,t})}; \quad \text{where} \quad F1_{v,t} = E_t R_{1,t+v-1} + \Psi_{k,t}$$

(A.5B.3)

$F1_{v,t}$ is the implied forward rate at time t of the one-period spot rate for the period $t + v - 1$. This leads to the key variable in the analysis, the forward rate revision, $\Delta F1_{v,t}$:

$$\Delta F1_{v,t} = F1_{v,t} - F1_{v+1,t-1} = E_t R_{1,t+v-1} - E_{t-1} R_{1,t+v-1} + \Lambda_{k,t}. \quad \text{(A.5B.4)}$$

This equation asserts that the forward rate revision is the change in expectations from time $t - 1$ to time t of the rate of the same one-period bond beginning in period $t + v - 1$, plus the change in the term premium ($\Lambda_{k,t}$). With respect to the change in the term premium, Plosser (1982, 1987) notes that relative to the variation in the spot rate, any stochastic variation in $\Lambda_{k,t}$ is likely to be a small component of the variation in expected returns. Therefore, following Plosser as well as Baxter (1989) $\Lambda_{k,t}$ will be treated as a constant.[29]

The expected one-period spot rate at time t, $E_t R_{1,t+v-1}$ can be thought of as the combination of the time $t + v - 1$ expected one-period real return $r^e_{1,t+v-1|t}$ and the expected one-period inflation rate $\pi^e_{1,t+v-1|t}$ or

$$E_t R_{1,t+v-1} = r^e_{1,t+v-1|t} + \pi^e_{1,t+v-1|t}$$

(A.5B.5)

Combining (A.5B.4) and (A.5B.5) arrives at

$$\Delta F1_{v,t} = (r^e_{1,t+v-1|t} - r^e_{1,t+v-1|t-1}) + (\pi^e_{1,t+v-1|t} - \pi^e_{1,t+v-1|t-1}) + \Lambda_{k,t}$$

(A.5B.6)

which states that the forward rate revision consists of innovations in expected future real rates, expected future inflation, and the term premium.

Returning to the results of the rational partisan theory developed in chapter 3, the rate of inflation expected after the election can be characterized as

$$\pi^e_{t+v-1|t} = (P^D_{t+v-1|t})\pi^D + (1 - P^D_{t+v-1|t})\pi^R \qquad \text{(A.5B.7)}$$

with $P^D_{t+v-1|t}$ the subjective probability party D will win the election and thus be in power (at time $t + v - 1$), given all information available before the election (at time t).

Combining the results of our models of the term structure of interest rates and the rational partisan theory (equations (A.5B.6) and (A.5B.7)) and reducing the expression produces the following testable hypothesis:

$$\Delta F1_{v,t} = (r^e_{1,t+v-1|t} - r^e_{1,t+v-1|t-1}) + (P^D_{t+v-1|t} - P^D_{t+v-1|t-1})(\pi^D - \pi^R) + \Lambda_{k,t}.$$
$$\text{(A.5B.8)}$$

This equation represents the fundamental model of how preelectoral political information should affect forward-looking bond yields.

Appendix C

Forward Rate Revision Calculation

To facilitate comprehension of figure 5.3 and the data analysis, the following notation is utilized:

$$Fn_{(v+1),(t-1)} = E_{t-1}R_{n,(t-1)+(v+1)-1} = E_{t-1}R_{n,t+v-1};$$

$$\Rightarrow \Delta Fn_{v,t} = Fn_{v,t} - Fn_{(v+1),(t-1)} = E_t R_{n,t+v-1} - E_{t-1}R_{n,t+v-1} \qquad \text{(A.5C.1)}$$

with $Fn_{(v+1),(t-1)}$ the forward rate, calculated at time $t-1$, for the n-month nominal interest rate starting at time $t + v - 1$. This forward rate is equivalent to the time $t - 1$ expectation of the yield on an n-month bond starting at time $t + v - 1$. Therefore, the forward rate revision, $\Delta Fn_{v,t}$ is the change in expectations from time $t - 1$ to time t

of the n-month interest rate starting at time $t + v - 1$. An enumeration of this notation yields

$$\Delta F24_{12,t} = F24_{12,t} - F24_{13,t-1} = E_t R_{24,t+11} - E_{t-1} R_{24,t+11}. \qquad \text{(A.5C.2)}$$

Thus $\Delta F24_{12,t}$ is the forward rate revision of the twenty-four-month spot, or nominal interest rate, starting eleven months from now (at time $t + 11$). That is, one month ago, at time $t - 1$, $F24_{13,t-1}$ was the implied forward rate of a two-year bond starting one year from then, or eleven months from now. Therefore, today (at time t), this same implied forward rate has now become $F24_{12,t}$, the rate of a two-year bond starting eleven months from now. Hence, $\Delta F24_{1,t}$ identifies the change in expectations for the same two-year bond from time $t - 1$ to time t.

6 Political Cycles in Industrial Economies

6.1 Introduction

The United States is not exceptional. In this chapter and the next, we argue that the evidence on eighteen OECD countries for the period 1960–93 is broadly consistent with our results in chapter 4 for the United States.

A priori, one can identify both similarities and differences when comparing the United States to other industrial democracies. On the one hand, incentives to manipulate the economy before elections as well as ideological and partisan differences among political parties may be as common in other industrial democracies as they are in the United States.[1] In terms of partisan differences, political polarization is at least as prevalent in other industrial countries as it is in the United States. Evidence suggests that social and economic conflicts about the distribution of wealth and income and the explicit gap in economic ideology between left-wing and right-wing parties may be even more significant in several OECD countries than they are in the United States.[2]

As for the differences, two come immediately to mind. First, in most OECD democracies, we do not observe a pure two-party system as in the United States. Specifically, in many countries, proportional electoral systems result in fragmented legislatures with several parties forming coalition governments. Partisan differences in economic policies should be more prevalent in two-party systems where the majority party has full control of executive and legislative powers and less pronounced in countries where broad-based coalitions are the rule. Second, in contrast to the United States, where election dates are fixed, in most industrial democracies the election date can be chosen.[3] This feature may give the incumbent administration a strategic incentive to choose the election date so as to maximize its reelection chances: Elections might be called early if the economy is doing well to capitalize on the government popularity or postponed as long as possible if the ruling government is unpopular. We attempt to take these differences into account in our empirical analysis.

When one considers evidence on a relatively large multicountry sample (eighteen countries) for relatively long time periods (more than three decades), one has to worry about cross-country institutional differences and stability in the parameters, that is, structural breaks at certain points in time. As for institutional differences, we are particularly concerned with the contrast between multiparty systems typical of proportional electoral systems and two-party or two-bloc systems, more common in majoritarian electoral systems. As for structural breaks, we consider the pre- and post-1973 periods as two (possibly) different samples; we consider the hypothesis that the degree and extent of political manipulation of the economy might have fallen since the 1980s because of a greater concern for the inflationary consequences of discretionary policy making in coincidence with the return to a system of semipegged parities in the European countries participating in the European Monetary System (EMS). In other words, we test whether one can find less evidence of political cycles in the latter part of our sample period.

The empirical methodology used in this and the next chapter is similar to that used in chapter 4, and this chapter's main results are consistent with those found for the United States. First, we find no evidence of an electoral cycle in growth and unemployment. In contrast to the evidence for the United States, however, we observe an electoral cycle on the inflation rate, with an upsurge in inflation after elections. Second, as in the case of the United States, the evidence on growth and unemployment for our panel of countries is consistent with the implications of the rational partisan theory and inconsistent with the implications of the Hibbs's partisan model with permanent effects. Third, this evidence in favor of the rational partisan theory is particularly strong for countries with a two-party system or with at least clearly identifiable left- and right-wing governments. Finally, as for the United States there are systematic differences in inflation rates between left- and right-wing regimes that are in accordance with the partisan model.

This chapter is organized as follows. In section 6.2 we present a survey of the empirical literature on the subject. In section 6.3 we describe the data and the empirical methodology used. Section 6.4 presents the results of tests of the rational partisan theory. Section 6.5 presents the results for the traditional partisan theory; section 6.6 then discusses some possible objections to our results. In section 6.7 we present the tests for the political business cycle models. Section 6.8 presents tests of an alternative model of passive opportunistic behavior of policymakers in the presence of endogenous elections. Section 6.9 summarizes the chapter's main results and conclusions.

6.2   Previous Empirical Results

Multicountry studies on political cycles are relatively rare. Hibbs (1977) considers a large sample of industrial countries and provides evidence in favor of the partisan theory. Alt (1985) finds evidence consistent with the partisan model looking at unemployment in twelve OECD countries. Paldam (1989a,b) reports favorable evidence of partisan effects using annual data on output and unemployment in several OECD countries. Alesina (1989) provides some qualitative tests with annual data using the same sample of countries; his results suggest that the rational partisan theory is broadly consistent with the evidence. Alvarez, Garrett, and Lange (1989) suggest that the degree of success of partisan policies may depend on the characteristics of labor market institutions and of unions' behavior; while Garrett and Lange (1991) suggest that partisan differences in industrial democracies persist in spite of the changes imposed on the partisan behavior of conservative and left-leaning governments by the increasingly higher degree of international interdependence. On the contrary, Sheffrin (1989) finds inconclusive results for the rational partisan theory, although his definition of "unexpected change" of governments is somewhat questionable. In fact, Sheffrin disregards the fact that in several countries the same party or coalition was elected repeatedly with no electoral uncertainty.[4]

The direct multicountry evidence on the political business cycle models is quite weak: Paldam (1979) finds very weak evidence (if any at all) of Nordhaus's political business cycle on output and unemployment using a sample of seventeen OECD countries; Alesina (1989), Alesina and Roubini (1992), and Alesina, Cohen, and Roubini (1992, 1993) reject the main implication of the political business cycle model on output and unemployment and find only some postelectoral effects on inflation. Frey and Schneider (1978, 1989) argue that preelectoral manipulations of the economy and pursuit of partisan goals are not incompatible. They contend that the evidence for many OECD economies suggests that partisan goals (especially in fiscal policy) will be pursued only as long as the incumbent parties have high degrees of popularity and are likely to be reelected. When election dates become closer or the ruling parties lose their popularity in the polls, they will follow fiscal policies aimed at maximizing their reelection chances.

In this chapter we consider the various theories in a unified framework. Furthermore, unlike most of the previous research, we use quarterly rather than annual data and employ more robust statistical tests. The use of quarterly data is important because the precise timing of cyclical fluctuations in relation to elections is crucial for the theories. In this regard, the contributions methodologically closest to this chapter are our previous studies (Alesina and Roubini 1992, Alesina, Cohen and Roubini 1992, 1993), in which we found evidence in favor of the rational partisan theory for a sample of OECD countries for 1960–1987.

6.3 Data and Specification of Empirical Tests

6.3.1 Data

We consider the OECD countries that have been democracies in the sample period, 1960 to 1993. The extent of the sample is limited by availability of quarterly data; in fact for some countries not all the series are available even for this period.[5] The countries included are Australia, Austria, Belgium, Canada, Denmark, Finland, France, Germany, Japan, Ireland, Italy, the Netherlands, New Zealand, Norway, Sweden, Switzerland, the United Kingdom, and the United States.

The economic data are quarterly observations on inflation rates, output growth, and unemployment rates. Inflation is defined as the yearly rate of change of CPI from IMF, IFS data. Output growth is obtained as the rate of change of real GNP (or GDP), also from IMF, IFS. For unemployment we use the total standardized unemployment rate from the OECD main economic indicators. More details on country-specific data issues can be found in table 6.A.1 in the appendix to this chapter. The political data are the election dates, the dates of changes of governments, and the political orientation of various governments. Dates of regime changes and elections do not always coincide in parliamentary systems in which changes of coalitions take place after elections and at other times as well. Table 6.A.2 in the appendix to this chapter summarizes this information. Sources for these political data are Alt 1985 and Banks 1994.

The identification of the changes of the political orientation of governments is usually unambiguous. Whenever ambiguities occur in the case of coalition governments, we have followed Alt's and Banks's conventions. The classification of the political orientation of the government is more difficult. In bipartisan political systems (such as these of the United States, the United Kingdom, Canada, Australia, and New Zealand), the classification of governments as relatively left and right (or relatively progressive and conservative) is quite simple. In another group of countries (France, Germany, and Sweden) there are usually more than two leading parties, but the coalition governments may still be classified rather unambiguously along the left-right divide. In the remaining countries, multiparty coalitions form governments, and the classification along partisan lines is more difficult; the ruling coalition can be centrist, center-left, or center-right and is often without a clear-cut partisan or ideological bent. Although in most of the analysis we have made a decision and have classified these governments as on either the left or the right, we have also derived finer measures of the degree of partisanship and tested the robustness of our results for these more subtle classifications of the government's ideological orientation. It should be noted that positive results for the partisan theory are found for those countries in which there are no ambiguities about the classification of the government's political orientation. Also, the classification is made on a priori ground and is never changed after the first regression is run.

6.3.2 Specification of Empirical Tests

The simplest and most direct way of testing the various theories is to run panel regressions of time-series cross-section data. For instance, for output growth:

$$y_t = \alpha_0 + \alpha_1 y_{t-1} + \alpha_2 y_{t-2} \ldots + \alpha_n y_{t-n} + \alpha_{n+1} y w_i + \alpha_{n+2} \text{PDUM}_t + \varepsilon_t$$

$$(6.1)$$

where y_t is the stacked vector of time-series data on output growth for the countries in the sample (this rate of growth is defined as $y_{it} = (x_{it} - x_{it-4}/x_{it-4})(100)$ where x_i is the level of real GDP in country i at time t); and $y w_t$ is a proxy for the growth of the world economy (this proxy is obtained as the average growth in the seven largest economies in our sample, weighted by each country's share of GDP over the total).[6] An analogous definition is used to construct proxies for OECD unemployment and inflation. PDUM is a dummy variable that captures the implication of different theories. We made use of Aikake and Schwartz tests to find the optimal lag structure in the autoregressive specification for the dependent variable.[7] In many respects, this is a generalization for a panel data set of the regressions for the United States economy discussed in chapter 4.

Because the sample includes open economies (most of which are small), we must control for the effect of the world economy on domestic economies, for two reasons. First, politicians' partisan or opportunistic goals are likely to be defined, in small open economies, in relation to the rest of the world. Second, regardless of governments' goals, international trade and financial linkages make the OECD economies highly interdependent. There are three basic ways to control for the world business cycle. The first, described in equation (6.1), is to add a proxy for an OECD average of the same variable (yw) as a regressor in the equation. The second is to redefine each country's variable as the difference between the actual variable and the OECD proxy of the same variable. The third is to add time dummies in the regression that capture the years of the world business cycle with higher- or lower-than-average growth. Our results concerning the relative performance of various political variables are insensitive to the procedure used to control for the world business cycle.

In the remainder of this chapter we present results of panel regressions on the different political theories of the business cycle. We make use of a so-called fixed-effects model with constant slopes. The fixed effects are country-specific dummy variables controlling for cross-country differences in long-term growth, unemployment and inflation rates; these differences may be due to country-specific factors and institutions not captured by the models' other variables. The assumption of constant slopes implies that, apart from these country-specific level effects, all the other parameters of the model are constant and equal across countries.[8]

6.4   Evidence on the Rational Partisan Theory

6.4.1   Description of the Test

We start with tests of the rational partisan theory. We construct a DRPTN political dummy variable equivalent to the one used in chapter 4 for the United States. Again, we consider $N = 4, 6, 8$ consistently with the idea that the transitory output effects might last between one and two years. This dummy variable assumes values different from zero only after actual changes in governments' partisan orientation. The theory suggests that only policy "surprises" should have real effects. Ideally, one would want to construct, for every country, a SURPRISE variable similar to the one used in chapter 5 for the United States. This task goes beyond the scope of the present volume and presents rather challenging difficulties.[9] Lacking an explicit measure of SURPRISE, one must choose between two alternatives: code only actual changes of governments, as we do, or code every election and every new government (even if it is the same coalition of parties). Several arguments speak in favor of the first choice. First, in several countries, particularly until the mid-1970s, several parties (or coalitions) were routinely reappointed with virtually no political uncertainty. Thus, coding each election as a surprise would vastly overestimate the amount of uncertainty. Second, in parliamentary democracies, coalition reshufflings may occur even without elections. Finally, elections can be called at (almost) any time. Thus, in theory, one should measure a certain amount of surprise in every period, not only when elections are actually called. For these reasons we adopt the first choice, albeit an imperfect one.

6.4.2 Tests for the Rational Partisan Theory

Column (1) of table 6.1 reports the result of the dynamic panel OLS regressions for the entire sample of countries and the time period 1960 to 1993. The dependent variable y is the rate of GNP growth; the AR(1) specification has been chosen as the optimal according to the Aikake and Schwartz test;[10] the regression includes fixed effects in the form of country dummies. The political dummy DRPT6 has the expected sign and is statistically significant at the 1 percent confidence level: A change in government to the right (left) leads to a transitory fall (increase) in output growth. The one-quarter lag in the political dummy is consistent with a reasonable interval between a change in regime (in quarter t) and change in policy (in period $t + 1$). The regressions with DRPT4 and DRPT8 (columns (2) and (3)) yield analogous results: the pattern of the coefficients suggests that partisan effects are observable from about the second to the eighth or ninth quarter after a government change. In terms of coefficient values and their significance, for the full sample of eighteen countries the coefficient estimate is largest (in absolute value) for DRPT4 (0.40), followed by DRPT6 (0.35), and smallest for DRPT8 (0.25). In terms of statistical significance, however, DRPT6 has a higher t-statistic (3.26) than DRPT4 (3.09) or DRPT8 (2.71). These results are consistent with our findings on U.S. data discussed in chapter 4.

Columns (4) to (6) present the results of the same regressions for a subset of countries that have either a pure two-party system or at least more clearly identifiable left and right coalitions: Australia, Canada, France, Germany, New Zealand, Sweden, the United Kingdom and the United States. The other countries in the sample have more fragmented political systems with governments formed from large coalitions of parties (often center-left) that are sometimes short-lived and unstable. In the regressions for the bipartisan systems, in fact, the coefficients on the political dummy are much larger in absolute value and have t-statistics systematically higher than those in first three

Table 6.1
Rational partisan theory
Dependent variable: rate of growth of output (y)

Independent variables	(1) Coefficient (t-statistics)	(2) Coefficient (t-statistics)	(3) Coefficient (t-statistics)	(4) Coefficient (t-statistics)	(5) Coefficient (t-statistics)	(6) Coefficient (t-statistics)
$y(-1)$	0.67 (45.8)	0.67 (46.0)	0.68 (45.8)	0.67 (30.1)	0.68 (30.6)	0.67 (29.7)
y_w	0.36 (12.5)	0.36 (12.4)	0.36 (12.6)	0.26 (8.10)	0.26 (7.9)	0.26 (8.07)
DRPT4(-1)	—	−0.40 (3.09)	—	—	−0.48 (3.20)	—
DRPT6(-1)	−0.35 (3.26)	—	—	−0.53 (4.35)	—	—
DRPT8(-1)	—	—	−0.25 (2.71)	—	—	−0.40 (3.75)
US	−0.41 (1.94)	−0.41 (1.93)	−0.41 (1.96)	−0.04 (0.22)	−0.04 (0.25)	−0.03 (0.17)
UK	−0.55 (2.65)	−0.55 (2.64)	−0.54 (2.55)	−0.20 (1.19)	−0.21 (1.20)	−0.20 (1.16)
France	−0.15 (0.71)	−0.15 (0.70)	−0.16 (0.74)	0.15 (0.87)	0.14 (0.80)	0.15 (0.85)
Germany	−0.35 (1.67)	−0.35 (1.66)	−0.35 (1.67)	−0.01 (0.06)	−0.02 (0.05)	−0.02 (0.01)
Sweden	−0.45 (1.93)	−0.46 (1.96)	−0.46 (1.93)	−0.16 (0.89)	−0.18 (0.97)	−0.16 (0.86)

Canada	0.02 (0.08)	0.02 (0.10)	0.02 (0.09)	0.35 (2.06)	0.35 (2.00)	0.36 (2.00)
Australia	-0.05 (0.24)	-0.06 (0.22)	-0.05 (0.26)	0.28 (1.64)	0.28 (1.60)	0.29 (1.68)
New Zealand	-0.45 (2.16)	-0.45 (2.15)	-0.44 (2.08)	-0.11 (0.63)	-0.11 (0.66)	-0.10 (0.60)
Belgium	-0.37 (1.79)	-0.37 (1.76)	-0.38 (1.79)	—	—	—
Ireland	0.68 (3.16)	0.68 (3.15)	0.67 (3.11)	—	—	—
Austria	0.12 (0.59)	0.12 (0.56)	0.17 (0.80)	—	—	—
Denmark	-0.32 (1.56)	-0.32 (1.53)	-0.32 (1.56)	—	—	—
Italy	-0.01 (0.03)	-0.01 (0.01)	-0.01 (0.07)	—	—	—
Netherlands	-0.07 (0.32)	-0.07 (0.31)	-0.07 (0.32)	—	—	—
Norway	-0.03 (0.18)	-0.03 (0.15)	-0.06 (0.19)	—	—	—
Finland	-0.24 (1.00)	-0.25 (1.06)	-0.25 (1.02)	—	—	—
Switzerland	-0.47 (2.24)	-0.47 (2.73)	-0.47 (2.26)	—	—	—
Japan	0.77 (3.63)	0.77 (3.61)	0.81 (3.81)	—	—	—
R^2	0.64	0.64	0.64	0.64	0.63	0.63

columns. The values of the coefficients in column (4) imply that about eighteen months after a change of regime to the right (left) the rate of growth of GNP is about 1.1 percent below (above) its steady-state value. Thus the difference in the rate of growth between the beginning of a left-wing government and the beginning of a right-wing government reaches a peak of about 2.2 percent, a rather large value considering that the average growth in the sample is 3.4 percent per year. Even the value of these coefficients is quite similar to those in our findings for the United States. The world dummy is significant, both statistically and economically. We obtain results on the political dummies that are very similar to those in table 6.1, however, even when we do not correct for the world business cycle.[11]

We move next to consider the tests of the rational partisan theory model on the unemployment rate. One has to be cautious because of the empirical high persistency of the unemployment rate, especially in European countries: Numerous studies suggest that the behavior of the U.S. unemployment rate is quite different from that of other OECD countries. Specifically, whereas there is some evidence that the U.S. unemployment rate is stationary and mean reverting, the high unemployment rates in the European countries appear to be highly persistent over time and possibly characterized by a nonstationary behavior.[12] One way of controlling for possible nonstationarities in the unemployment process is to take deviations of the unemployment rate of a particular country from the average unemployment rate in the OECD region; this approach also allows a control for the components of a country's unemployment rate not due to world business cycle movements. Therefore, in table 6.2 we consider the difference (UDIFF) between the domestic unemployment rate (U) and the OECD unemployment rate (UW) defined analogously to the average world GNP growth. Table 6.2 shows that by considering such differences, nonstationarity issues are somewhat mitigated but not completely eliminated; the coefficients on the lags of the UDIFF variable add up to 0.98, showing that this variable is still highly persistent over time.[13]

Table 6.2
Rational partisan theory
Dependent variable: unemployment rate (relative to OECD average) (UDIFF)

Independent variables	(1) Coefficient (t-statistics)	(2) Coefficient (t-statistics)
UDIFF(-1)	1.10 (49.7)	1.09 (33.2)
UDIFF(-2)	-0.12 (5.29)	-0.11 (3.39)
DRPT6(-2)	0.08 (4.00)	0.13 (4.47)
US	0.003 (0.09)	0.01 (0.47)
UK	0.05 (1.39)	0.05 (1.64)
France	0.06 (1.54)	0.07 (1.75)
Germany	0.007 (0.19)	-0.01 (0.20)
Sweden	-0.01 (0.24)	-0.04 (0.97)
Canada	0.04 (1.01)	0.06 (1.57)
Australia	0.05 (1.41)	0.06 (1.60)
New Zealand	-0.03 (0.57)	-0.06 (1.14)
Belgium	0.03 (0.80)	—
Ireland	0.13 (2.67)	—
Austria	-0.03 (0.68)	—
Denmark	0.10 (2.32)	—
Italy	0.05 (1.30)	—
Netherlands	0.07 (1.62)	—

Table 6.2 (continued)

Independent variables	(1) Coefficient (t-statistics)	(2) Coefficient (t-statistics)
Norway	−0.01 (0.36)	—
Finland	0.07 (2.10)	—
Switzerland	−0.04 (0.70)	—
Japan	−0.07 (1.61)	—
R^2	0.98	0.97

Because the unemployment rate in many countries is close to being nonstationary and only mildly correlated with the world business cycle, the difference variable is mean-reverting but remains very persistent.

The table shows results consistent with those on GDP growth. The political dummy DRPT6 is significant at the 1 percent level, and the fit is even stronger when the sample is restricted to seven bipartisan countries (column (2)). The dummy DRPT6 is lagged two quarters to capture the slower response of unemployment to policy changes relative to output growth. In any case, analogous results (available upon request) are obtained if this variable is lagged only one quarter or when DRPT4 or DRPT8 are used. The values in the second column of table 6.2 imply that about six quarters after a change of regime toward the right (left), the unemployment rate is about 1.3 percentage points above (below) normal.

We should note that, since the variable UDIFF shows a high level of persistence, even a temporary policy shock has rather persistent effects over time. Although this implies that partisan shocks may lead to persistent effects on the unemployment rate even after the policy surprise has disappeared, as we discuss in section 6.5, these effects do not imply evidence in favor of the traditional partisan theory. In fact, we provide evidence that partisan dummies for the second half of an administration do not significantly affect the unemployment rate. This means that even if one finds that the unemployment rate is on average lower in the second half of a left-wing administration than it is in a right-wing one, this effect may be due simply to the persistent temporal propagation of the original partisan shock in the first half of the administration rather than a further impulse of a partisan variable in the second half of these administrations.

We consider next the evidence on the inflation rate. We define two political dummies. One, RADM, is the panel data equivalent of the dichotomous dummy for Democratic/Republican administrations defined in chapter 4. Here it classifies the governments of the eighteen countries in the sample in terms of pure right- and left-wing regimes. The other dummy, ADM, tries to distinguish more finely the center-right and center-left governments from those more clearly rightist and leftist. Thus, the ADM variable is defined as follows:

$$ADM = \begin{cases} 1 \text{ if a right-wing government is in office, including the} \\ \quad \text{quarter of the change in government} \\ 1/2 \text{ if a center-right government is in office, including the} \\ \quad \text{quarter of the change in government} \\ -1/2 \text{ if a center-left government is in office, including the} \\ \quad \text{quarter of the change in government} \\ -1 \text{ if a left-wing government is in office, including the} \\ \quad \text{quarter of the change in government} \end{cases}$$

In table 6.3, the dependent variable is domestic inflation (π) defined as the yearly rate of change of the consumer price index (CPI), i.e., $\pi = ((CPI_t - CPI_{t-4})/CPI_{t-4})100$. The variable for world inflation (πw) is defined analogously to the world average growth.

The results in table 6.3 show that the coefficients on ADM always have the expected sign for both the eighteen-country and eight-country samples and are statistically significant at the 10 percent confidence

Table 6.3
Partisan theory
Dependent variable: inflation rate (π)

Independent variables	(1) Coefficient (t-statistics)	(2) Coefficient (t-statistics)	(3) Coefficient (t-statistics)	(4) Coefficient (t-statistics)
$\pi(-1)$	1.13 (5.58)	1.22 (40.2)	1.13 (55.8)	1.22 (40.3)
$\pi(-2)$	−0.15 (4.90)	−0.26 (5.58)	−0.14 (4.90)	−0.26 (5.59)
$\pi(-3)$	−0.11 (5.82)	−0.08 (3.11)	−0.11 (5.82)	−0.09 (3.11)
πw	0.11 (13.1)	0.12 (9.82)	0.11 (13.1)	0.11 (9.78)
ADM(−1)	−0.05 (1.80)	−0.05 (1.67)	—	—
RADM(−1)	—	—	−0.03 (1.46)	−0.04 (1.39)
US	−0.06 (0.63)	−0.05 (0.55)	−0.05 (0.69)	−0.05 (0.57)
UK	0.39 (3.89)	0.38 (3.87)	0.39 (3.86)	0.38 (3.81)
France	0.19 (1.93)	0.18 (1.93)	0.18 (1.85)	0.18 (1.88)
Germany	−0.20 (2.01)	−0.20 (2.19)	−0.21 (2.15)	−0.21 (2.30)
Sweden	0.22 (2.23)	0.21 (2.18)	0.23 (2.33)	0.21 (2.26)
Canada	0.03 (0.36)	0.02 (0.26)	0.03 (0.36)	0.03 (0.79)
Australia	0.22 (2.22)	0.21 (2.21)	0.21 (2.16)	0.21 (2.16)
New Zealand	0.46 (6.40)	0.44 (4.33)	0.64 (6.32)	0.66 (6.26)
Belgium	−0.01 (0.18)	—	−0.02 (0.23)	—
Ireland	0.44 (6.36)	—	0.43 (4.24)	—
Austria	−0.07 (0.75)	—	−0.07 (0.70)	—

Table 6.3 (continued)

Independent variables	(1) Coefficient (t-statistics)	(2) Coefficient (t-statistics)	(3) Coefficient (t-statistics)	(4) Coefficient (t-statistics)
Denmark	0.22 (2.24)	—	0.21 (2.15)	—
Italy	0.52 (5.14)	—	0.52 (5.01)	—
Netherlands	−0.06 (0.63)	—	−0.05 (6.54)	—
Norway	0.18 (1.88)	—	0.18 (1.82)	—
Finland	0.27 (2.76)	—	0.27 (2.70)	—
Switzerland	−0.09 (0.92)	—	−0.08 (0.82)	—
Japan	0.07	—	0.06 (0.58)	—
R^2	0.94	0.95	0.96	0.95

level or better (columns (1) and (2)). The coefficients are not statistically significant, however, when we use the RADM classification (columns (3) and (4)).[14] The value of the coefficients in the regressions in column (1) imply a difference in the steady-state inflation rate between a left- and a right-wing regime of about 0.8 percent for both the eight-country and the full sample of countries. This relatively low value reflects the fact that our sample includes the 1960s, with a low and stable inflation, and countries, such as Germany, with a low inflation rate throughout the sample period.

In the regressions of table 6.3 several coefficients on the country dummies are statistically significant, indicating that different countries have had substantially different average inflation rates in the sample period considered here. Specifically, if we consider the results in column 1, we can identify three groups of countries. A first group, including Italy, Ireland, New Zealand and the United Kingdom, shows, in the sample, inflation rates significantly above average (both in absolute terms and statistically). In a second group (the United States, Germany, Canada, Belgium, Austria, the Netherlands, Switzerland and Japan), the country dummy is statistically insignificant (or, in the case of Germany, negative and statistically significant). This group has inflation rates significantly below those of the first group. A third group includes France, Sweden, Australia, Denmark, and Norway: These countries have inflation rates (statistically) higher than the second group but also (statistically) lower than the high inflation first group. An often cited explanation for these country differences is the degree of central bank independence (see Alesina 1989; Grilli, Masciandaro, and Tabellini 1991; Alesina and Summers 1993; and Cukierman 1992). More independent central banks appear to have been associated with lower average inflation rates. We could add as a regressor in the inflation equation one of the indexes of central bank independence. However, such an index assigns numerical values to different countries, and these numbers do not vary over time. Therefore, the country dummies already included in the regression capture the same effect. For more discussion of the effects of central bank independence in a partisan model, see chapter 8.

6.4.3   Stability and Robustness of the Rational Partisan Theory Effects over Time

An important issue is the robustness of the results over time. For a start, political cycles might have been mitigated in the last decade. Many OECD countries have shown a greater concern for the inflationary consequences of discretionary policy making, and a number of European countries moved to a system of semipegged parities (the EMS) in the 1980s as a way to commit to stable low-inflation monetary policies; other countries (most notably New Zealand) have increased the independence of their central banks as a way of enforcing low-inflation policies. It is therefore quite interesting to test whether

Table 6.4
Rational partisan theory
Dependent variable: rate of growth of output (y), 1960–1980

Independent variables	(1) Coefficient (t-statistics)	(2) Coefficient (t-statistics)	(3) Coefficient (t-statistics)	(4) Coefficient (t-statistics)
$y(-1)$	0.67 (35.0)	0.67 (34.9)	0.62 (19.9)	0.61 (19.5)
yw	0.38 (9.57)	0.38 (9.56)	0.29 (6.59)	0.30 (6.73)
DRPT4(-1)	−0.46 (2.48)	—	−0.56 (2.67)	—
DRPT6(-1)	—	−0.33 (2.13)	—	−0.62 (3.51)
R^2	0.61	0.61	0.56	0.56

there is less evidence of political cycles in the last decade. Although the choice of any point as the moment of the presumed shift from a discretionary policy-making regime with high inflation to an anti-inflation regime is arbitrary, we pick 1980 as the presumed shift point. Sensitivity analysis shows that the results do not depend on the choice of 1980 as the break point; similar results are obtained using 1983, 1985 or 1987.[15]

Table 6.4 presents the results of regressions similar to those in table 6.1, but using the sample period 1960–1980 instead of 1960–1993.[16] As a comparison of table 6.4 with table 6.1 shows, there is no systematic evidence of a less pronounced partisan cycle in the 1980s; both the coefficient estimate and the statistical significance of the DRPT variable are as high in 1960–1993 as in 1960–1980 (or higher). If anything, the results for the period including the 1980s and 1990s are even stronger than those for the previous period. Therefore, the evidence suggests that political cycles in output have not dampened in the post-1980 period.

A related hypothesis regarding regime shifts is that political cycles are more prevalent under flexible exchange regimes than under fixed

Table 6.5
Rational partisan theory
Dependent variable: rate of growth of output (y), 1960–1972

Independent variables	(1) Coefficients (t-statistics)	(2) Coefficients (t-statistics)
	18-country sample	8-country sample
$y(-1)$	0.65 (23.9)	0.60 (14.2)
yw	0.26 (2.71)	0.12 (1.18)
DRPT6(-1)	-0.21 (0.81)	-0.30 (1.03)
R^2	0.53	0.43

exchange rates, such as the Bretton Woods period that ended in 1973.[17] Table 6.5 shows the results of regressions for 1960–1972. Partisan cycles appear mostly as a post-1973 phenomenon associated with the more discretionary economic policies that followed the switch to a flexible exchange rate: Although the coefficients on the DRPT variable have the expected sign in the pre-1973 period, they are not statistically significant.[18] These results are significant in that they show that macroeconomic manipulation of the economy seemed to be less systematic before 1973. Sensitivity analysis (available upon request) regarding the temporal stability of the unemployment results is consistent with the results on output growth.

We consider next the robustness of the results on the inflation rate. The results on partisan effects in inflation rates presented in table 6.3 were somewhat weaker than those we found in our previous work that considered the shorter sample period 1960–1987 (see Alesina and Roubini 1992). It is possible that the convergence of inflation rates in the last decade has reduced partisan differences in inflation rates among industrial countries. Moreover, since the middle of the 1980s, the increasing credibility (and reduced number of realignments) of the European Monetary System has been instrumental in leading to a

Table 6.6
Partisan theory: 1960–87
Dependent variable: inflation rate (π)

Independent variables	(1) Coefficient (t-statistics)	(2) Coefficient (t-statistics)	(3) Coefficient (t-statistics)	(4) Coefficient (t-statistics)
	18-country sample		8-country sample	
$\pi(-1)$	1.12 (50.1)	1.12 (50.1)	1.24 (36.4)	1.24 (36.4)
$\pi(-2)$	−0.15 (4.65)	−0.15 (4.66)	−0.31 (5.89)	−0.31 (5.90)
$\pi(-3)$	−0.11 (5.14)	−0.11 (5.15)	−0.07 (2.14)	−0.07 (2.15)
πw	0.12 (12.3)	0.12 (12.3)	0.12 (9.64)	0.12 (9.56)
ADM(−1)	−0.07 (2.15)	—	−0.09 (2.46)	—
RADM(−1)	—	−0.05 (1.66)	—	−0.07 (2.05)
R^2	0.93	0.93	0.95	0.95

greater convergence of inflation rates in Europe. To test whether partisan differences in inflation rates have dampened since the 1980s, we run the regressions in table 6.3 on the 1960–1987 sample used in our previous work. Table 6.6 reports the results. The coefficient on the ADM variable is now statistically significant at the 5 percent confidence level or better for both the eighteen-country and the eight-country samples, whereas the coefficient on the RADM is significant at the 5 percent confidence level for the eight-country sample and at the 10 percent level for the eighteen-country sample. A comparison of table 6.6 with table 6.3 also shows that the results for 1960–1987 are stronger than those for 1960–1993 in terms of both the statistical significance of the coefficients and the absolute value of the coefficients representing the partisan effects on inflation. The values of the coefficients in the regressions in table 6.6 (columns (1) and (3)) imply a difference in the steady-state inflation rate between a left- and a right-wing regime of about 1.3 percent for the eight-country sample and 1.1 percent for the full sample of countries.

To test for the role of the exchange rate regime in constraining governments' inflationary policies, we run the same regressions of tables 6.3 and 6.6 for the period before and after the Bretton Woods regime of fixed exchange rates, that is, before and after 1973. In these regressions (available upon request) the coefficient on the RADM and ADM dummy are not statistically significant in the 1960–1972 period of fixed exchange rates; in the post–1972 period of flexible exchange rates, the results are statistically comparable to those in table 6.3. Therefore, in the post–1972 period, the coefficient estimates imply a difference in the inflation rate across political regimes significantly larger than under fixed rates.[19]

In summary, the regressions on all the macroeconomic variables improve in the post-1972 period because in the fixed exchange rate period (1960–72 in our sample) the macroeconomic policies of each country were more constrained and integrated; systematically, the t-statistics on the political dummies improve and the value of the coefficients increase in absolute value in the post-1972 sample. The problem in pursuing this comparison, pre- and post-1972, however, is that very few regimes changed in the pre-1973 period (see table 6.A.2 in the appendix); many countries had no changes of regimes in the 1960s. Thus, the political dummies in pre-1973 regressions are very imprecisely estimated and hard to compare with the post-1972 sample.

An important difference between the results obtained here and those found for the United States in chapter 4 is the evidence of a regime change in the OECD countries after the move to floating exchange rates in 1973, a shift which was not found for the United States. This difference is not surprising but, on the contrary, reassuring. In fact, the United States was the leader of the Bretton Woods system and thus maintained a large degree of monetary autonomy in spite of the existence of fixed exchange rates. Up to 1973, the discipline of fixed exchange rates was instead more binding on the other small open economies in the OECD region; thus, their ability to pursue independent monetary policies was much more limited.

6.5   Traditional Partisan Theory

Hibbs's partisan theory implies permanent differences in growth and unemployment in addition to permanent differences in inflation across governments. Thus, one way of comparing the Hibbs's traditional partisan theory with the rational partisan theory is to run the same regressions of table 6.1 (on output) and table 6.2 (on unemployment) using the "permanent" partisan dummies RADM or ADM rather than the "transitory" political dummy DRPT. Tables 6.7 and 6.8 show the results of these regressions. In the growth regressions, the coefficients on the political dummy are insignificant, even though with the expected sign. In the unemployment regressions, the coefficients have the expected sign but are not statistically significant in the eight-country regression. Quite surprisingly, in the full sample, the coefficient on the permanent partisan dummy is significant at the 10 percent confidence level when we use the RADM dummy and at the 5 percent level when we use the ADM dummy.[20] This last result for the full sample is surprising because it is the only evidence in favor of permanent partisan differences in economic activity, as suggested by the traditional partisan hypothesis of Hibbs. As we argued for the case of the United States, this result may be spurious and due to a number of factors: first, in the first half of an administration, the RADM variable overlaps with the DRPT variable so that the RADM variable might be capturing the effects of the DRPT variable rather than permanent effects; second, because the unemployment rate is highly persistent in most OECD countries, such effects from the first half of the term might propagate through the second half even if the partisan effect is due only to the original electoral surprise.

Table 6.7
Traditional partisan theory
Dependent variable: rate of growth of output (y)

Independent variables	(1) Coefficient (t-statistics)	(2) Coefficient (t-statistics)	(3) Coefficient (t-statistics)	(4) Coefficient (t-statistics)
	18-country sample		8-country sample	
$y(-1)$	0.68 (46.4)	0.68 (46.4)	0.69 (31.0)	0.69 (31.0)
yw	0.36 (12.3)	0.36 (12.3)	0.25 (7.72)	0.25 (7.72)
RADM(-1)	−0.01 (0.23)	—	−0.04 (0.70)	—
ADM(-1)	—	−0.03 (0.45)	—	−0.04 (0.71)
R^2	0.64	0.64	0.63	0.63

Table 6.8
Traditional partisan theory
Dependent variable: unemployment rate (relative to OECD average) (UDIFF)

Independent variables	(1) Coefficient (t-statistics)	(2) Coefficient (t-statistics)	(3) Coefficient (t-statistics)	(4) Coefficient (t-statistics)
	18-country sample		8-country sample	
UDIFF(-1)	1.11 (49.9)	1.11 (49.9)	1.11 (33.7)	1.11 (33.7)
UDIFF(-2)	−0.13 (5.55)	−0.12 (5.52)	−0.13 (3.87)	−0.13 (3.85)
RADM(-1)	0.02 (1.74)	—	0.01 (1.18)	—
ADM(-1)	—	0.02 (2.07)	—	0.02 (1.29)
R^2	0.98	0.98	0.97	0.98

An additional test shows that the results of table 6.8 in favor of the traditional partisan theory are in fact spurious. We define a new dummy variable SEC, the "complement" of the DRPT variable; that is, it takes the value of 1 during right-wing governments *after* the first N quarters, and −1 *after* the first N quarters of left-wing governments. We add this new variable in our panel regressions of tables 6.1 and 6.2. The coefficient on this variable has the opposite sign to the DRPT dummies and is statistically insignificant.[21] The coefficients on the DRPT dummies, instead, remain statistically highly significant. This test confirms that the effects of changes of governments on growth and unemployment are transitory rather than permanent. These results also suggest that any persistent unemployment effect of a partisan shock (captured by the results for RADM in table 6.8) is due only to the initial policy shock that persists over time because of the intrinsic dynamics of the unemployment rate. The effect deriving from the original partisan shock instead does not have further impulse effects on the unemployment (or growth) rate after a few quarters.

The results on the rational and traditional partisan theories, viewed together, indirectly provide some empirical support for the inflation bias model of Kydland and Prescott (1977) and Barro and Gordon (1983a), where the equilibrium inflation rate depends on the degree to which policymakers attempt to reduce the unemployment rate from its natural rate. In fact, our regressions show that a permanent difference in inflation rate is associated with temporary deviations of output and unemployment from trend; consistently with the models of inflation bias, real effects occur only when there are unexpected policy shocks, in our case as a result of electoral surprises. The results also suggest that administrations more concerned about growth and unemployment than inflation are caught in the suboptimal equilibrium with an inflation bias after the temporary initial expansion. In fact, inflation remains high even though economic activity returns to its natural level. This is precisely the feature of the suboptimal time-consistent equilibrium of models where policymakers have an incentive to boost output above its natural level: There is no permanent gain in output or unemployment and the attempt to affect real output results only in a higher inflation rate.

6.6 Level versus Growth Effects

Some authors[22] have suggested that the results found in this chapter as well as in chapter 4 can be interpreted as consistent with the traditional partisan theory rather than the rational partisan theory. The criticism takes different forms that must be addressed separately. First, these authors argue, even temporary growth effects have permanent effects on the level economic activity, a result consistent with the traditional partisan theory hypothesis. This argument forgets that although in a world without growth, output is stationary and the standard aggregate supply function relates the level of economic activity to unexpected inflation shocks, in a world with positive trend growth of output, inflation surprises will have transitory effects on the growth rate of output. So what is crucial for the rational partisan theory is not whether a transitory shock has a permanent effect on the level of economic activity but rather whether a political shock has transitory or permanent effects on the unemployment rate of the economy or the growth rate of the economy in a world with trend growth. The results above suggest that these effects are only transitory: policymakers cannot exploit a permanent unemployment (growth)– inflation trade-off because the Phillips curve shifts upward as a result of attempts to permanently affect the economy's unemployment or growth rate.

Second, critics say, because the unemployment rate (and less so the growth rate) shows a high level of temporal persistency, any transitory partisan shock will have long-lasting effects even after the political influence has ceased to occur. It is true that, becasue the unemployment rate has a high level of persistence, even a temporary policy shock has rather persistent effects over time. These effects do not, however, imply evidence in favor of the partisan theory with permanent effects. In fact, we have provided evidence that partisan dummies for the second half of an administration do not significantly affect the unemployment rate or the growth rate. This means that any persistent unemployment effect of the partisan shock is due only to the initial policy shock that persists over time solely as a consequence of the unemployment rate's intrinsic dynamics. The dynamic effect deriving from the partisan dummy instead ceases to have further impulse effects on the unemployment (or growth) rate after a few quarters: Any persistent effect is due only to the propagation effects of the initial policy impulse.

6.7   Evidence on Political Business Cycles

Nordhaus's (1975) political business cycle model can be tested on growth and unemployment by constructing for the panel data set a preelectoral dummy NRDN equivalent to the one defined in chapter 4 for the United States. Again we have chosen $N = 4, 6$, and 8 because a relatively short preelectoral output expansion is consistent with this theory, which views the electorate as short sighted. Furthermore, because in many countries in the sample several elections occurred at less than four-year intervals, a longer specification of the preelectoral period appears unreasonable.

Table 6.9 reports the results on output and unemployment for the eighteen-country and eight-country samples, using NRD4. (The fixed-effect coefficients are not reported.) Consider first the eighteen-country sample. On both variables the coefficients of NRD4 are insignificant. Several alternative specifications with NRD6 and NRD8, using the difference of domestic growth from the world as the dependent variable and alternative lag structures, yield no support for the theory. In fact, the coefficient on the political dummy has a sign inconsistent with the theory in several of the regressions. For the sample of eight bipartisan countries, again on both variables the coefficients of NRD4 are

Table 6.9
Political business cycle theory
Dependent variables: rate of growth of output (y) (Columns (1), (2)) unemployment rate (UDIFF) (columns (3), (4))

Independent variables	(1) Coefficient (t-statistics) 18-country sample	(2) Coefficient (t-statistics) 8-country sample	(3) Coefficient (t-statistics) 18-country sample	(4) Coefficient (t-statistics) 8-country sample
$y(-1)$	0.68 (45.8)	0.68 (30.3)	—	—
yw	0.36 (12.2)	0.26 (7.77)	—	—
UDIFF(-1)	—	—	1.10 (48.1)	1.10 (32.5)
UDIFF(-2)	—	—	-0.12 (5.09)	-0.12 (3.51)
NRD4	0.01 (0.09)	0.13 (1.14)	-0.01 (0.39)	-0.01 (0.56)
R^2	0.63	0.62	0.98	0.97

insignificant. An alternative specification with NRD6 and NRD8 shows coefficients of the right sign. In the case of the unemployment regression, the coefficients on NRD6 and NRD8 are not statistically significant; however, they have the right sign and are statistically significant (at the 5 percent confidence level) in the growth regression. These results are the only case in which we find some statistical evidence of a political business cycle effect on the level of economic activity. Although the result is significant, it should be considered with caution for a number of reasons. First, we find no such effect for the eight-country unemployment regression. Second, evidence of preelectoral manipulation up to two years before an election (as suggested by NRD8) is surprising; standard political business cycle theories suggest that a manipulation of the economy will affect growth rates in the months before an election or at most a year before it. Third, if manipulation of the economy was already affecting output growth six to eight quarters before an election, it is surprising that no effect is found in election year (the coefficient on NRD4 is insignificant). We therefore conclude that the results for NRD6 and NRD8 in the growth regression for the eight bipartisan countries cannot be taken with much confidence as showing a systematic political business cycle effect on output. We also tested whether the NRD dummy approaches statistical significance when partisan effects are held constant. Regressions including both the DRPT6 and the NRD ($N = 4, 6, 8$) dummies were run, with no support for the political business cycle, but the DRPT dummy remained statistically significant.[23]

We tested for electoral cycles on inflation using the same variable NPOST5 defined, as in chapter 4, as equal to one in the four quarters following an election and in the election quarter:

$$\pi_t = 1.12\,\pi_{t-1} \quad - 0.14\,\pi_{t-2} \quad - 0.11\,\pi_{t-3} \quad + 0.11\,\pi w_t \quad + 0.14\,\text{NPOST5}_t$$
$$\quad (55.9) \qquad (4.88) \qquad \quad (5.75) \qquad \quad (13.2) \qquad \quad (3.08)$$

$$R^2 = 0.93 \qquad\qquad\qquad\qquad\qquad\qquad\qquad\qquad (6.2)$$

The dummy NPOST5 is significant at the 1 percent level. Additional regressions (available upon request) confirm that the upward jump in inflation does not occur before the election but only in the election quarter and lasts three to five quarters.[24] If confirmed by direct findings on policy instruments, this result would suggest that around elections, monetary and fiscal policy instruments may be manipulated, even though these policies do not seem to affect real economic activity, as implied by the models of Rogoff and Sibert (1988) and Rogoff (1990). This is one of the issues that we tackle in the next chapter.

Up to this point, the different theories have been tested separately, that is by including only one political dummy variable in each regression. Our results were also confirmed when we ran a general nesting model. Specifically, we estimated regressions on growth and unemployment in which all three dummy variables, DRPT, RADM, and NRD, were included. Only the DRPT variable remained significant. We also calculated an F-test comparing the unrestricted model with all three political variables and the restricted model with only the DRPT: For both samples of countries we could not reject the restricted model, at very high levels of significance.

As far as inflation is concerned, we tested whether the two dummies ADM and NPOST remain jointly significant when used as regressors in the same equation; the NPOST dummy is statistically significant at the 5 percent level and the ADM variable at the 10 percent level for both the larger and the smaller country samples. Formal F-tests reject the hypotheses that either one or both variables are zero.[25]

6.8   Endogenous Elections and Opportunistic Policymakers

A few recent contributions to the political business cycle literature consider the implications of endogenous timing of elections. Specifically, Ito (1990a) and Terrones (1989) suggest that policymakers may be opportunistic in a somewhat passive way: In the presence of endogenous timing of elections, they may call an election earlier if the economy is doing well on its own (inflation is low and growth is high) to increase their reelection probability.

Using Ito's simple but insightful framework, suppose for simplicity that governments have no control over real economic activity and that voters are naive and retrospective and judge the incumbent government by evaluating positively high growth, low unemployment and low inflation. Then, if high growth occurs soon after an election, the incumbent may choose to call another election; if, instead, growth is low, he may wait: He has a better chance of capitalizing on a faster growth period by calling an election later in their term of office. As time elapses from the previous election, however, the date at which an election must be called, according to the law, approaches. Then, even an average level of growth may spur the incumbent to call an election, because he wants to avoid the risk of reaching the last period with low growth possibly even lower. Thus, the probability that an election is called should be an increasing function of the time elapsed from the previous election and the state of the economy.

An empirical test of Ito's (1990a) model is as follows. Define Q_t as the probability that an election is called at time t and assume that an election was held in period τ and that, according to the law, an election must be held at least every n periods; Ito's model implies that $\beta_i > 0$, $i = 1, 2, 3$ in:

$$Q_i = \beta_0 + \beta_1(t - \tau) + \beta_2 y_t - \beta_3 \pi_t; \quad \text{for } \tau < t < \tau + n \qquad (6.3)$$

Equation 6.4 displays this panel probit regression for all the countries in the sample in which the timing of elections is endogenous.

$$Q_t = -2.96 \quad +0.17\,\text{TL} \quad -0.004\,y_{t-1} \quad +0.02\,\pi_{t-1}$$
$$ (11.5) \quad (12.6) \quad\quad (0.33) \quad\quad\quad (1.79) \qquad\qquad (6.4)$$

Following Ito, the variable TL is defined as the number of quarters elapsed from the preceding election; the other two regressors are output growth (y) and inflation (π). We use a standard panel probit model with fixed effects. The fixed effects are country dummies capturing institutional factors (such as electoral laws determining the normal length of a legislature) making elections more or less frequent on average in different countries. The TL variable as well as several country dummies (not reported) are significant.[26] The growth variable is not statistically significant, but quite surprisingly, the inflation variable has the wrong sign and is statistically significant at the 10 percent confidence level. One interpretation of this result is that reverse causation may also be important (especially for weak coalition governments): When the economy is doing poorly, inflation is high and the coalition cannot agree on what to do, governments may collapse and elections may have to be called early (see Robertson 1983).

Because the endogenous manipulation of elections may occur more often in some countries than in others, we also performed single-country regressions. These results are not supportive of the theory: the only variable that is systematically significant is again the time from the last election. In Finland, the growth variable is of the right sign and borderline significant. For Japan, the results are different from those found by Ito (1990a) on a shorter sample: We find no evidence that elections are more likely when growth is high and inflation is low. No other country in the sample supports the theory; in fact, there are at least as many signs inconsistent with the theory as consistent, although in either case they are all insignificant. Various sensitivity tests confirm the nature of these results.

These negative results on the hypothesis of passive opportunism should not be interpreted as a total rejection of the basic idea of strategic choice of election timing, for several reasons. First, the economy is only one of the many variables that may influence the choice of calling an election. The incumbent may use strategically a major success in foreign policy or various events that negatively affect the opposition's public image. Second, the model of strategic timing of elections is probably more applicable to countries like Japan or the United Kingdom with unified control rather than coalition governments. In fact, different members of a coalition government may disagree on the optimal time for calling an election, because their expectations, based on their relative popularity, may diverge. In countries with large coalitions and frequent elections (such as Belgium, Italy and the Netherlands) coalition collapses are probably the result of more complex politico-economic factors than the short-run state of the economy.

6.9   Conclusions

One way of summarizing this chapter's results is that the more recent models of political cycles significantly outperform their predecessors. The rational partisan model by Alesina (1987) and the rational opportunistic model by Rogoff and Sibert (1988) are generally more consistent with the overall pattern of evidence for several countries than previous traditional models. Also, the main findings of this chapter are remarkably consistent with those obtained for the United States in chapters 4 and 5. More specifically we found:

1. No evidence of a systematic opportunistic cycle of the Nordhaus type, either for growth or unemployment.

2. No evidence of a passive opportunistic electoral behavior, where elections are called early when the macroeconomy is performing well.

3. An electoral cycle on the inflation rate, consistent with the models of budget cycles of Rogoff and Sibert (1988); although this results holds for the panel of OECD countries, we did not find a similar post-electoral surge in inflation in the United States in chapter 4.

4. Evidence consistent with the rational partisan theory for growth, unemployment and inflation, particularly for a subset of countries with a bipartisan system or with clearly identifiable political changes from the left to the right and vice versa. This theory is less applicable to, and in fact tends to fail for, countries with large coalition governments with frequent government collapses.

5. No evidence of permanent partisan effects on growth and unemployment.

Thus, a political cycle that seems to appear fairly consistently in several countries is the following: Left-wing governments expand the economy when elected; for a while (about two years) they succeed, then inflation expectations adjust and the economy returns to its natural rate of growth. At this point, left-wing governments are trapped into the time-consistent equilibrium with an inflation bias à la Barro and Gordon (1983a). Note that, when left-wing governments approach the new election with this inflationary bias, they may try to reduce inflation, particularly if the latter is perceived as the main economic problem at the time (Lindbeck 1976). When right-wing governments are elected, they fight inflation, therefore causing a recession or a growth slowdown. Later in their term, the economy returns to its natural rate of growth and inflation remains low.

Appendix

Table 6.A.1
Economic data for the OECD countries in the sample

Inflation rate: The inflation rate is obtained as the annual rate of change of the Consumer Price Index (CPI) as described in the text. For all countries, the sample is 1960:1–1993:3, and the CPI is taken from line 64 of the International Monetary Fund, International Financial Statistics (IMF-IFS).

Output growth: The output growth is derived, when data are available, from quarterly GDP data in the IMF-IFS data set. When not available, other output measures (described below) are used. Country details and samples are provided below.

Unemployment rate: The unemployment rate is derived, when data are available, from OECD Main Economic Indicators data set (OECD-MEI). Country details and samples are provided below.

Australia
Output: Real quarterly GDP. Sample: 1960:1–1993:3. Source: IMF-IFS.
Unemployment: Quarterly unemployment rate, adjusted. Sample: 1965:1–1993:4. Source: OECD-MEI.

Austria
Output: Real quarterly GDP. Sample: 1960:1–1993:2. Source: IMF-IFS.
Unemployment: Quarterly unemployment rate, total, adjusted. Sample: 1969:1–1993:3. Source: OECD-MEI.

Table 6.A.1 (continued)

Belgium
Output: Quarterly industrial production. Sample: 1960:1–1993:4. Source: IMF-IFS.
Unemployment: Quarterly unemployment rate, total insured, adjusted. Sample: 1960:1–1993:4. Source: OECD-MEI.

Canada
Output: Real quarterly GDP. Sample: 1960:1–1993:4. Source: IMF-IFS.
Unemployment: Quarterly unemployment rate, total, adjusted. Sample: 1960:1–1993:4. Source: OECD-MEI.

Denmark
Output: Real annual GDP (converted into quarterly data by assuming that quarter-to-quarter annual change corresponds to year-to-year change). Sample: 1960:1–1992:4. Source: IMF-IFS.
Unemployment: Quarterly unemployment rate, registered unemployed, adjusted. Sample: 1970:1–1993:4. Source: OECD-MEI.

Finland
Output: Real quarterly GDP. Sample: 1970:1–1993:4. Source: IMF-IFS.
Unemployment: Quarterly unemployment rate, total, adjusted. Sample: 1960:1–1993:4. Source: OECD-MEI.

France
Output: Real quarterly GDP. Sample: 1965:1–1993:3. Source: IMF-IFS.
Unemployment: Quarterly unemployment rate, total, adjusted. Sample: 1967:1–1993:4. Source: OECD-MEI.

Germany
Output: Real quarterly GDP. Sample: 1960:1–1993:4. Source: IMF-IFS.
Unemployment: Quarterly unemployment rate, adjusted. Sample: 1965:1–1993:4. Source: OECD-MEI.

Ireland
Output: Quarterly industrial production. Sample: 1960:1–1993:4. Source: IMF-IFS.
Unemployment: Quarterly unemployment rate, adjusted. Sample: 1975:1–1993:4. Source: OECD-MEI.

Italy
Output: Real quarterly GDP. Sample: 1960:1–1993:3. Source: IMF-IFS.
Unemployment: Quarterly unemployment rate, adjusted. Sample: 1960:1–1993:4. Source: OECD-MEI.

Japan
Output: Real quarterly GDP. Sample: 1960:1–1993:3. Source: IMF-IFS.
Unemployment: Quarterly unemployment rate, adjusted. Sample: 1965:1–1993:4. Source: OECD-MEI.

Netherlands
Output: Quarterly industrial production. Sample: 1960:1–1993:4. Source: IMF-IFS.
Unemployment: Quarterly unemployment rate, registered unemployed. Sample: 1971:1–1993:4. Source: OECD-MEI.

Table 6.A.1 (continued)

New Zealand
Output: Real annual GDP (converted into quarterly data by assuming that quarter-to-quarter annual change corresponds to year-to-year change). Sample: 1960:1–1992:4. Source: IMF-IFS.
Unemployment: Quarterly unemployment rate, adjusted. Sample: 1970:1–1985:4. Source: OECD-MEI.

Norway
Output: Quarterly industrial production. Sample: 1960:1–1993:4. Source: IMF-IFS.
Unemployment: Quarterly unemployment rate, adjusted. Sample: 1972:1–1993:4. Source: OECD-MEI.

Sweden
Output: Real quarterly GDP. Sample: 1969:1–1993:3. Source: IMF-IFS.
Unemployment: Quarterly unemployment rate, total insured, adjusted. Sample: 1969:1–1993:4. Source: OECD-MEI.

Switzerland
Output: Quarterly industrial production. Sample: 1960:1–1993:4. Source: IMF-IFS.
Unemployment: Quarterly unemployment rate, total, adjusted. Sample: 1974:1–1993:3. Source: OECD-MEI.

United Kingdom
Output: Real quarterly GDP. Sample: 1960:1–1993:2. Source: IMF-IFS.
Unemployment: Quarterly unemployment rate, registered, civilian, adjusted. Sample: 1960:1-1993:4. Source: OECD-MEI.

United States
Output: Real quarterly GDP. Sample: 1960:1–1993:4. Source: IMF-IFS.
Unemployment: Quarterly unemployment rate, total, adjusted. Sample: 1960:1–1993:4. Source: OECD-MEI.

Table 6.A.2
Elections and regime change

Legend:

E   = Election Date

CH L = Administration change towards the left

CH R = Administrations change towards the right

AUSTRALIA: Endogenous Timing of Elections, 3 Years

1961:4	E	RIGHT	a)
1963:4	E		
1966:4	E		
1969:4	E		
1972:4	E	CH L	
1974:2	E		(*) b)
1975:4	E	CH R	
1977:4	E		
1980:4	E		
1983:1	E	CH L	
1984:4	E		(*)
1987:3	E		
1990:1	E		
1993:1	E		

AUSTRIA: Endogenous Timing, 4 Years

1959:2	E	RIGHT	
1962:4	E		
1966:1	E	CH R	
1970:1	E	CH L	
1971:4	E		(*)
1975:4	E		
1979:2	E		
1983:2	E	CH R	
1986:4	E	CH R	
1990:4	E		

Table 6.A.2 (continued)

BELGIUM: Endogenous Timing, 4 Years

1961:1	E	RIGHT	
1965:2	E		
1968:1	E	CH L	
1971:4	E		
1973:1		CH R	
1974:1	E		
1977:2	E	CH L	
1978:4	E		(*)
1981:4	E	CH R	
1985:4	E		
1987:4	E		
1988:2		CH L	
1991:4	E		

CANADA: Endogenous Timing, 5 Years

1962:2	E	RIGHT	
1963:2	E	CH L	(*)
1965:4	E		
1968:2	E		
1972:4	E		
1974:3	E		(*)
1979:2	E	CH R	
1980:1	E	CH L	(*)
1984:3	E	CH R	
1988:4	E		
1993:4	E	CH L	

DENMARK: Endogenous Timing, 4 Years

1960:4	E	LEFT	
1964:3	E		
1966:4	E		
1968:1	E	CH R	(*)
1971:3	E	CH L	
1973:4	E	CH R	

Table 6.A.2 (continued)

1975:1	E	CH L	(*)
1977:1	E		
1979:4	E		
1981:4	E		
1982:3		CH R	
1984:1	E		
1987:3	E		
1990:4	E		
1993:1		CH L	

FINLAND: Endogenous Timing, 4 Years

1962:1	E	LEFT
1963:4		CH R
1966:1	E	CH L
1970:1	E	
1972:1	E	
1975:3	E	CH R
1977:2		CH L
1979:1	E	
1983:1	E	
1987:1	E	CH R
1991:1	E	CH R

FRANCE: Endogenous Timing, 5 Years

1962:4	E	RIGHT	
1967:1	E		
1968:2	E		(*)
1973:1	E		
1978:1	E		
1981:2	E	CH L	
1984:3		CH R	
1986:1	E	CH R	
1988:2	E	CH L	
1993:1	E	CH R	

Table 6.A.2 (continued)

GERMANY: Endogenous Timing, 4 Years

1961:3	E	RIGHT
1965:3	E	
1966:4		CH L
1969:3	E	CH L
1972:4	E	CH R
1976:4	E	
1980:4	E	
1982:4		CH R
1983:1	E	
1987:1	E	
1990:4	E	

IRELAND: Endogenous Timing, 5 Years

1961:4	E	RIGHT	
1965:2	E		
1969:2	E		
1973:1	E	CH L	
1977:2	E	CH R	
1981:2	E	CH L	
1982:1	E	CH R	(*)
1982:4	E	CH L	(*)
1987:1	E	CH R	
1989:3	E		
1992:4	E	CH L	

ITALY: Endogenous Timing, 5 Years

		RIGHT
1962:4		CH L
1963:2	E	
1968:2	E	
1972:2	E	
1974:4		CH R
1976:2	E	CH L

Table 6.A.2 (continued)

1979:2	E		
1983:2	E		
1987:2	E		
1989:2	E		
1992:2	E		

JAPAN: Endogenous Timing, 4 Years

1960:4	E	RIGHT	
1963:4	E		
1967:1	E		
1969:4	E		
1972:4	E		
1976:4	E		
1979:4	E		
1980:2	E		(*)
1983:4	E		
1986:3	E		
1990:1	E		
1993:3	E	CH L	

NETHERLANDS: Endogenous Timing, 4 Years

1959:1	E	RIGHT	
1963:2	E		
1965:2		CH L	
1967:1	E	CH R	
1971:1	E		
1972:4	E		(*)
1973:2		CH L	
1977:2	E		
1977:4		CH R	
1981:2	E	CH L	
1982:3	E	CH R	(*)
1986:2	E		
1989:3	E	CH L	

Table 6.A.2 (continued)

NEW ZEALAND: Endogenous Timing, 3 Years

1960:4	E	RIGHT
1963:4	E	
1966:4	E	
1969:4	E	
1972:4	E	CH L
1975:4	E	CH R
1978:4	E	
1981:4	E	
1984:3	E	CH L
1987:3	E	
1990:4	E	CH R

NORWAY: Exogenous Timing, 4 Years

1961:3	E	LEFT
1965:3	E	CH R
1969:3	E	
1971:4		CH L
1972:4		CH R
1973:3	E	CH L
1977:3	E	
1981:3	E	CH R
1985:3	E	
1986:2		CH L
1989:3	E	CH R
1990:4		CH L

SWEDEN: Exogenous Timing, 3 Years
Sweden switched from endogenous to exogenous elections in the middle of the 1970s.

1960:3	E	LEFT
1964:3	E	
1968:3	E	
1970:3	E	
1973:3	E	
1976:3	E	CH R

Table 6.A.2 (continued)

1979:3	E		
1982:3	E	CH L	
1985:3	E		
1988:3	E		
1993:3	E	CH R	

SWITZERLAND: Exogenous Timing, 4 Years

1959:4	E	RIGHT
1963:4	E	
1967:4	E	
1971:4	E	
1975:4	E	
1979:4	E	
1983:4	E	
1987:4	E	
1991:4	E	

UNITED KINGDOM: Endogenous Timing, 5 Years

1959:4	E	RIGHT	
1964:4	E	CH L	
1966:1	E		(*)
1970:2	E	CH R	
1974:1	E		
1974:3	E	CH L	(*)
1979:2	E	CH R	
1983:2	E		
1987:2	E		
1992:2	E		

United States: Exogenous Timing, 4 Years

		RIGHT
1960:4	E	CH L
1964:4	E	
1968:4	E	CH R
1972:4	E	

Table 6.A.2 (continued)

1976:4	E	CH L	
1980:4	E	CH R	
1984:4	E		
1988:4	E		
1992:4	E	CH L	

a) RIGHT or LEFT indicates the type of government in power at the beginning of the sample, which is 1959:1. We also indicate for each country whether election dates are endogenous or exogenous and the official number of years between elections.

b) Elections denoted with an * are not included in tests of the political business cycle theory because they are too close (less than two years) to previous elections. They are, however, included in tests of the opportunistic endogenous election model.

Source: For data until 1987, election dates are obtained from Banks 1989 and dates of changes of government and their classification of Right and Left are obtained from Alt 1985 and Banks 1989. For data after 1987, the source is the Europa Yearbooks (various years).

7

Political Cycles and Macroeconomic Policies: Evidence from Industrial Democracies

7.1 Introduction

Partisan and opportunistic cycles on growth, unemployment and inflation must originate from manipulations of policy instruments, namely monetary and fiscal policy. For the opportunistic model, manipulations of policy instruments can be motivated by two goals. First, expansionary policies can create a temporary surge of growth before an election. Second, some policies, such as a tax cut or an increase in transfers, may have a direct beneficial effect for the incumbent government at the polls. Thus, electoral manipulations of policy instruments could be observed, even without any effect on the aggregate economy. As for the partisan theory, note that it does not make a precise prediction on which policy instrument is used to achieve partisan goals: It could be monetary policy, fiscal policy, or a combination of the two. Also this combination could change over time and across countries.

In this chapter we study political cycles in macroeconomic instruments using the same sample of countries as in chapter 6; our main findings are the following:

1. One can observe some cases of expansionary monetary policy in election years. This result is somewhat mixed, however: although we find electoral cycles on monetary aggregates, similar tests for short- and long-term interest rates fail to find statistical evidence of monetary loosening before elections. Generally, the evidence on these oppor-

tunistic cycles is not overwhelming: Electoral monetary cycles occur frequently, but not always, and their size is small.

2. Fiscal policy is relatively loose in election years.

3. Inflation tends to increase after elections, probably because of the preelectoral loose monetary and fiscal policies, an opportunistic timing of increases in publicly controlled prices, or indirect taxes.

4. We find systematic partisan differences in monetary policy between left- and right-wing governments.

5. Finally, we find no evidence of partisan effects in budget deficits. On average, left-wing governments run no larger budget deficits than right-wing ones, after accounting for other political and economic determinants of deficits.

The chapter is organized as follows. Section 7.2 presents the data and specification of the empirical tests for monetary policy. Section 7.3 discusses tests of the implications of partisan models for monetary policy. Section 7.4 evaluates the evidence concerning preelectoral manipulation of monetary policy. Section 7.5 considers political cycles in fiscal policy, namely budget deficits, spending and taxes. The final section suggests an interpretation of our results in the broader context of the literature on political cycles.

7.2 Data and Specification of Empirical Tests for Monetary Policy

7.2.1 Data

The sample of countries is as in chapter 6; the economic data are quarterly observations on money supply growth rates and short- and long-term interest rates. Money supply growth is defined as the yearly rate change of M1 from IMF-IFS data. Short- and long-term interest rates are also from IMF-IFS. More details on country-specific data issues can be found in table 7.A.1 in the appendix to this chapter. For the political data, we use the same data set as in chapter 6, summarized in table 6.A.2.

7.2.2 Specification of the Empirical Tests

As discussed in chapter 4, the critical issue for a specification of empirical tests on monetary policy concerns the identification of the correct monetary policy instrument. Should we use monetary aggregates or interest rates as the measures of monetary policy in the OECD countries in the sample? In general, apart from a period in the 1970s when monetary growth targeting became popular as an intermediate instrument of monetary policy, short-term interest rates have been and are the most common instrument of monetary policy in most OECD countries. In this chapter we use both monetary supply measures and interest rates in our empirical tests.

We run the following panel regressions of time-series cross-section data, for instance for money growth:

$$m_{it} = \alpha_0 + \alpha_1 m_{it-1} + \alpha_2 m_{it-2} + \alpha_n m_{it-n} + \alpha_{n+1} \text{PDUM}_t + \varepsilon_t \qquad (7.1)$$

where m_{it} is the stacked vector of time-series data on money growth for the countries in the sample; this rate of the money supply is defined as $m_{it} = (M_{it} - M_{it-4})/M_{it-4}(100)$ where M_{it} is the level of the monetary aggregate in country i at time t; PDUM is again a political dummy capturing the dynamic implications of different theories.[1] We consider potential country differences in long-term money growth rates and interest rates by also presenting results of a fixed-effects model.[2] Conceptually, it is not obvious whether or not country variables should be included in the regressions for the policy instruments. On the one hand, one can argue that different countries may have different long-run money growth rates, for instance, because they suffer credibility problems to different degrees; this would lead to including country dummies to control for these country specific effects. On the other hand, one can argue that these credibility problems are due to precisely the political factors we are studying, for instance, to differing vulnerability of a country's politicians to political business cycle pressures or to differences in the degree of ideological partisanship of politicians across countries. In this case, including country dummies might lead to incorrectly imputing to an unspecified country effect differences in money growth rates that are due to political factors in the first place. Thus, we present results that both include and exclude the country dummies.

7.3   Evidence on Partisan Effects in Monetary Policy

In this section we start with tests of the partisan theory. Both the rational and the traditional version of the partisan theory imply that monetary policy will be more expansionary (contractionary) during a left-wing (right-wing) government. We now test that the growth rate of the money supply and the level of short- and long-term interest rates will be higher (lower) during a left-wing (right-wing) administration.

For money growth, we run the following panel regression:

$$m_{it} = \beta_0 + \beta_1 m_{it-1} + \beta_2 m_{it-2} + \cdots + \beta_n m_{it-n} + \beta_{n+1} \text{ADM}_{it} + \varepsilon_t$$

$$(7.2)$$

where m_{it} is the rate of growth of money (or the level of the short- and long-term interest rate) for country i at time t. ADM_{it} is the partisan dummy variable described in chapter 6.[3] Money growth is defined as the quarterly observations of the yearly rate of change of M1. This definition is used to remove seasonality from the money data. Tests with the quarterly rate of change of M1 as well as other methods of seasonally adjusting the data reveal no modification of the results. The best auto-regressive specification for the dependent variable was found to be an AR(9); however, our results are not dependent on the model's lag specification. For brevity, the coefficients on the lags are not displayed.[4]

Table 7.1 presents the results for the full eighteen-country and eight bipartisan country samples. The coefficient on the ADM variable (lagged one period to account for a delay in policy change) has the

Table 7.1
Partisan theory
Dependent variable: rate of growth of money (m)

Independent variables	(1) Coefficient (t-statistics)	(2) Coefficient (t-statistics)	(3) Coefficient (t-statistics)	(4) Coefficient (t-statistics)
	18-country sample		8-country sample	
Constant	1.46 (8.76)	—	1.59 (6.66)	—
ADM(−1)	−0.17 (1.82)	−0.18 (1.67)	−0.17 (1.43)	−0.18 (1.43)
United States	—	1.30 (3.66)	—	1.27 (3.58)
United Kingdom	—	1.86 (4.91)	—	1.81 (4.56)
France	—	1.81 (4.65)	—	1.80 (4.36)
Germany	—	1.59 (4.30)	—	1.58 (4.09)
Sweden	—	1.61 (4.14)	—	1.60 (3.95)
Canada	—	1.76 (4.71)	—	1.74 (6.62)
Australia	—	1.87 (5.04)	—	1.83 (4.71)
New Zealand	—	1.66 (4.47)	—	1.64 (4.21)
Belgium	—	1.13 (3.07)	—	—
Ireland	—	1.97 (5.20)	—	—
Austria	—	1.33 (3.71)	—	—
Denmark	—	1.97 (5.12)	—	—
Italy	—	2.65 (6.24)	—	—
Netherlands	—	1.56 (4.28)	—	—

Table 7.1 (continued)

Independent variables	(1) Coefficient (t-statistics)	(2) Coefficient (t-statistics)	(3) Coefficient (t-statistics)	(4) Coefficient (t-statistics)
	18-country sample		8-country sample	
Norway	—	2.33 (5.93)	—	—
Finland	—	2.05 (5.24)	—	—
Switzerland	—	1.12 (3.16)	—	—
Japan	—	2.48 (5.63)	—	—
R^2	0.73	0.73	0.73	0.73

expected sign (*i.e.*, money growth rates are higher during a left-wing administration) and is significant at the 10 percent confidence level for both the model without fixed effects and the model with fixed country effects. The *t*-statistic is, however, a slightly higher in the model without fixed effects (column (2)). In the sample of eight bipartisan countries the coefficient on ADM has the expected sign but is not statistically significant. The coefficient estimate in the full sample implies that in the steady state the yearly difference in the growth rate of the money supply between a left- and a right-wing administration is around 2.4 percent. This difference is consistent with the inflation differential between left- and right-wing administrations found in chapter 6. We tested whether the weakness of the results on money growth, particularly on the eight bipartisan countries, might be due to the inclusion in the sample of the Bretton Woods period of fixed exchange rates. Although differences in money growth rates were found not to be significant in the period before 1973, the estimation of the model for the 1973–1993 period of flexible exchange rates yielded results similar to those for the full sample in table 7.1.[5]

We consider next the evidence on partisan differences in the levels of short- and long-term interest rates. The specification is similar to that used for the money growth regressions, but now the dependent variable and the regressors are short- and long-term interest rates. Tables 7.2 and 7.3 present the results of these regressions. In each table we present the results obtained with and without country fixed effects. The best autoregressive specification is found to be an AR(10) for the short-term interest rates and AR(6) for the long-term interest rate.[6] As for the case of the money regressions, we considered whether we should include in the interest rate regressions a world variable. On one side, world financial conditions might affect the choice or determination of short- and long-term interest rates in a country; on the other, imposing the restriction that world interest rates affect all countries similarly (as implied by a common coefficient on the world variable) might be more arbitrary than assuming that world business cycle conditions affect similarly most countries' growth rates. We therefore present results that include and exclude a world variable. The world variable that we chose in the interest rate regressions is the average inflation rate of the G-7 countries.

Consider first the results for the eighteen-country sample. In table 7.2, the results for the long-term interest rate show that the coefficient on ADM has the expected negative sign (i.e., long-term interest rates are higher (lower) during a left-wing (right-wing) administration). In three out of four cases (columns (1) to (3)) the coefficient is also statistically significant at the 5 percent confidence level or better. The coefficient is not significant only when we add to the regression both the country dummies and the world variables (column (4)). In table 7.3 we present the corresponding result for short-term interest rates. Here the coefficients are always of the expected sign and significant at the 5 percent level or better.

The results in tables 7.2 and 7.3 broadly confirm the hypothesis that permanent differences in nominal interest rate levels reflect permanent differences in monetary and inflation policies between left- and right-wing governments. From an economic point of view, the estimated coefficients in column (2) of tables 7.2 and 7.3 imply that the steady-state difference in the short-term (and long-term) interest rates between

Table 7.2
Partisan theory
Dependent variable: long-term interest rates (LR)

Independent variables	(1) Coefficient (t-statistics)	(2) Coefficient (t-statistics)	(3) Coefficient (t-statistics)	(4) Coefficient (t-statistics)
Constant	0.18 (5.85)	—	0.08 (2.33)	—
ADM	−0.04 (2.85)	−0.04 (2.67)	−0.03 (2.18)	−0.02 (1.53)
πw	—	—	3.64 (9.78)	4.21 (10.9)
United States	—	0.21 (4.00)	—	0.09 (1.70)
United Kingdom	—	0.28 (4.69)	—	0.23 (3.79)
France	—	0.24 (4.31)	—	0.17 (2.95)
Germany	—	0.20 (3.80)	—	0.09 (1.64)
Sweden	—	0.23 (4.05)	—	0.17 (3.05)
Canada	—	0.23 (4.17)	—	0.16 (2.81)
Australia	—	0.26 (4.46)	—	0.19 (3.23)
New Zealand	—	0.26 (4.44)	—	0.18 (3.06)
Belgium	—	0.23 (4.19)	—	0.14 (2.63)
Ireland	—	0.30 (4.87)	—	0.25 (4.10)
Austria	—	0.19 (2.90)	—	0.06 (0.97)
Denmark	—	0.29 (4.71)	—	0.25 (4.10)
Italy	—	0.28 (4.65)	—	0.16 (4.34)
Netherlands	—	0.20 (3.84)	—	0.10 (2.00)

Table 7.2 (continued)

Independent variables	(1) Coefficient (t-statistics)	(2) Coefficient (t-statistics)	(3) Coefficient (t-statistics)	(4) Coefficient (t-statistics)
Norway	—	0.21 (3.90)	—	0.13 (2.46)
Finland	—	0.32 (4.35)	—	0.24 (3.32)
Switzerland	—	0.14 (2.99)	—	−0.006 (0.08)
Japan	—	0.19 (3.05)	—	0.01 (0.16)
R^2	0.97	0.97	0.97	0.97

a left- and a right-wing administration is around 2.5 percent (3.0 percent for the long-term interest rate). This difference is consistent with the money growth differential between left- and right-wing administrations (2.4 percent) found earlier in this section and with the partisan inflation differentials found in chapter 6. The results for the sample of eight bipartisan countries (available upon request) are similar to those obtained for the full sample but slightly weaker. The results for the short-term interest rate are statistically significant at the 5 percent confidence level or better (with the exception of the one specification where the world variable is included but the country effects are not). The results for the long-term interest rate are statistically significant at least at the 10 percent confidence level and sometimes better.

We also tested whether political effects on interest rates are different before and after the Bretton Woods period of fixed exchange rates. We found that the coefficient on the political dummy ADM was insignificant for both the short- and long-run interest rates equations in the period before 1973. Conversely, the estimation of the model for the 1973–1993 period of flexible exchange rates yielded results similar to those for the full 1960–1993 sample in tables 7.2 and 7.3.[7]

One final observation: The rational partisan theory implies that the output effects associated with a government change toward the left

Table 7.3
Partisan theory
Dependent variable: short-term interest rates (SR)

Independent variables	(1) Coefficient (t-statistics)	(2) Coefficient (t-statistics)	(3) Coefficient (t-statistics)	(4) Coefficient (t-statistics)
Constant	0.69 (6.53)	—	0.20	—
ADM	−0.10 (2.82)	−0.11 (2.79)	−0.07 (2.03)	−0.08 (1.94)
πw	—	—	5.57 (5.78)	5.86 (6.04)
United States	—	0.63 (4.58)	—	0.31 (2.16)
United Kingdom	—	0.82 (5.48)	—	0.56 (3.59)
France	—	0.79 (5.40)	—	0.52 (3.39)
Germany	—	0.56 (4.36)	—	0.26 (1.90)
Sweden	—	0.74 (4.90)	—	0.48 (3.06)
Canada	—	0.65 (4.62)	—	0.39 (2.64)
Australia	—	0.79 (5.36)	—	0.53 (3.41)
New Zealand	—	0.94 (5.81)	—	0.68 (4.04)
Belgium	—	0.61 (4.64)	—	0.33 (2.40)
Ireland	—	1.07 (5.14)	—	0.79 (3.70)
Austria	—	0.57 (3.75)	—	0.26 (1.61)
Denmark	—	1.00 (4.98)	—	0.69 (3.35)
Italy	—	1.26 (5.92)	—	1.00 (4.68)
Netherlands	—	0.60 (4.37)	—	0.31 (2.16)

Table 7.3 (continued)

Independent variables	(1) Coefficient (t-statistics)	(2) Coefficient (t-statistics)	(3) Coefficient (t-statistics)	(4) Coefficient (t-statistics)
Norway	—	0.99 (5.15)	—	0.69 (3.49)
Finland	—	1.01 (4.41)	—	0.80 (3.50)
Switzerland	—	0.46 (2.65)	—	0.16 (0.89)
Japan	—	0.68 (4.63)	—	0.35 (2.26)
R^2	0.88	0.88	0.89	0.88

derive from the surprise inflation; a new government will increase the rate of growth of the money supply leading to higher inflation and, for a given real interest rate, to a higher nominal interest rate, a transitory reduction in real wages and an output increase. This output stimulus will persist as long the wage adjustment process is subject to inertia because of staggered or overlapping labor contracts. Partisan output effects might also derive, however, from a transitory reduction in real interest rates generated by the expansionary monetary policy followed by the government. In fact, although money growth rates, inflation rates and nominal interest rates should be on average higher during left-wing administrations, the partisan hypotheses are also consistent with a view that a looser monetary policy will lead to an increase in economic activity (transitory according to the rational partisan theory, permanent in the Hibbs version of the model) via a (transitory or permanent) real interest rate effect. In other terms, while nominal short-term interest rates should be higher because of the partisan effects on inflation and money growth, a successful partisan monetary expansion leading to output effects may be also associated, for any given inflation rate, with real interest rates lower than what they would otherwise be. If this is the case, in a partisan cycle short-term real interest rates may be relatively low and contribute to the positive output effect.

We tested for real interest rate effects in the data but found no evidence of permanent or temporary partisan differences in real interest rates. The lack of permanent real interest rate differences across partisan lines is consistent with the evidence in chapter 6 of no permanent partisan differences in economic activity. Concerning the rational partisan theory, the lack of transitory real interest rate effects after a change in administration can be explained as follows. First, the transitory output effects found in the data may be due mostly to other channels rather than a real interest rate effect. Second, a monetary expansion would at first lead to a reduction in short-term real interest rates but, if economic activity were successfully stimulated, nominal and real interest rates would start to rise rather than fall. In fact, the regularity with which real interest rates tend to be procyclical suggests that a successful partisan growth expansion will be associated with an increase in real interest rates as the stimulus to economic activity puts upward pressure on interest rates.

In summary, the evidence from money growth rates and short- and long-term nominal interest rates is consistent with the view of systematic partisan differences in monetary policies between left- and right-wing administrations.

7.4   Evidence on Political Business Cycle Effects in Monetary Policy

7.4.1   Tests of the Political Business Cycle Model on Monetary Aggregates

Our tests of the political business cycle model adopt a methodology analogous to that used in section 7.2: we run the panel regression (7.1) where the dependent variable is m_{it} and the political variable is the electoral dummy variable NRDN (with N = 4, 6) discussed in chapter 6.

Table 7.4
Political business cycle theory
Dependent variable: rate of growth of money (m)

Independent variables	(1) Coefficient (t-statistics)	(2) Coefficient (t-statistics)	(3) Coefficient (t-statistics)	(4) Coefficient (t-statistics)	(5) Coefficient (t-statistics)	(6) Coefficient (t-statistics)	(7) Coefficient (t-statistics)	(8) Coefficient (t-statistics)
	18-country sample		8-country sample		18-country sample		8-country sample	
	Without country dummies				With country dummies			
Constant	0.90 (3.07)	0.83 (2.79)	0.64 (1.52)	0.69 (1.59)				
mw	0.06 (1.43)	0.04 (1.39)	0.06 (1.85)	0.06 (1.72)	0.05 (1.88)	0.05 (1.82)	0.08 (2.11)	0.07 (2.02)
NRD4	0.48 (2.64)	—	0.85 (3.34)	—	0.48 (2.63)	—	0.87 (3.38)	—
NRD6	—	0.44 (2.66)	—	0.53 (2.27)	—	0.42 (2.56)	—	0.54 (2.29)
R^2	0.73	0.73	0.73	0.73	0.73	0.73	0.73	0.73

Table 7.4 reports the results of the panel regressions for NRD4 and NRD6 for the full sample of countries and the subsample of eight bipartisan countries. The table, which includes specifications with and without country dummies, indicates that in each case, the coefficient on the electoral dummy is both of the expected sign and significantly different from zero at least at the 5 percent confidence level.[8] These results are consistent with the implications of the political business cycle model: ceteris paribus, money growth is higher for the twelve to eighteen months before an election. All of the reported results were found to be invariant to tests of robustness such as leading or lagging the political dummy or excluding individual countries that might be thought to be driving the results. In addition, excluding the world average money growth variable as a regressor did not change the results.[9]

Note that the coefficient estimates and statistical significance for the NRD6 regressions are slightly lower than those for NRD4, especially in the eight-country sample. Opportunistic models indicate that the office holder wishes to boost the economy right before the election, without any concurrent inflation. Given the long-run inflationary implications of monetary policy, expansionary monetary policy too far in advance will result in an a boom too early and high levels of inflation before the election.

7.4.2   Interaction of Opportunistic and Partisan Cycles in Monetary Policy

We next investigated a "partisan-opportunistic" interaction term. As emphasized by Lindbeck (1976), Hibbs (1987a) and Alesina (1989), preelectoral opportunistic behavior for left-wing governments may be different than that for right-wing governments. More specifically, left-wing governments pursuing expansionary monetary policies at the beginning of their term to lower unemployment may be willing to reduce money growth at the end of their terms to reduce the inflation caused by their initial policies. Opportunistic left-wing governments may want to strengthen their anti-inflation policies to appeal to the median voter in election years. Conversely, right-wing governments that undertook contractionary monetary policy to lower inflation may be more willing to expand monetary growth at the end of their terms to face elections in a period of economic expansion.

A formal test of this hypothesis can made by running the following panel regressions:

$$m_{it} = \gamma_0 + \gamma_1 m_{it-1} + \gamma_2 m_{it-2} + \cdots + \gamma_n m_{it-n}$$
$$+ \gamma_{n+1} \text{ADM}_{it} + \gamma_{n+2} \text{PBCNL}_{it} + \gamma_{n+3} \text{PBCNR}_{it} + \varepsilon_t \qquad (7.3)$$

ADM is the dummy that captures the partisan differences in monetary policy, and PBCNL and PBCNR are interaction terms between NRDN and the left- and right-wing government dummies respectively.[10] If partisan or opportunistic political manipulation of monetary policy exists, one expects the coefficients on the left- and right-wing interaction terms to be different. The strong form of this theory, as described above, suggests that the coefficients should in fact be of opposite sign.

Table 7.5 reports the results of the panel regressions with M1. For PBC4 (excluding country dummies), we find that the coefficient estimates for right- and left-wing governments are very similar in magnitude. Moreover, the coefficient for right-wing governments is significantly different from zero at the 5 percent level, whereas that of left-wing governments is significant only at the 10 percent level for the eighteen-country sample. In the eight-country sample, both coefficients are significant. Therefore, we cannot reject the hypothesis that the left- and right-wing interaction terms are of the same magnitude.

7.4.3 Tests of the Political Business Cycle Model on Interest Rates

We consider next tests of the political business cycle theory on interest rates. Because the previous evidence suggests that monetary growth rates are above average before elections, we now test whether short- or long-term interest rates are lower than average during election

Table 7.5
Tests of partisan business cycle with partisan effects
Dependent variable: rate of growth of money supply (m)

Independent variable	(1) Coefficient (t-statistics)	(2) Coefficient (t-statistics)	(3) Coefficient (t-statistics)	(4) Coefficient (t-statistics)
	18-country sample		8-country sample	
Constant	0.85	0.83	0.57	0.69
	(2.82)	(2.69)	(1.32)	(1.55)
mw	0.03	0.03	0.06	0.06
	(1.32)	(1.27)	(1.70)	(1.61)
ADM	−0.24	−0.13	−0.31	−0.16
	(1.25)	(0.62)	(1.15)	(0.51)
PBC4L	0.49	—	0.87	—
	(1.78)		(2.22)	
PBC4R	0.47	—	0.85	—
	(1.98)		(2.51)	
PBC6L	—	0.58	—	0.77
		(2.32)		(2.17)
PBC6R	—	0.33	—	0.35
		(1.52)		(1.13)
R^2	0.73	0.73	0.73	0.73

years. Specifically, we run political business cycle regressions similar to those in equation (7.2) where the dependent variable is now an interest rate measure instead of a money growth rate. The results for both the eighteen- and eight-country samples, presented in table 7.6, reject the idea that interest rates are lower in election years. The coefficients on NRD4 have mostly the expected sign but are not statistically significant at any standard confidence level. We tested the robustness of these results by testing for a longer preelectoral effect (NRD6 instead of NRD4), by excluding the country dummies and by adding a world variable; in each case we did found no preelectoral reduction in interest rates. Finally, given the evidence (in tables 7.2 and 7.3) in favor of partisan differences in short- and long-term interest rates, we tested whether the electoral dummies became significant after we controlled

Table 7.6
Political business cycle theory
Dependent variable: short-term (SR) and long-term (LR) interest rates

Independent variables	(1) Coefficient (t-statistics)	(2) Coefficient (t-statistics)	(3) Coefficient (t-statistics)	(4) Coefficient (t-statistics)
	18-country sample		8-country sample	
	Long Rate	Short Rate	Long Rate	Short Rate
Constant	0.15	0.54	0.22	0.57
	(2.56)	(3.92)	(3.49)	(3.69)
NRD4	−0.005	−0.03	−0.02	0.02
	(0.21)	(0.44)	(0.49)	(0.24)
R^2	0.97	0.89	0.97	0.90

for the partisan dummies. We found that although the partisan dummies remained significant (as in tables 7.2 and 7.3), the electoral dummy did not.

7.5   Electoral and Partisan Determinants of Fiscal Policy and Budget Deficits

In this section we consider the effects of elections and partisan factors on fiscal policy. The recent political economy literature on budget deficits (see Alesina and Perotti 1995a for a survey) suggests that there may be several political biases in fiscal policy. In this chapter we will concentrate on partisan and electoral factors, and we will postpone to chapter 9 the analysis of other political economy aspects.

For electoral effects in fiscal policy, both traditional and recent rational versions of political business cycle models imply that we should observe fiscal deficits before elections. However, these theories are vague about whether the preelectoral fiscal expansion will occur through a reduction in taxes, an increase in government spending, or both. In principle, the actual combination of preelectoral tax cuts and fiscal spending increases may change over time and across countries.

We therefore start our analysis of preelectoral budget cycles by con-
centrating on public-sector fiscal deficits. We will subsequently consider the two components of the fiscal balance (spending and taxes).

As discussed for the case of the United States, the fiscal implications
of partisan models are less clear-cut. On one hand, left-wing governments should be more willing to use government spending to achieve
policy objectives. This is the source of the conventional view that fiscal
deficits will be larger under left-wing governments than under right-
wing governments. On the other hand, although left-wing governments may be more willing to increase government spending, they
may also be relatively more inclined to increase taxes than right-wing
governments. It is therefore not obvious, on a theoretical basis, whether
the bias toward fiscal deficits will be larger under left- or right-wing
governments.

In analyzing empirically the effects of elections and partisan factors
on fiscal deficits, we use (as in chapter 4 for the United States) a structural model of budget deficits to control for the economic determinants
of budget deficits. We rely upon the structural model used by Roubini
and Sachs (1989a) to study the effects of political instability on budget
deficits. The specification is similar to the one used for the United
States but somewhat simpler; the simplification is needed because of
the nature of the sample, which is a panel of several countries.

We estimate a pooled cross-section time-series regression where the
left-hand side variable is the annual deficit, measured as the change in
the debt-to-GDP ratio, $d(b_{it})$. The panel includes thirteen countries, and
the sample period is 1961–1993 (whenever the data are available).[11]
The basic explanatory variables are (1) the lagged deficit, db_{it-1}; (2) the
change in the unemployment rate, dU_{it}; (3) the change in the GDP
growth rate, denoted dy_{it}; (4) the change in the real interest rate minus
the growth rate times the lagged debt-to-GDP ratio, $b_{it-1}d(r-y)_{it}$;[12]
(5) an electoral dummy, ELE_{it}, to be defined below; and (6) a dummy
that identifies left-wing governments, $LEFT_{it}$. Finally, v_{it} is an error
term. The basic structure of the pooled regression model is the follow-

ing (i denotes country, t denotes time, and dx denotes the change in variable x):

$$db_{it} = \delta_0 + \delta_1\, db_{it-1} + \delta_2\, dU_{it} + \delta_3\, dy_{it} + \delta_4\, b_{it-1}\, d(r-n)_t$$

$$+ \delta_5\, \text{ELE}_{it} + \delta_6\, \text{LEFT}_{it} + v_{it} \tag{7.4}$$

We expect the following: $0 < \delta_1 < 1$ (to allow for any slow adjustment and persistence of budget deficits); $\delta_2 > 0$ (because a rise in the unemployment rate reduces tax revenues and may raise government spending above its permanent value in the short-term); $\delta_3 < 0$ (because a rise in GDP growth increases government revenues and may lower government spending below its permanent value in the short-term); $\delta_4 > 0$ (because a rise in the real interest rate directly raises the real deficit, which if transitory should be accommodated by a temporary rise in the budget deficit).[13]

Before introducing and discussing the electoral partisan determinants of budget deficits, in column (1) of table 7.7 we present the results of the regression when we include only the economic variables. This specification provides a rather successful account of the role of economic shocks in inducing budget deficits in the industrial countries. In particular, a rise in unemployment raises the budget deficit; a rise in the debt-servicing cost raises the budget deficit; and an acceleration of GDP growth lowers the budget deficit. Note that the variable measuring this slowdown in growth is highly significant.[14] Finally, the coefficient on the lagged deficit (db_{t-1}) suggests that about 76 percent of the lagged budget deficit persists to the following period.

In columns (2) through (4) we add to the basic regression a dummy ELE taking on value 1 in election years and 0 otherwise. We assign value 1 to the dummy in the preelectoral year ($t-1$) if the election occurs in the first or second quarters of year t; otherwise we assign value 1 in the electoral year t if the election occurs in the third or fourth quarter of year t. We also run regressions using ELX, which takes value 1 in the election year regardless of whether the election

Table 7.7
Political effects on fiscal policy
Dependent variable: real budget deficit (% of GDP) (*db*)

Independent variable	(1) Coefficient (t-statistics)	(2) Coefficient (t-statistics)	(3) Coefficient (t-statistics)	(4) Coefficient (t-statistics)	(5) Coefficient (t-statistics)
Constant	−0.0005 (0.41)	−0.002 (1.44)	−0.002 (1.30)	−0.003 (1.63)	−0.001 (0.84)
$db(-1)$	0.76 (20.5)	0.77 (20.7)	0.74 (17.4)	0.76 (20.5)	0.76 (20.3)
dU	0.23 (3.76)	0.23 (3.84)	0.23 (3.91)	0.24 (2.91)	0.23 (3.82)
dy	−0.50 (10.0)	−0.50 (10.2)	−0.50 (10.1)	−0.51 (10.2)	−0.50 (10.0)
$b_{-1}d(r-y)$	0.52 (3.47)	0.50 (3.35)	0.49 (3.29)	0.49 (3.26)	0.51 (3.39)
ELE	—	0.006 (2.22)	0.005 (1.94)	0.006 (2.23)	—
dbELE	—	—	0.10 (1.41)	—	—
LEFT	—	—	—	0.002 (0.81)	0.002 (0.80)
R^2	0.66	0.66	0.67	0.67	0.67

occurs in the first second half of the year. The results of the estimations are shown in columns (2) through (4). After controlling for the economic determinants, the electoral dummy, ELE, has the expected sign and is statistically significant at the 5 percent confidence level. The estimated coefficients on ELE in column (2) imply that real fiscal deficits will be higher in election years by more than 0.5 percent of GDP. The results are similar using ELX. In column (3), we investigate an interaction term of the electoral variable with the lagged deficit (termed *db*ELE), with the view that the speed of adjusting to an inherited level of the deficit might be lower in election years. The sign on the interaction variable *db*ELE is positive as expected (deficits are more persistent in election years, i.e., fiscal adjustment to past deficits is slower during election periods) but it is not statistically significant (the *t*-statistic is 1.41).[15]

Column (4) of table 7.7 adds the left-wing government dummy (LEFT). After controlling for the election year effect, the coefficient on the left-wing government dummy has a positive sign (i.e., deficits are higher during left-wing administrations) but is not statistically significant. We obtain the same result even if we do not control for ELE in our regressions (see column (5)). Therefore, there is no statistical evidence in favor of the hypothesis that left-wing governments have a greater bias toward deficits. In a shorter (1961–1985) sample we found evidence that, in addition to ELE, the left-wing dummy variable was statistically significant, indicating higher budget deficits during these regimes.[16] The extension of the sample from 1985 to 1993 eliminates this result. An interpretation of this might be that, in the last decade, even left-wing governments have become fiscally more conservative. In fact, the worldwide recession of the early 1980s left a legacy of high deficits and large debt-to-GDP ratios in many industrial countries and led to a general trend toward fiscal retrenchment in the second half of the decade. This fiscal adjustment was accomplished in most countries regardless of the partisan nature of the ruling coalition.[17] The interpretation of this result (and the result itself) is consistent with the evidence of Alesina and Perotti (1995b). They show that left- and right-wing governments have been about equally likely to implement significant fiscal adjustments, defined as large reductions of primary deficits. Although these authors consider a 1960–1993 sample, a majority of major fiscal adjustments occurred in the last decade, after the large accumulation of debts that occurred in several countries in the decade following the first oil shock.[18]

Does this electoral budget cycle found in the results displayed in table 7.7 derive from increased spending before elections or reduced taxes? Conceptually, the issue is ambiguous. The choice of whether to reduce taxes or increase spending in any single country may vary over time and over different elections. We do not necessarily expect to find

Table 7.8
Political business cycle determinants of fiscal spending and revenues
Dependent variable: dgy (Columns (1), (2)), dty (Columns (3), (4))

Independent variable	(1) Coefficient (t-statistic)	(2) Coefficient (t-statistic)	(3) Coefficient (t-statistic)	(4) Coefficient (t-statistic)
Constant	0.006 (6.84)	0.0057 (6.53)	0.0032 (4.85)	0.0032 (4.59)
dU	0.089 (2.72)	0.091 (2.78)	−0.069 (−2.64)	−0.068 (−2.62)
dy	−0.36 (−14.3)	−0.36 (−14.4)	−0.04 (−2.31)	−0.047 (−2.30)
ELE	0.0011 (0.77)	—	−0.0014 (−1.22)	—
ELX	—	0.0020 (1.45)	—	−0.0008 (−0.70)
R^2	0.47	0.47	0.05	0.04

a strong effect of elections on government spending or taxes in a large panel of countries.

Despite these caveats, we test whether there is any electoral cycle in government spending and revenues.[19] Given the strong persistence of the ratio of government spending and government revenues over GDP, we take as our dependent variables the first difference of the ratio of government expenditures (dgy) and taxes (dty) over GDP.[20] We ran the two variables over our measures of the business cycle, the change in unemployment (dU), the change in growth rate (dy), and our electoral dummies (ELE and ELX). Table 7.8 presents the results of these regressions. Columns (1) and (2) display the results for government spending (dgy). As expected, the change in the ratio of government spending to GDP has a strong cyclical component (it increases when unemployment goes up and when there is a growth slowdown). The electoral dummies ELE and ELX enter with the appropriate sign, that is, government spending relative to GDP tends to increase before elections; however, the coefficient estimates are not statistically significant (the highest *t*-statistic is 1.45 and is obtained when we use ELX as our electoral dummy). Columns (3) and (4) show a strong cyclical impact of unemployment on tax revenues; surprisingly, however, an acceleration of growth rates leads to a reduction in the revenues-to-GDP ratio. The electoral dummy has the expected sign (i.e., tax revenues are lower before elections) but it is not statistically significant (the highest *t*-statistic is 1.22 and is obtained when ELE is used as the electoral dummy).

Finally, we tested systematically whether particular subcomponents of spending and revenues have a more pronounced electoral cycle (such as government transfers or social security payments), but we found no stronger effects than the ones shown in table 7.8. In particular, Rogoff's (1990) hypothesis that preelectoral signalling leads to a reduction in public investment spending and an increase in government consumption (or transfers) does not seem to be supported by the data. (All these results are available upon request). Further work along these lines may prove quite worthwhile.

7.6 Conclusions

In this chapter we examined the evidence of political business cycles and partisan cycles in macroeconomic policy instruments in a large set of OECD countries. The results of the regressions are quite interesting. We found stronger evidence in favor of partisan cycles than electoral cycles in monetary policy. The evidence suggests the existence of partisan differences in monetary growth rates and short- and long-term interest rates that, together with the results on output growth, unemployment rates and inflation in chapter 6, are consistent with the rational partisan theory.

For the political business cycle model, the evidence on monetary growth is consistent with the idea of a preelectoral monetary expansion. There is stronger evidence of an electoral cycle in fiscal policy; budget deficits appear to be higher during election years.

The results of this chapter together with those in chapter 6 reject Nordhaus's formulation of the political business cycle, but do not reject the rational political cycles models of Rogoff and Sibert (1988) and Persson and Tabellini (1990). In fact, even though in chapter 6 we found no evidence of cycles on GDP and unemployment, here we found evidence of electoral cycles on monetary and fiscal policy instruments and on inflation. Our interpretation of these results is that, in general, politicians try to avoid restrictive monetary and fiscal policies in election years, and occasionally they are openly expansionary. This view is consistent with the overall significance of the electoral dummy in the full sample of countries and with its lack of significance in many subsamples (i.e., specific countries). In summary, our results suggest that monetary and budget cycles occur frequently, and in several countries, but in no country do they occur in every election or are they of very large dimensions.

Appendix

Table 7.A.1
Monetary and fiscal data for the OECD countries in the sample

---

Data for monetary regressions. Frequency: quarterly.

Money growth: The money growth rate is obtained as the annual rate of change of the M1 definition of money as described in the text; M1 is taken from line 34 of the International Monetary Fund, International Financial Statistics (IMF-IFS). The sample is 1960:1–1993:3 for all countries but two:
United Kingdom: 1960:1–1992:4; Belgium: 1960:1–1990:4.

Short rate: The short-term interest rate is obtained from either line 60b (money market rate) or line 60c (treasury bill rate) of the IMF-IFS data set; choice was based on the length of available series. For all countries but those below the sample is 1960:1–1993:3; the exceptions are

Sweden: 1961:1–1993:3
Ireland: 1973:1–1993:3
Austria: 1967:1–1993:3
Denmark: 1972:1–1993:3
Italy: 1971:1–1993:3
Norway: 1971:4–1993:3

Table 7.A.1 (continued)

Finland: 1978:1–1993:3
Switzerland: 1975:4–1993:3

Long rate: The long-term interest rate is obtained from line 63 of the IMF-IFS data set. For all countries but four the sample is 1960:1–1993:3; the exceptions are

Austria: 1970:1–1993:3
Italy: 1960:1–1992:2
Finland: 1972:1–1993:1
Japan: 1966:1–1993:3.

Data for fiscal regressions. Frequency: annual.

For the period until 1985, the data are the same as those used in Roubini and Sachs 1989; and Alesina, Cohen and Roubini 1992, 1993; for 1986–1993, the variables in the fiscal deficit regressions were updated with raw data from IMF-IFS and OECD-MEI.

The panel for the fiscal deficit regressions is unbalanced because data for some variables were missing for some countries. The sample for each country is as follows:

Austria: 1970–1993
Belgium: 1960–1993
Denmark: 1971–1993
France: 1960–1993
Finland: 1970–1993
Germany: 1960–1993
Japan: 1964–1993
Italy: 1964–1993
Netherlands: 1970–1993
Norway: 1970–1993
Sweden: 1970–1993
United Kingdom: 1960–1993
United States: 1960–1993

8   Political Cycles and Central Bank Independence

8.1   Introduction

In the previous seven chapters, we have largely ignored the institutional complexities of macroeconomic policy making. In fact, we have assumed that in a two-party (or two-bloc) election, the winner takes all and has full control over policy. This is, of course, a simplification. In this chapter we move toward integrating theory and evidence of political business cycles in a richer institutional framework by focusing on the issue of the interaction of elected politicians and semi-independent central banks in charge of monetary policy.

In reality, central banks, not politicians, control monetary policy. Governments and legislatures have an indirect influence on monetary policy through a variety of channels that differ according to the central bank's institutional structure: presence of government representatives on central banks' boards, explicit or implicit obligations for the central bank to accommodate fiscal policy, informal contacts between the treasury and the central bank, direct pressures from the prime minister (or president) on the governor of the central bank, the executive's power to appoint the central bank's board and governor, and ultimately the desire of central banks not to displease the politicians too much for fear of losing their prerogatives and autonomy. Which channel of influence is more important may vary from country to country.[1]

A large theoretical and empirical literature has highlighted the benefits of central banks' political independence. The idea is that by insulating monetary policy from the politicians' direct control and by appointing a conservative (i.e., inflation-averse) central banker, one can reduce inflation from a level that is too high because of the policy-makers' fruitless attempts to reduce average unemployment. In other words, independent central banks are a means of achieving credibility in policy making, thus reducing the average and variability of inflation, possibly at low cost in increased real fluctuations.

The first generation of papers discussed the benefits and costs of independence in models that essentially ignored the political arena, because policymakers were modeled as social planners. A welcomed development has followed, with several papers that have incorporated political incentives (partisan and opportunistic) in models where the central bank has some degree of independence. This step forward is important, because if one wants to derive policy prescriptions for institutional reforms, one must take into account that institutions operate in a world of partisan and opportunistic politicians, not in a world of social planners.

If one explicitly accounts for politicians' incentives, in general one finds that the benefits of central bank independence are even higher. The reason is that independent central banks can, up to a point, insu-late monetary policy from politically induced monetary volatility due to partisan or opportunistic motivations. From a positive, predictive point of view, we also argue that these political models are quite con-sistent with the empirical evidence and can explain empirical regu-larities that escape the literature on central bank independence in nonpolitical models.

This chapter is organized as follows. Section 8.2 reviews the basic model that emphasizes the benefits of central bank independence. Sec-tion 8.3 introduces politics in to this model by focusing, in particular, on the effects of central bank independence in a rational partisan model. Section 8.4 discusses other relevant literature, particularly the recent contracting approach to central banks. The last section concludes.

8.2   Independent Central Banks

To address the issue of Central Bank independence in an interesting way, we need to introduce a motive for stabilization, to obtain a meaningful trade-off between output stabilization and average inflation. For this purpose, we adopt a simplified version of the model by Rogoff (1985). Consider the following supply function:

$$y_t = \pi_t - \pi_t^e + \varepsilon_t \tag{8.1}$$

where ε_t is a random shock uncorrelated over time with mean zero and variance σ_ε^2. With this shock we intend to capture in the simplest possible way all the random perturbations that monetary policy might be interested in counteracting.[2]

For the moment we consider the case of a social planner who has the following utility function in each period:

$$U = -\frac{1}{2}\pi_t^2 - \frac{b}{2}(y_t - k)^2$$

$$k > 0 \quad b > 0 \tag{8.2}$$

Equation (8.2) is a generalization of (3.4) and (3.5): The difference is that in (8.2), growth enters quadratically. We need this complication to create an incentive for stabilization policies.[3] The target on growth, k, is greater than the natural level, which, as always, is normalized at zero. We discussed the reasons why the policymaker would like to increase output about the market level in chapter 3. The target on inflation is normalized at zero with no loss of generality; b represents the weight on output variability.

The sequence of events within each period is as follows. First expectations (i.e., nominal wages) are set, then the shock (ε_t) is realized and publicly observed, then inflation is chosen. Therefore, monetary policy can react more quickly to random shocks than the wage setters can, and as a result, monetary policy can have a stabilizing role.

Substituting (8.1) in (8.2), taking the first-order condition with respect to π_t, solving for rational expectations and dropping time subscripts, one obtains[4]

$$\pi = bk - \frac{b}{1+b}\varepsilon, \tag{8.3}$$

$$\pi^e = bk, \tag{8.4}$$

$$y = \frac{1}{1+b}\varepsilon. \tag{8.5}$$

The policy rule (8.3) includes an inflation bias (bk) and a stabilization term ($b/(1+b)\,\varepsilon$). In fact, from (8.3) through (8.5), one obtains

$$E(\pi) = bk, \qquad E(y) = 0 \tag{8.6}$$

$$\mathrm{var}(\pi) = \left(\frac{b}{1+b}\right)^2 \sigma_\varepsilon^2, \qquad \mathrm{var}(y) = \frac{1}{(1+b)^2}\sigma_\varepsilon^2 \tag{8.7}$$

Equation (8.6) shows, again, the time inconsistency problem we illustrated in the appendix to chapter 3: Average inflation is higher than its desired level (zero) without any improvement on average growth. When, as in this case, there is a role for stabilization policies, the story does not end here: Equation (8.7) shows that, although this policy implies the inflation bias described above, it also reduces the variance of growth, because it stabilizes some of the shock's variance. In summary, the policy rule in (8.3) reduces output variance relative to the shock's variance but induces a positive level of average inflation without increasing average growth.

An important question of institutional design is whether one can improve on this outcome. First of all, one way of eliminating the inflation bias would be for the policymaker to commit ex ante to following the first best policy rule, given by:

$$\pi^* = -\frac{b}{1+b}\varepsilon \tag{8.8}$$

This policy rule reduces output variability, obtaining the same variance of growth as in (8.7) without introducing an inflation bias, because with this rule average inflation is zero. The problem is that this rule is "time inconsistent" and therefore not credible, for the same reasons discussed in the appendix to chapter 3. That is, if the public expects this policy, the policymaker has an incentive, ex post, once expectations are formed, to deviate from this rule and create an inflation shock to increase the level of economic activity. Thus, the public would expect this behavior and would not form expectations based on (8.8). As a result, the economy reverts to the equilibrium described in (8.3) to (8.7), which is often labeled the "discretionary equilibrium."[5]

One possible way of enforcing the optimal rule (8.8) is to write a law prescribing that rule. Even laws can be changed ex post, but constitutional laws, for instance, are relatively difficult to change, certainly more difficult than adjusting the course of day-to-day in a discretionary regime. The problem is that policy rules sanctioned as laws must be simple, otherwise monitoring and implementation become problematic.[6] The rule embodied in (8.8) is, indeed, theoretically relatively simple: It is contingent on the realization of one single, publicly observable, shock. In practice, however, the first best policy rule might have to be contingent on the realization of many shocks, not all of which are immediately and publicly observable. This problem is particularly severe when certain relationships between monetary instruments and targets become unstable and unreliable, as often happened in the last decade in several countries.

If complicated monetary rules cannot be turned into laws, one may ask whether simple rules can improve on the discretionary outcome (i.e., no rules) characterized by (8.3). In our model, the only rule simpler than (8.3) and, therefore, the unique and obvious choice is to set the inflation target at the optimal level—zero in our model.[7]

$$\tilde{\pi} = 0 \qquad\qquad\qquad (8.9)$$

Then, the question is whether this simple rule ($\tilde{\pi}$) given in (8.9) is preferable to the discretionary policy in (8.3). To answer this question, the two policies must be evaluated according to the utility function (8.2). Therefore, one must substitute (8.3) into (8.2) and then take expectations over the shock (ε): In fact, the two rules have to be evaluated ex ante, before the realization of the shock, to measure how they work on average, not in a specific case. Pursuing these calculations, then repeating the same procedure for the rule (8.9), and after some algebra, one obtains that the simple rule in (8.9) is preferable to the discretionary outcome (8.3) if and only if:

$$\sigma_\varepsilon^2 \le k^2(1 + b) \tag{8.10}$$

The intuition of this result is simple: If the variance of the shock is low relative to the parameters influencing the inflation bias (b and k), little is lost by giving up stabilization completely. On the contrary, if the variance of the shock is high, the benefits of stabilization more than compensate for the cost of the inflation bias. Equation (8.10) succinctly captures important aspects of the traditional debate of rules versus discretion. Those who favor simple rules believe that the benefits of monetary stabilization are relatively small, for instance because of the "long and variable lags" made famous by Milton Friedman. These economists believe that the output variance affected by monetary policy (σ_ε^2) is low relative to the inflationary costs of a stabilization policy (b and k). Thus these economists believe that (8.10) holds. On the contrary, Keynesian economists believe that the benefits of stabilization are high—σ_ε^2 is high and (8.10) does not hold.

The institution of an independent central bank can generate an outcome superior to both (8.3) and (8.9). Rogoff (1985) notes that social welfare increases if the policymaker delegates, ex ante, the choice of monetary policy to an independent agent. Suppose that the policymaker has the option of selecting an agent with a preference parameter $\hat{b}$ different from his own, if he so wishes. That is, the policymaker can choose an agent who is more (or less) inflation averse than he, that is,

$\hat{b} < b$ (or $\hat{b} > b$). The sequence of events is as follows: First the policy-maker chooses an agent, then expectations are formed, then the shock ε is realized, and finally the agent chooses policy. In the next period, the policymaker can change the agent, but because all periods are identical, the policymaker's optimal choice is always the same in every period. *Independence means that the agent cannot be dismissed ex post, after the shock has occurred and before the policy is chosen.*

To find the optimal $\hat{b}$, we begin to note that once he has been appointed, the central banker will choose the policy characterized in (8.3), with $\hat{b}$ instead of b. This implies that, when in office, the central banker cannot commit (credibly) to any policy rule other than the dis-cretionary policy, given his preferences. This is reasonable, because we are studying precisely whether the institution of central bank indepen-dence can help in situations where credible rules of policy (like (8.9)) are not enforceable because a credible commitment is impossible. Ex ante, the policymaker will choose the central banker (i.e., the $\hat{b}$) who maximizes his utility, knowing that the central banker will follow the policy given in (8.3). The policymaker maximizes over $\hat{b}$ his expected utility function; note that the policymaker's utility will depend on his preferences, specifically on b, and on the parameter $\hat{b}$, because the latter determines the policy rule the central banker follows, once appointed.

$$\max E(U(b,\hat{b})) = E\left[-\frac{1}{2}\left(\hat{b}k - \frac{\hat{b}}{1+\hat{b}}\varepsilon \right)^2 - \frac{b}{2}\left(\frac{1}{1+\hat{b}}\varepsilon - k \right)^2 \right] \qquad (8.11)$$

The solution of this problem (8.11) implies that $0 < \hat{b} < b$, as shown originally by Rogoff, and as we derive in the appendix to this Chapter. *The policymaker improves his own utility (and social welfare if they coin-cide) by delegating monetary policy to an independent agent more inflation averse, i.e., more "conservative," than the policymaker himself.*[8]

The crucial point is that the agent is independent, that is, he cannot be removed ex post. In fact, after expectations are set, the policymaker has an incentive to remove the agent and choose monetary policy directly, thus causing unexpected inflation. This behavior would revert the system to the no-commitment equilibrium with an inflation bias.

Using (8.6) and (8.7), it is important to verify that with an independent and conservative central banker, namely with $\hat{b} < b$, average inflation is lower and growth variability is higher than without an independent central bank. In fact, the price to pay to achieve lower average inflation is that the conservative central banker is less responsive to output shocks.[9] Alesina and Summers (1993) test precisely these two implications in a sample of OECD countries. They find that, in fact, the degree of central bank independence is inversely related to inflation; that is, more independent central banks have been associated with lower average inflation. On the other hand, and contrary to the model's prediction, the variance of real economic activity, measured by the variance of growth and unemployment, is not related to the degree of central bank independence.[10]

The next section tackles this empirical puzzle, merging the partisan theory with this model of central bank independence.

8.3   Political Cycles and Central Bank Independence

Governments and political parties supporting them appoint central bankers, not social planners as assumed in the previous section. Waller (1989) first incorporated the previous discussion of central bank independence into a model with partisan politicians, arguing that instituting central bank independence should reduce politically induced fluctuations in growth and inflation because partisan politicians do not control monetary policy directly. Waller also studies how the sequences of appointments to the central bank board may reduce the inflation bias in monetary policy. The same author (1992) analyzes more precisely the nature of the bargaining process between the two parties in a stylized confirmation process of members of the central bank's board. He studies how the timing of appointments, relative to the timing of elections, influences the two parties' relative bargaining power and therefore the appointees' characteristics (more or less partisan).

We illustrate some of these points, and in particular the role of the central bank as a mitigator of partisan shocks on monetary policy, following the paper by Alesina and Gatti (1995), which addresses issues quite similar to those in Waller 1989. Consider a slight modification of the model of chapter 3, where the output equation is as in (8.1) and the two parties' utility functions are as follows:

$$U^L = -\frac{1}{2}\pi_t^2 - \frac{b^L}{2}(y-k)^2 \tag{8.12}$$

$$U^R = -\frac{1}{2}\pi_t^2 - \frac{b^R}{2}(y-k)^2 \tag{8.13}$$

where $0 < b^R < b^L$. Thus, generalizing our analysis of chapter 3, party L cares more about output stabilization relative to inflation than party R. To keep things simple and with no loss of generality, we assume here that both parties have the same target on inflation, namely zero; that is, using the same notation as in chapter 3 we are imposing $\bar{\pi}^L = \bar{\pi}^R = 0$. The timing of events is as follows: First, expectations (wages) are set; then elections take place; party L wins with exogenous probability P, party R wins with probability $1 - P$. After the election, the shock ε occurs; finally, the party in office chooses policy.[11] Thus, a term of office lasts one period, which also coincides with the duration of a wage contract. Nothing hinges on this assumption, however: The model could easily be extended to multiperiod terms of office.

The critical point is that, as in the model in chapter 3, inflation expectations embody electoral uncertainty, namely:

$$\pi^e = PE(\pi^L) + (1-P)E(\pi^R) \tag{8.14}$$

We can solve the model with the same methodology used in chapter 3. First, we compute the first-order conditions, maximizing U^L and

U^R, taking π^e as given. We then impose rational expectations, using (8.14) on the first-order condition, rearrange and obtain:

$$\pi^L = \frac{b^L(1+b^R)}{(1+b^L) - P(b^L - b^R)}k - \frac{b^L}{1+b^L}\varepsilon, \tag{8.15}$$

$$\pi^R = \frac{b^R(1+b^L)}{(1+b^L) - P(b^L - b^R)}k - \frac{b^R}{1+b^R}\varepsilon. \tag{8.16}$$

Thus, using (8.16) and (8.1) it follows that, if party L is elected:

$$y^L = \frac{(1-P)(b^L - b^R)}{(1+b^L) - P(b^L - b^R)}k + \frac{1}{1+b^L}\varepsilon. \tag{8.17}$$

If, instead, party R is elected, we obtain:

$$y^R = -\frac{P(b^L - b^R)}{(1+b^L) - P(b^L - b^R)}k + \frac{1}{1+b^R}\varepsilon. \tag{8.18}$$

From (8.17) and (8.18), we then obtain our main result:

$$\text{var}(y) = \frac{P(1-P)(b^L - b^R)^2 k^2}{[(1+b^L) - P(b^L - b^R)]^2} + \left[\frac{P}{(1+b^L)^2} + \frac{(1-P)}{(1+b^R)^2}\right]\sigma_\varepsilon^2. \tag{8.19}$$

The variance of output in (8.19) is decomposed in two parts. The first term reflects the fluctuations of output induced by the electoral uncertainty. The second term is the economically induced variance due to the effect of the economic shock's variance, σ_ε^2. The politically induced variance vanishes for $P = 1$ or $P = 0$, namely when there is no political uncertainty. Also, it is increasing in $(b^L - b^R)$, namely in the difference between the two parties' preferences. This is very intuitive: The more different are the two parties' policies, the more the electoral uncertainty influences real economic activity throughexpectation uncertainty. Even though electoral uncertainty creates growth variability, both parties reduce the amount of economic variability induced by the shock ε. The second term in (8.19) captures this effect.

We now ask the following question: Can the two parties improve on the outcome described above by agreeing before the election to appoint an independent central banker who, after the election, chooses policy and cannot be removed from office? More precisely, consider the following timing: First the two parties appoint a Central Banker, namely, they agree on an agent characterized by a certain $\hat{b}$ in his loss function; expectations are formed, then elections take place; ε is realized; finally, the independent agent chooses policy. In this context, the meaning of "independence" becomes even clearer and very consistent with empirical measures of this concept: An independent central banker is one who cannot be easily removed by a newly appointed government and replaced by a different central banker, more sympathetic to the new executive's point of view.

Under an independent central banker with $\hat{b}$ in his utility function, we obtain, solving the model with the usual procedure:

$$E(\pi) = \hat{b}k, \tag{8.20}$$

$$\text{var}(\pi) = \left(\frac{\hat{b}}{1+\hat{b}}\right)^2 \sigma_\varepsilon^2, \tag{8.21}$$

$$E(y) = 0, \tag{8.22}$$

$$\text{var}(y) = \frac{1}{(1+\hat{b})^2} \sigma_\varepsilon^2. \tag{8.23}$$

Using (8.16) and (8.17), one can easily verify that without an independent central bank we have instead

$$E(\pi) = \frac{b^R(1+b^L) + P(b^L - b^R)}{(1+b^L) - P(b^L - b^R)} k \tag{8.24}$$

$$\text{var}(\pi) = \frac{P(1-P)(b^L - b^R)^2 k^2}{[(1+b^L) - P(b^L - b^R)]^2}$$

$$+ \sigma_\varepsilon^2 \left[P\left(\frac{b^L}{1+b^L}\right)^2 + (1-P)\left(\frac{b^R}{1+b^R}\right)^2 \right] \tag{8.25}$$

$$E(y) = 0 \tag{8.26}$$

$$\text{var}(y) = \frac{P(1-P)(b^L - b^R)^2 k^2}{[(1+b^L) - P(b^L - b^R)]^2} + \left[\frac{P}{(1+b^L)^2} + \frac{(1-P)}{(1+b^R)^2}\right]\sigma_\varepsilon^2. \quad (8.27)$$

The question is whether one can find a range of values for $\hat{b}$ such that both parties are better off with an independent central banker than with the noncooperative outcome characterized by (8.24) to (8.27). Alesina and Gatti (1995) suggest that one can easily identify a range of $\hat{b}$ that satisfies this requirement.[12] For our purposes, four observations are important:

1. The variance of output is not necessarily larger with an independent central bank; in fact the variance of output in (8.27), without an independent central bank, can easily be larger than the variance of output with an independent and inflation-averse central banker, as in (8.23). To see this, start from the extreme case in which $b^R = b^L = b$, and $\hat{b} < b$. Now consider a small increase in b^L, to make it slightly larger than b^R. In this case the two parties have very similar preferences, and only a very little political uncertainty is introduced into the system. As $(b^L - b^R)$ increases, the role of the political variances also increases. For $(b^L - b^R)$ sufficiently large (relative to σ_ε^2), the first term in (8.27) becomes predominant, and the variance of output is significantly lower with an independent central bank. Thus, although we should find an empirical correlation between average (and variance of) inflation with the degree of central bank independence, the model implies no correlation between average and variance of real economic activity and degree of central bank independence. These results are consistent with the empirical findings by Alesina and Summers (1993).

2. The second point, closely related, is that explicit consideration of political factors enhances the benefits of central bank independence. In fact, central bank independence, in addition to the benefits pointed out in the literature inspired by Rogoff (1985), insulates the economy from the policy variability and expectation uncertainty caused by partisan cycles.

3. Central bank independence may also insulate the economy from opportunistic political cycles, not only from partisan ones. In election years, independent central banks can more easily resist political pressures for loose money. However, even very independent central banks can resist accommodating governments' desires only up to a point. For example, central bankers may fear decreasing the prospect of their own reappointment. Thus, they may wish to be particularly accommodating to the incumbent executive, if the government and the central banker's future in office are linked.[13]

4. In this model, the longer the central banker's term of office, the better, because this model does not allow for the possibility of changes in preferences that may require an adjustment in the desired central banker. Waller and Walsh (1996) study precisely this problem of accountability. They emphasize an important trade-off: Long terms of office for central bank board members reduce the inflation surprise and therefore the economy's policy-induced variability. Long terms of office are costly, however, if society's preferences change or, one may add, if central bankers' marginal productivity decreases with the time they spend in office.

8.4 A Note on the "Contracting" Approach

The previous discussion has focused on the institutional arrangement of delegating monetary policy to an independent agent. In a recent paper Walsh (1995b) has proposed a different solution.[14] He suggests a "contracting" approach in which the "principal" (i.e., the legislature) sets up a contract with the "agent" (i.e., the central banker). The idea is that one can set up a contract so that the central banker behaves as if he had an additional linear cost of inflation in his objective function. As a result, one can achieve the optimal solution characterized in (8.8).[15] Thus it is relatively easy, in the context of this model with a single observable shock, to achieve the optimal outcome with simple contracts between the central bank and the legislators. In fact, some recent institutional reforms toward "inflation targeting," particularly in New Zealand, Canada, Great Britain, Sweden and Finland, have moved in this direction.[16] The idea of (more or less flexible) inflation targeting can be interpreted as a way of increasing the costs to the Central Banker of deviating from the optimal policy. Although, the simplicity of the contracting approach is impressive in theory, however, the reality of multiple and unforeseeable contingencies makes the implementation of this approach more problematic.

A thorough discussion of alternative monetary rules is outside the boundaries of this book. The only point we intend to make is that this contracting model still awaits a discussion in a framework that explicitly accounts for political incentives. Walsh (1995b), Persson and Tabellini (1994) and Svensson (1995) all consider models where the principal is a social planner who embodies social preferences. What if instead, partisan or opportunistic politicians can modify the central bank's contract? In this case, would the contracting approach be superior to the Rogoff-style conservative independent central banker? How binding should these contracts be for successive governments? Should one require qualified majorities in the legislature to change them? These are fascinating (and still unanswered) questions from both an academic and policy perspective.

8.5   Conclusions

The critical point we hope we have conveyed in this chapter is that, in evaluating alternative institutional arrangements in monetary policy, it is important to view the policymakers as elected politicians with partisan and opportunistic incentives rather than social planners. The institutional choices that are optimal with a social planner may be suboptimal in the world of politics.

In general, institutions put implicit constraints on the government's day-to-day influence on monetary policy are desirable. Independence of the central bank and inflation rules are therefore all the more attractive in the world of real political conflict, relative to the hypothetical word of social planners. A critical point, however, is the trade-off between independence and accountability. On the one hand, one would want a central bank insulated from day-to-day partisan and opportunistic influences; on the other hand, monetary authorities cannot be totally detached and impenetrable to society's preferences.

Appendix

Solution to problem (8.11):

$$\max_{\hat{b}} E(U(b, \hat{b})) = E\left[-\frac{1}{2}\left(\hat{b}k - \frac{\hat{b}}{1+\hat{b}}\varepsilon\right)^2 - \frac{b}{2}\left(\frac{1}{1+\hat{b}}\varepsilon - k\right)^2\right] \qquad \text{(A.8.1)}$$

The first-order condition is the following:

$$E\left[-\left(\hat{b}k - \frac{\hat{b}}{1+\hat{b}}\varepsilon\right)\left(k - \frac{\varepsilon}{(1+\hat{b})^2}\right) + b\left(\frac{\varepsilon}{1+\hat{b}} - k\right)\left(\frac{\varepsilon}{(1+\hat{b})^2}\right)\right] = 0$$
$$\text{(A.8.2)}$$

Rearranging terms and taking expectations, one obtains:

$$\frac{\sigma_\varepsilon^2}{(1+\hat{b})^3}(b - \hat{b}) = \hat{b}k^2 \qquad \text{(A.8.3)}$$

where $\sigma_\varepsilon^2 = E(\varepsilon^2)$ is the variance of ε. From (A.8.3) it follows that $b = \hat{b}$ cannot be a solution of this problem, since in this case the left hand side of (A.8.3) is zero and the right hand side is positive. The solution must imply

$$b > \hat{b} \qquad \text{(A.8.4)}$$

Equation (A.8.4) shows that the social planner chooses a central banker more inflation averse (i.e., more conservative) than himself.

9

Political Parties, Institutions, and Budget Deficits

9.1 Introduction

One of the most striking observations in the recent economic history of OECD countries is the emergence of very large and persistent deficits in many (but not all) industrialized countries, starting approximately in the mid-1970s. Table 9.1 highlights both the very high current debt-to-GDP ratios in many countries and the large cross-country variance. In the early 1990s, the debt-to-GDP ratios vary from more than 120 percent (in Italy and Belgium) to less than 40 percent (in Australia). Until the early 1970s, the debt-to-GDP ratios were relatively low as a result of a steady decline since the end of World War II, and the cross-country variance was moderate. Since the early 1970s, both the average and the variance of debt-to-GDP ratios in OECD countries have increased tremendously.

These observations lead immediately to two questions:

1. Why do we observe large and persistent deficits in peacetime, and why have these deficits increased so dramatically in the last two decades?

2. Why do we observe large debts in certain countries and not in others?

The relevant economic framework that one should use to begin addressing these questions is the "tax-smoothing" model of optimal

Table 9.1
Public debt in OECD countries

	1965	1975	1990	1994
Australia	N.A.	N.A.	23.5%	36.1%
Austria	19.4%	23.9%	58.3	65.7
Belgium	67.49	61.1	128.5	135.0
Canada	58.79	43.1	73.1	95.6
Denmark	11.30	11.9	68.0	81.1
Finland	17.70	8.56	16.8	62.3
France	53.1*	41.1	40.4	54.7
Germany	17.3	25.1	43.4	51.5
Greece	14.1	22.4	77.7	119.0
Ireland	N.A.	64.4	97.4	92.3
Italy	35.4	60.4	106.4	123.9
Japan	.07	22.4	66.0	75.6
Netherlands	52.2	41.4	78.8	79.1
Norway	47.0*	44.7	32.5	43.5
Portugal	N.A.	N.A.	68.6	70.5
Spain	N.A.	N.A.	50.3	68.2
Sweden	30.5	29.5	44.3	79.5
Switzerland	N.A.	N.A.	N.A.	N.A.
United Kingdom	81.8	63.7	39.3	54.5
United States	52.1	42.7	55.7	63.0

Source: OECD. Figures represent gross debt as a share of GDP.
* 1970 Observation.

taxation proposed by Barro (1979) and Lucas and Stokey (1983).[1] According to this approach to fiscal policy, budget deficits and surpluses should be used to minimize the distortionary effects of taxation. Thus, tax rates should be relatively constant, and deficits and surpluses should be used as a buffer to "smooth" spending and revenue shocks. Thus, budget deficits should be observed only when tax revenues are temporarily low (for instance, during recessions) or public spending is temporarily high (for instance, during wars—"cold" or "hot," national calamities, or other exceptional circumstances).

As a normative theory of the government budget, the importance of the tax-smoothing model cannot be overemphasized. As a "positive" (i.e., explanatory and predictive) model of fiscal policy, the success of the tax-smoothing model is more questionable. Barro (1979, 1986, 1987) shows that the tax-smoothing model provides a convincing explanation of U.S. and British fiscal history in the last 200 years. In fact, it is quite remarkable how much of these two important cases this theory can explain.

However, the tax-smoothing model alone cannot answer the two questions we raised above. First, the OECD countries have similar recent economic histories and, except perhaps for the United States, have not been involved in major wars since the end of World War II; thus it is unclear how the tax-smoothing model can explain this cross-country variance. Second, a rapid increase of debt-to-GDP ratios over two decades with no wars is inconsistent with the tax-smoothing model. Note that this growth of debt-to-GDP ratios has been so high in some countries in the late 1980s and early 1990s that some countries (particularly Belgium, Greece, and Italy) seemed to violate a long-run public-sector solvency, as discussed, for instance, in Buiter, Corsetti, and Roubini 1993. Once again, this does not mean that the tax-smoothing theory is wrong, simply that not all governments follow the principles of optimal taxation.

Because economic theory alone cannot answer our two questions, one must turn to politics. Alesina and Perotti (1995b, 1996) review the political economy literature that has addressed budget deficits and evaluate it on its ability to answer the two questions raised above. They conclude that the two most important institutional variables that help explain actual fiscal policies are the structure of government (coalition versus single-party governments) and budgetary procedures, namely all the rules and regulations determining how budgets are prepared, approved and implemented. These institutional differences can explain budget deficits' cross-country variance. The interaction of these institutional features with the large economic shocks of the early 1970s can explain why large and persistent deficits in peacetime have started to appear in the last twenty years and not before.

In this chapter we discuss whether, after controlling for some of these institutional differences, partisan and opportunistic motivations affect the timing and patterns of budget deficits. Unfortunately, an empirical literature based on cross-country samples that covers the last, say, thirty years of OECD fiscal policies is just beginning, thus the available results are still not quite settled. Our reading of the literature and our own tests discussed below lead to a few tentative conclusions. First, opportunistic motivations lead to relatively loose fiscal policies in election years, after controlling for institutional differences across countries. This electoral effect is not very large, however, and does not appear to be the main determinant of major changes in fiscal policy.

Second, partisan effects on budget deficits appear in some specifications but not in others, depending upon what one controls for. This point needs further research. In fact, from a theoretical point of view, it is not obvious whether left-wing parties should favor deficits more than right-wing parties. After all, running a deficit means choosing to tax tomorrow rather than today for given expenditures. One may argue that the crucial partisan distinction is not on the level of deficits but on the level of spending.

This chapter is organized as follows. Section 9.2 briefly reviews politico-economic models of budget deficits and the relevant empirical evidence. Section 9.3 presents our results and those of others on the specific question of opportunistic and partisan effects on budget deficits. Section 9.4 discusses some normative implications for institutional design. Section 9.5 concludes.

9.1   Political Models of Budget Deficits

To discuss explanations of why budget deficits are "too high" (or "too low," or "just right"), one needs a benchmark. Most of the literature reviewed in this section takes, more or less explicitly, the tax-smoothing model as its benchmark. Thus, the political models considered attempt to explain which institutional features may explain deviations from the tax-smoothing model. Alesina and Perotti (1995b) classify these models into six groups:

1. models based upon the idea of "fiscal illusion";
2. models of debt as a strategic variable;
3. models of intergenerational redistributions;
4. models of distributional conflict;
5. models of geographically dispersed interests;
6. models of budgetary institutions.

The first type of model, developed by the public choice school[2] is based on two crucial assumptions: Policymakers are opportunistic and use budget deficits to increase their chances of reelection; and voters do not understand the government's intertemporal budget constraint; in particular, they overestimate the benefits of current expenditures and underestimate current and especially future tax burdens. As a result, voters do not punish politicians for the opportunistic policies that generate excessive deficits. Alesina and Perotti (1995a) argue that although these models of fiscal illusion can certainly contribute to explaining loose fiscal policies in election years, they are vastly insufficient as an explanation of the large accumulation of debts in some countries and not in others, as documented in table 9.1. In particular, it is unclear how this theory can explain the very large differences between countries, unless one argues that voters are intrinsically more prone to illusion in one country than another. Furthermore, it is unclear why the interaction between fiscal illusion and opportunistic politicians should have created large budget deficits from the mid-1970s onward, but not before. As we show in the next section, opportunistic motivations may explain some preelectoral distortions in fiscal policy, but it is difficult to argue that the electoral motivation is the only answer to the two questions we raised above, and more generally, the sole explanation of the long-run behavior of budget deficits in OECD countries.

The second type of model views the stock of debt as a strategic variable linking the current government to future governments. By manipulating current fiscal policy, today's government can influence the choices of its successors, who may have a different preference on fiscal policy.[3] This conflict implies that the current government does not fully internalize the cost of running budget deficits today. This deficit bias is increasing in the degree of political polarization (reflected in the difference in spending priorities between current and future governments) and in the degree of electoral uncertainty. Suppose, for example, that the current administration would like to reduce the size of government, measured by the ratio of spending to GDP. If the current administration knows that the next would, instead, increase government spending, it may cut taxes today, thereby bequeathing a large debt to its successors. The next government will have to use tax revenues to service the debt and will be forced to reduce, up to a point, its plan of increasing primary spending. Clearly, the two critical components of this type of models are different preferences among different parties in office at different points in time and some alternation in office. In related work, Aghion and Bolton (1990) show that budget deficits can be strategically used to influence electoral results by causing individuals to change their preferences on fiscal policy as a result of changes in their asset holding: the more government debt the public holds, the more averse it will be to inflation, default and other nonconservative macroeconomic policies.

This setup has been used to explain certain specific episodes, most importantly the Reagan deficits in the early 1980s, viewed as a maneuver to constrain the welfare spending of future Democratic administrations. A *New York Times* editorial of January 25, 1987, states, referring the budget deficits of the early to mid-1980s: "This deficit is no despised orphan. It is President Reagan's child and secretly he loves it: *The deficit rigorously discourages any idea of another dime for social welfare*" (emphasis added). Persson and Svensson (1989) suggest that these models are consistent with the Swedish experience of the fiscally loose conservative government in 1976–82. However, despite this anecdotal evidence, these models still lack a consistent and rigorous empirical test.

The third type of model emphasizes that public debt can redistribute the tax burden across generations and can be used by the current generation to leave negative bequests to future generations. That is, by increasing debt today, the current generation can switch the tax burden to future generations. The current generation can vote and choose the policy while the future ones cannot; thus today's electorate has an obvious political advantage.[4]

Although intergenerational conflicts are clearly important, it is not obvious that they can explain the large differences across countries, because this same type of conflict should then be present everywhere. Secondly, it is not a priori obvious why the intergenerational conflict should have appeared in the early 1970s. Clearly, aging populations straining social security systems have a lot to do with persistent budget deficits. But the very large cross-country differences shown in table 9.1 cannot be easily linked to differences in the population's age structure.

The fourth type of model focuses on the conflict among policy makers or parties which have a simultaneous influence on budgetary decisions. An obvious example of this situation would be a coalition government. One way of studying the behavior of coalition governments in fiscal matters is to use a "war of attrition" model as proposed by Alesina and Drazen (1991). In this model, an initial, exogenous, permanent fiscal shock creates budget deficits. A social planner would react immediately to the shock by raising tax revenues to balance the budget.[5] Consider instead the case of two groups or political parties that have to agree on a fiscal policy.[6] Thus, whereas in the partisan model discussed above, different parties are in office at different times, in this model both parties have a veto power over the adoption of a fiscal stabilization, defined as a change of policy that stabilizes the debt-to-GDP ratio.

In other words, the two groups must decide how to share the fiscal burden of the stabilization. The longer they wait, the higher are the costs, since the prestabilization fiscal distortions persist over time and the debt accumulates. An immediate agreement on how to share the fiscal burden of stabilization makes both groups better off compared with the same agreement reached after a delay. However, rational delays occur under two conditions: either when the proposed stabilization is "inequitable," so one group has to bear a disproportionate share of the fiscal burden; or when the two groups are not informed about how costly it is for the opponent to postpone the fiscal stabilization.

These costs of delaying stabilizations include lobbying, filibustering, and direct political actions necessary to prevent the opponent from enacting a stabilization plan tilted in his or her favor. An alternative, non–mutually exclusive interpretation of these costs emphasizes the economic costs of the prestabilization economic instability. Both groups want to avoid being the "loser," the group that is taxed proportionally more when the fiscal stabilization comes. Generally, neither group will accept being the loser immediately, because it hopes the other group will do so. The optimal concession time for each group is determined by equating the marginal cost of waiting with the marginal benefit of waiting. The former is the utility cost of living another instant in the unstable economy. The latter is given by the conditional probability that the other group will concede in the next instant multiplied by the difference in utility between being the winner and the loser, that is, between paying the lower and the higher share of the fiscal burden. Thus, this model's message is simple: after an exogenous fiscal shock, stabilization is delayed when multiparty politics attributes, formally or informally, a veto power to various members of a coalition that influences fiscal policy.

Spolaore (1993) develops these ideas and applies them more directly to different government structures. In doing so, he formalizes the trade-off between single-party and coalition governments. Coalition governments delay stabilizations because of a war of attrition, as discussed above. In Spolaore's model, however, single-party governments have the opposite problem: They stabilize too much! That is, they overreact to shocks, because they do not fully internalize the costs of stabilizations. In fact, they know that they can shield their supporting constituency from the fiscal burden of the stabilization. Thus, we have a trade-off between the relative inaction of coalition governments and the partisan overreaction of majority single-party governments.

In related work, Velasco (1995) models a deficit bias in coalition governments with a "tragedy of the commons" game. He views spending ministers in a coalition government as drawing from a common pool of fiscal revenues. Lacking a strong unitary leadership such as that provided by, say, the prime minister in a single-party majority government, no spending minister internalizes the budget constraint. So in equilibrium, the government as a whole overdraws on fiscal revenues, generating budget deficits. In summary, these studies point toward government fragmentation as a critical institutional variable that distinguishes high-debt countries from low-debt countries. More specifically, the argument is that coalition governments delayed the structural fiscal adjustments that became necessary after the buildup of budget deficits started in the mid-1970s, following the first oil shock.

Empirical evidence on this type of models is quite promising. Work by Roubini and Sachs (1989a,b) and Grilli, Masciandaro, and Tabellini (1991) shows that coalition governments and, in particular, fragmented and unstable coalitions, react more slowly to fiscal shocks and, as a result, lead to accumulation of public debt. The next section reviews some of this evidence.

The fifth type of model emphasizes the interaction between the organization of legislatures and fiscal decisions.[7] Those advancing such a model argue that the political representatives of geographically-based constituencies overestimate the benefits of public expenditures in their district relative to their financing costs, because these costs are borne not only by the legislator's constituents but by taxpayers of every constituency. This failure to internalize the tax costs of spending programs leads to government spending in excess of the optimal level.

From the perspective of our two questions, these models have two problems. First, they are static. Therefore, although they can explain the size of government spending, they are not well equipped for explaining the intertemporal allocation of taxes and expenditures which generates budget deficits. In fact, current fiscal revenues could completely finance large expenditures on pork barrel projects. Second, the type of discretionary government spending (pork barrel projects) on which these models focus, has not grown more rapidly in the last two decades. Transfers and entitlement programs have grown more than proportionally relative to total government spending in the last two decades, are they are typically not geographically based.

The last type of model emphasizes the role of budgetary institutions, defined as all the rules and regulations according to which budgets are drafted, approved and implemented. These rules vary greatly across countries, thus they can potentially explain cross-country variance. One can identify three components of procedures: formal laws which prescribe numerical targets on the deficits, such as balanced budget laws; voting procedures in the preparation and implementation of the budget; and transparency of the budget document.[8]

Balanced budget laws are virtually nonexistent for national governments. However, U.S. states have a variety of restrictions on their fiscal balance, from rather stringent balanced budget prescriptions to virtually no restrictions. A recent lively research has shown that these restrictions do indeed affect different states' fiscal positions. Regulations that limit the ability of states to run deficits generate lower average deficits and quicker responses to adverse shocks.[9]

As for voting procedures, one can identify two phases in the budget process: the formulation of a budget proposal within the executive, and the presentation and approval of the budget in the legislature. The literature on the influence of voting procedures on the budget outcome has been developed mostly in the context of the models of geographically dispersed interests briefly reviewed above and has addressed two questions: What procedural rules make the choice of projects, given a certain total budget, more or less efficient? How do different procedural rules influence the final allocation of net benefits among districts?

Two issues have been emphasized: the timing of votes and the rules concerning admissible amendments to the budget. As for the timing, an important question from the point of view of fiscal discipline is whether one should vote first on the aggregate size of the budget (total spending, deficit and taxation) and then, after the first binding vote, decide on the allocation of spending programs. The alternative procedure is to vote first on various programs and then determine the aggregate spending and deficit as a residual.

Intuitively, one might think that the first type of voting procedure should lead to more budget discipline. However, Ferejohn and Kreibel (1987) show (theoretically) that the size of the budget is not always smaller when legislatures vote first on its size and then on its composition. In fact, forward-looking legislators, when voting first on the budget's composition, calculate how their first vote affects the final outcome, both in terms of size and composition. Conversely, when voting on the size of the budget first, rational legislators can compute how a certain size will then lead to a certain composition in the following sequence of votes on various budget components.[10] Despite these caveats, the empirical literature reviewed below shows that in general, to vote first on the size and then on the composition favors fiscal discipline.

As for amendment rules, Baron (1989, 1991) and Baron and Fere-john (1989) study how different procedures lead to different budget outcomes, in terms of size and allocation of pork barrel projects. They distinguish between closed rules and open rules. A *closed rule* is one in which the legislature must vote immediately either for or against the proposal made by a member of the legislature. If the proposal is ap-proved, "the game is over" and the budget approved; if it is rejected, a new member of the legislature can make another proposal, which, again is voted up or down. An *open rule* is one in which the proposal made by the member selected can be amended from the floor. That is, the first member selected makes a proposal. Another member is then selected, and he can either ask for a vote on the proposal as it is or propose an amendment. In the second case, the amendment is balloted against the proposal. The winner becomes the new proposal on the floor and a new member is selected, and so forth. Alesina and Perotti (1996b) summarize the results of this literature in four points as follows:

1. An open rule creates delays in the approval of a proposal, where "delays" means that more than one vote is needed for a budget to pass.

2. A closed rule leads to the adoption of more inefficient budgets, namely budgets where the ratio of aggregate benefits to aggregate taxation is lower.

3. A closed rule leads to the adoption of "majoritarian" allocation rules. That is, the benefits are allocated to a "50 percent plus one" fraction of the legislature. An open rule may lead to a distribution of benefits in which more than "the minimum majority" of legislators receive positive net benefits.

4. With an open rule the distribution of benefits within the winning majority are more egalitarian than with a closed rule.

Therefore, with closed rules, voting procedures are more hierarchical, with open rules they are more collegial. Hierarchical procedures attribute more power to the first agenda-setter and have a top-bottom nature. For simplicity and tractability, in the formal literature the agenda-setting power is attributed randomly to a member of the legislature. In reality, in parliamentary democracies the executive has the agenda-setting power vis-à-vis the legislature, and one member of the executive (typically the treasury minister) has the agenda-setting power within the government. Thus, hierarchical procedures attribute strong powers to the treasury minister against spending ministers within intragovernmental negotiations on the formulation of the budget. Also hierarchical institutions limit the legislature's prerogatives to amend the budget the government has proposed. Collegial institutions have the opposite features; namely, they do not attribute a special status to the treasury minister vis-à-vis spending ministers, attribute vast amendment powers to the legislature, and generally emphasize collegiality in the budget process and protect the prerogatives of the minority not represented in the government coalition. A rather common limitation on legislatures' amendment prerogatives is the prohibition on increasing the deficit target (and sometimes the spending target) by the government has proposed. On the contrary, legislatures typically can amend the allocation of government-proposed spending programs. Thus, hierarchical procedures limit legislative amendments to the budget's composition but impose a closed rule on the size of the deficit and sometimes of total spending. Collegial institutions allow amendments not only on the composition but also on total spending and even on the deficit.

Finally, one should consider the issue of transparency. Having transparent budget documents and procedures should be considered as important as having appropriate voting and procedural rules. In fact, politicians do have no incentive to produce the most transparent budget, for two reasons. The theory of "fiscal illusion" (Buchanan and Wagner 1977) provides the first: Lack of budget transparency can increase voters' "illusion," namely their tendency to overestimate the benefits of public spending and underestimate the costs of current and future taxation. Opportunistic politicians facing naive voters have no incentive to inform them precisely about their short-termist and possibly suboptimal fiscal policies. Thus, the less transparent are budget procedures and budget documents, the easier it is for opportunistic politicians to engage in preelectoral fiscal manipulations and, more generally, favor one lobby group or the other. The second argument holds even in a model with rational voters. For instance, Cukierman and Meltzer (1986), Alesina and Cukierman (1990), Rogoff and Sibert

(1988), and Rogoff (1990) in a variety of different contexts emphasize the benefit of a certain amount of ambiguity in the policy process. In a few words, the idea is that by creating confusion and, in particular, by making it less clear how policies translate into outcomes, policy-makers can retain a strategic advantage over rational, but not fully informed voters. For instance, as we argued in chapter 2, rational opportunistic fiscal cycles can arise if the voters are not perfectly (and timely) informed about the budget. Nontransparent procedures are a critical ingredient in making electoralistic policies possible with rational voters. This informational advantage would disappear with transparent procedures.

Empirical work on cross-country samples on the effects of budgetary procedures is just beginning. Von Hagen (1992) and von Hagen and Harden (1994) study the twelve countries that are members of the European Union; Alesina, Hausmann, Hommes, and Stein (1996) focus on Latin American countries; Kountopoulos and Perotti (1996) study OECD countries. All these studies rely on the construction of some indexes of budgetary procedures, from the most hierarchical-transparent to the most collegial-nontransparent. All find that hierarchical-transparent procedures have positive effects on fiscal discipline, whereas countries with more collegial-nontransparent procedures run more persistent and larger deficits and take longer to react to adverse fiscal shocks.

9.3   Opportunistic and Partisan Effects on Fiscal Policy Revisited

In chapter 7 we studied opportunistic and partisan effects without explicitly allowing for differences in government structure or budget procedures. In this section we return to studying these influences but allow for cross-country institutional differences. As argued in the preceding sections, of all the institutional models of budget deficits, the two most successful empirically are those emphasizing the effects of government fragmentation (i.e., coalition governments) and budget procedures on fiscal outcomes.

We follow Roubini and Sachs (1989a,b), and consider the evidence of the last thirty years in OECD countries. These authors show that coalition governments have had a tendency to follow looser fiscal policies than single-party governments. The question that more directly concerns us here is whether partisan and opportunisitic effects, studied in chapter 7, survive once one has controlled for government structure. To answer this question we extend the results presented in table 7.7. We use basically the same model of deficits, but we add a variable, POL, that captures the degree of government fragmentation. Roubini and Sachs define this variable as follows:

POL = 0   in one-party majority governments or in a presidential system with the same party holding the presidency and the majority in the legislature;

POL = 1   in a coalition parliamentary government with two-parties in the coalition; or in a presidential system with the party holding the presidency without a majority in the legislature;

POL = 2   in coalition governments with two or more parties members of the coalition

POL = 3   in minority parliamentary governments.[11]

Clearly, this variable is increasing in the degree of fragmentation in the structure of government. In column (1) of table 9.2, the variable POL is the only political variable in addition to the economic determinants of deficits. The economic variables included in the regression are identical to those of table 7.7, and the reader is therefore referred to that table and the accompanying discussion of it for a more extensive treatment of these variables. The variable POL is statistically significant at the 5 percent level with the expected sign. In columns (2) and (3) we add our electoral variable (ELE) and a partisan variable (LEFT), defined as before. The former is significant, the latter is not, although it has the sign the theory predicts. These results confirm what we found

Table 9.2
Political effects on fiscal policy
Dependent variable: real budget deficit (% of GDP) (db)

Independent variable	(1) Coefficient (t-statistic)	(2) Coefficient (t-statistic)	(3) Coefficient (t-statistic)
Constant	−0.002 (2.02)	−0.005 (2.63)	−0.006 (2.68)
$db(-1)$	0.74 (19.6)	0.75 (19.7)	0.74 (19.6)
dU	0.20 (3.40)	0.21 (3.47)	0.21 (3.54)
dy	−0.49 (9.88)	−0.50 (10.0)	−0.50 (10.1)
$b_{-1}d(r-y)$	0.50 (3.39)	0.47 (3.17)	0.46 (3.08)
ELE	−	0.005 (2.16)	0.005 (2.19)
POL	0.0032 (2.40)	0.003 (2.31)	0.003 (1.41)
LEFT	−	−	0.002 (0.79)
R^2	0.66	0.67	0.67

in chapter 7, even after controlling for the government fragmentation variable, which remains significant.

Further results by Roubini and Sachs suggest that the effects of government fragmentation on government deficit occur mostly or exclusively after the first oil shock. As a matter of fact, budget deficits in OECD countries were uniformly lower before 1973, and more importantly, cross-country differences substantially increased after the major shocks of the mid-1970s. A suggested interpretation is that government fragmentation does not create deficits, but delays fiscal adjustments to external shocks.[12]

Alesina and Perotti (1995a) reach similar results using a different methodology. They study which types of government are more likely

Table 9.3
Government type and fiscal policy

	(1) Observations	(2) Frequency of "very loose"	(3) Frequency of "very tight"	(4) Probability of "success"	(5) Probability of "no success"
Single party	177	8.5%	10.2%	35.7%	64.3%
Coalition	223	12.1%	13.0%	8.7%	91.3%
Minority	109	10.1%	15.6%	46.7%	53.3%
Right	313	8.6%	10.9%	26.9%	73.1%
Center	65	15.4%	10.8%	0.0%	100%
Left	129	12.4%	17.8%	35.1%	64.9%

Source: Alesina and Perotti 1995a.

to engage in loose or tight fiscal policies and in more or less successful fiscal adjustments. They construct a measure of cyclically adjusted primary surplus (called BFI) and use the following definitions:

a. A very loose fiscal policy in year t occurs when the BFI decreases by more than 1.5 percent of GDP.

b. A very tight fiscal policy occurs when the BFI increases by more than 1.5 percent of GDP.

c. A successful adjustment in year t is a very tight fiscal policy in year t such that the gross debt-to-GDP ratio in year $t + 3$ is at least 5 percentage point lower than in year t.[13]

Table 9.3, reproduced from Alesina and Perotti 1995a, draws upon a sample of twenty countries for 1960–92. Governments are classified according to their structure (single party, coalition and minority) and according to their ideological orientation (left, right and center).[14] The first column of the table identifies the number of observations per year with the corresponding type of government. The other columns identify the frequency with which a certain fiscal outcome is observed per type of government. So, for instance, the first entry in column (2) says that in 8.5 percent of years of single-party governments, one observes a very loose fiscal policy, etc. The last two columns identify the probability of success of fiscal adjustments, defined as the frequency of success and failure over the total number of very tight policies.

Several interesting observations emerge. The first three columns of the table's top half show that there is little difference in the propensity of the three types of governments to engage in fiscal adjustments and fiscal expansions, that is, loose fiscal policies. However, a striking difference emerges from columns (4) and (5). Fiscal adjustments initiated by coalition governments are almost always unsuccessful. That is, although coalition governments try as often as single-party governments to initiate adjustments, they typically fail. A possible explanation of this result is that intracoalition disagreements together with the pressures exerted by various groups represented by different parties force a relaxation of the tight fiscal stance after an initial attempt. Somewhat surprisingly, minority governments have a fairly high success rate. Note, however, that in some cases minority governments are appointed with the specific goal of reducing budget deficits.

The table's bottom half shows that there is little difference between left- and right-wing governments. What is striking here is that center governments seem incapable of successfully adjusting the budget. This is in fact a confirmation of the coalition weakness argument, because center governments typically have a coalition structure.

In a recent paper, Kontopoulos and Perotti (1996) control for both the structure of government (as we did above) and for an index of budget procedures, similar to the one used for European countries only by von Hagen and Harden (1994). They find that both institutional variables are important determinants of budget deficits in a sample of OECD countries. In this respect they confirm (using a larger sample and more sophisticated procedures and indexes) the findings of some of the previous literature on the subject: The countries more likely to have protracted budget deficits and in particular to take longer in responding to adverse fiscal shocks, are those with coalition governments and collegial-nontransparent budget procedures. These authors also find that a partisan variable becomes significant, after controlling for both these institutional variables, namely the structure of governments (coalitions or not) and budget procedures. Specifically, according to their results, left-wing governments run on average larger deficits than right-wing governments, contrary to the previous finding described above.[15]

9.4 Normative Implications

The evidence presented in previous chapters confirms the hypothesis that there are significant political biases in fiscal policy, such as opportunistic behavior, coalition weakness and collegial-nontransparent budgetary procedures.

The growing awareness of the fiscal implications of political distortions has led to the normative suggestion that discretionary fiscal policy should be restricted by rules limiting the size of government deficits. In the United States, repeated calls for a balanced-budget constitutional amendment have often been motivated by the large deficits of the 1980s and early 1990s. Although a proposed constitutional amendment to balance the budget by the year 2002 was defeated by a narrow margin in 1995, the same goal of a balanced budget is still pursued in the fiscal plans of the U.S. Congress. In Europe, the framers of the Maastricht Treaty on Monetary Union were equally concerned with the possibility of excessive deficits. The treaty includes rules limiting the size of national debt and deficits that must be satisfied as a precondition for a country's admission to the European Monetary Union (EMU).[16]

Are these fiscal rules well grounded, or should fiscal policy be left to policymakers' discretion? As in the case of monetary policy, there is a trade-off between the benefits of rigid fiscal rules and those of fiscal discretion. The main argument in favor of rules is that, if they are enforceable, they would reduce or even eliminate political fiscal biases. The first disadvantage of rigid rules such as balanced-budget amendments is that they do not allow the necessary flexibility in fiscal policy required to react to various economic shocks.[17] As argued above, both neoclassical and Keynesian models of fiscal deficits advocate the optimality of deficit spending during recessions.

The empirical evidence that balanced budget rules have been effective in restraining the ability of American state governments to run large fiscal deficits has strengthened the arguments in favor of fiscal rules as tools for fiscal discipline.[18] For many reasons, however, these results cannot be used mechanically to argue that a national balanced-budget rule would be similarly effective. First, state rules often permit borrowing for capital expenditures, something ruled out by the recently proposed constitutional balanced-budget amendment. Second, states' rules often allow the accumulation of rainy-day reserves that can be used to run effective deficits during recessions, a form of actual tax-smoothing. Third, countercyclical federal transfers to the states' budgets improve states' ability to balance their budgets during recessions. No such mechanism would be at work at the federal level.[19] Fourth, the supply- and demand-side macroeconomic effects of the attempt to balance a federal budget during a recession via a cut in spending, an increase in taxes, or both would be much larger than those at the state level. In fact, states' revenues and spending as a share of the state income are much smaller than the federal spending and revenues as a fraction of the national income. Thus, one should be cautious in drawing lessons from the states' experiences with balanced-budget rules for national governments.

A second problem of balanced-budget rules is that they generate incentives to engage in creative accounting to circumvent them. These attempts, in addition to partially undermining the rule itself, generate negative side effects by making the budget less transparent, less controllable and easier to manipulate. For both these reasons—flexibility and transparency—we believe that governments should move away from the definition of numerical constraints and focus on the institutions and procedures involved in the process of preparing and approving the budget. In principle, reforms of institutions and procedural budget rules could provide effective fiscal discipline at low macroeconomic costs by enhancing the transparency and the democratic nature of the budget process.[20]

9.5 Conclusions

This chapter argues that, in addition to opportunistic and partisan motivations, several other institutional variables influence the behavior of budget deficits in OECD countries. In particular, the structure of government and budgetary institutions are two important political influences on fiscal policy.

Although an exhaustive treatment of this point is worth another volume, in this brief chapter we have simply emphasized that an appropriate evaluation of the extent of partisan and opportunistic cycles on budget deficits in a multicountry sample cannot ignore the effects of different institutional settings in different countries. After controlling for institutional differences, opportunistic effects appear as significant determinants of the fluctuations of budget deficits. Whether partisan effects are significant is not completely clear from the data.

Before closing, it is useful to make an important connection between the results of this chapter and the previous ones concerning the effect of coalition versus single-party governments. In this chapter we have argued that single-party governments are better suited to enforce fiscal discipline relative to coalition governments. Our results in the previous chapters, however, suggest that single-party governments are also more likely to create partisan cycles in macroeconomic management. Thus, in a sense, coalition governments achieve at the same time moderation and balancing of partisan policies and also gridlock in policy making, particularly in fiscal matters.

Single-party governments are the results of majoritarian electoral systems, whereas coalition governments typically emerge from proportional electoral systems. Which of the two systems is preferable is not then obvious, because both have advantages and disadvantages. In other words, one faces a trade-off in institutional design. It is quite unlikely that extreme choices on this trade-off are optimal, and the underlying distribution of preferences in the population must influence the choice. For example, in very polarized societies, proportional electoral systems and coalition governments may be a necessity to avoid the extremism of single-party governments. In less polarized societies, the risk of extremism is minimal and the benefits of single-party governments may outweigh their costs.

Appendix

In this appendix, we briefly review the tax-smoothing model. The original papers on this subjects are Barro 1979 and Lucas and Stokey 1983.

Consider a benevolent government that has to finance a stream of exogenously given expenditures, denoted $\{G_t\}$, $t: 0 \ldots \infty$. Expenditures are perfectly known in advance. Tax revenues (T_t) are equal to

$$T_t = \tau_t y_t \tag{A.9.1}$$

where τ_t is a tax rate and y_t is national income.

Assume that the interest rate (r) is exogenously given and define the discount factor $\beta = 1/(1+r)$. Then, the government budget constraint is

$$\sum_{t=0}^{\infty} \beta^t G_t + B_0 \leq \sum_{t=0}^{\infty} \beta^t \tau_t y_t \tag{A.9.2}$$

In (A.9.2), B_0 is the stock of outstanding government debt at time zero, where $B_0 \gtreqless 0$. Income taxes are distortionary. We assume that these costs of distortions (C_t) are convex, and to keep things simple, we assume that they are quadratic in the tax rate.

$$C_t = (\tau_t)^2 \tag{A.9.3}$$

The benevolent government's objective is to minimize the costs of tax distortions given its budget constraints. Thus, the government solves:

$$\min \sum_{t=0}^{\infty} \beta^t (\tau_t)^2 \tag{A.9.4}$$

$$\text{s.t.} \quad \sum_{t=0}^{\infty} \beta^t G_t + B_0 \leq \sum_{t=0}^{\infty} \beta^t \tau_t y_t$$

Because the right-hand side of the budget constraint is a constant, the solution of (A.9.4) is immediate:

$$\tau_{t+1} = \tau_t \quad \text{for} \quad t: 0, \ldots, \infty \tag{A.9.5}$$

Using the budget constraint, one obtains:

$$\tau_{t+1} = \tau_t = \bar{\tau} = \frac{\displaystyle\sum_{t=0}^{\infty} \beta^t G_t + B_0}{\displaystyle\sum_{t=0}^{\infty} \beta^t y_t} \tag{A.9.6}$$

Equations (A.9.5) and (A.9.6) capture the basic idea of tax smoothing. The tax rate must be constant at a level compatible with the intertemporal budget constraint. A few examples may help illuminate the intuition.

1. Suppose that income is constant and spending is usually low (G) except for a period of war when G is exceptionally and temporarily high. Figure 9.A.1 identifies the optimal tax-smoothing policy. In this example a (perfectly anticipated) war starts at $t = a$ and ends at $t = b$. The tax-smoothing policy requires the accumulation of a fiscal surplus before the war, an increasing debt during the war, and a reduction of the debt after the war. The level of debt reaches its peak at the end of the war.

2. Suppose that spending is always constant at $\bar{G}$, but income is high and low in alternative periods, that is, expansions and recessions in a stylized business cycle. Figure 9.A.2 illustrates the tax-smoothing

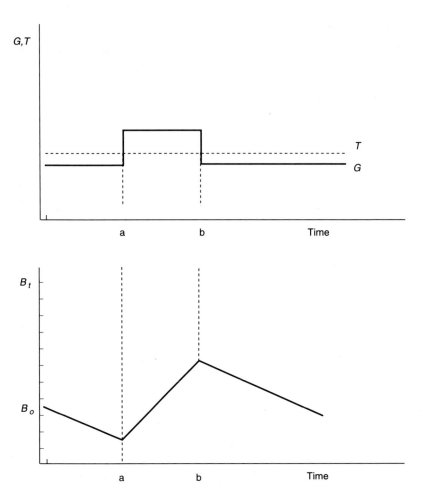

Figure 9.A.1
The tax-smoothing policy: Example 1

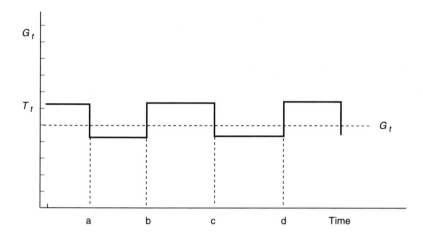

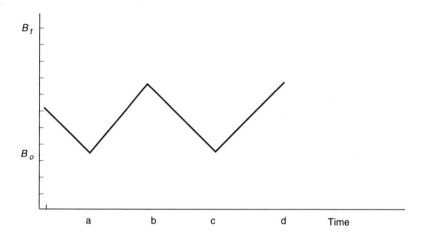

Figure 9.A.2
The tax-smoothing policy: Example 2

policy. The optimal policy implies deficits during recessions and surpluses during expansions.

These two examples capture the two most often cited results of this
model, namely that an optimal fiscal policy implies deficits during wars
and recessions. The corollary is that a policy prescribing a budget balanced in every period is not optimal.

The tax-smoothing theory can be extended in a variety of direc-
tions: a more general formulation of the tax distortions (Barro 1979);
a general equilibrium model where tax distortions are the result of
an endogenous labor supply decision (Lucas and Stokey 1983); a
model with uncertainty about future income and future expenditure
(Lucas and Stokey 1983). Although several of these extensions add
important qualifications to the basic result, the basic message of the
tax-smoothing theory briefly sketched above survives.

10   Conclusions

10.1   Summary of Results

10.1.1   The Success of Rational Models

Although important work in macro-political economics predates the rational expectations revolution in macroeconomics, a new literature emerged as a result of developments in the rational theory of economic policy. This literature emphasizes the constraints that the assumption of individual rationality imposes on the ability of policymakers to systematically, predictably, and permanently influence the state of the economy along an inflation-unemployment trade-off; and policymakers' ability to systematically fool the electorate. The empirical evidence accumulated in this book is quite supportive of the message of these rational models of macro-political economics.

10.1.2   Parties Are Not All Identical

Macroeconomic policies and outcomes are not independent of which party (or coalition of parties) holds office. Left-wing parties are typically associated with more expansionary and inflationary policies than right-wing parties. Because of the rationality constraint, however, these different policies have only short-run real effects. Only in the short run, left-wing governments manage to keep the economy below the natural level of unemployment (or above the natural rate of growth). Conversely, right-wing governments create short-run recessions in their anti-inflationary efforts.

These partisan effects are somewhat stronger on outcomes (growth, unemployment, inflation) than on policy instruments. The evidence on policy instruments is less systematic probably because different governments in different countries and in different time periods may have used different policy instruments to achieve the desired targets; for instance, the spending versus revenue side in fiscal policy, targeting monetary aggregates versus short-term interest rates, and so forth. By focusing on one policy instrument at a time, one obtains a blurred picture, because of the multitude of available instruments and their complex (and often over time unstable) relationship with policy outcomes, the ultimate goals of policymakers. For instance, if different left-wing governments use different policy instruments to reduce unemployment, one may find systematic short-run partisan effect on unemployment but a weak partisan effect on any single policy instrument examined in isolation.

10.1.3 Opportunistic Cycles Are Relatively Small and Unsystematic

We found virtually no evidence of systematic electoral cycles in which growth surges and unemployment falls in the year or two before elections. Two non–mutually exclusive arguments consistent with a rational view can explain this finding. First, policymakers do not have enough control over the economic cycle to be able to create a convenient expansion immediately before each election. Second, an excessively open and systematic preelectoral manipulation of the economy may be counterproductive at the polls, because voters may punish overly opportunistic policymakers.

This second observation raises the controversial issue of rationality of retrospective voting. Although there is ample evidence that high growth in the preelectoral year(s) favors the incumbent at the polls, it is not clear whether this voting behavior is rational. Do voters use all the available information when judging the incumbent on the basis of economic conditions? This is an important question, with empirically relevant implications. For example, should we expect that the electorate will punish an incumbent even when poor economic performance is clearly not due to the government's incompetence? Although this book helps in clarifying the nature and implications of this question, it does not even begin answering it empirically.

Even though we do not observe systematic electoral cycles on growth and unemployment, we document that monetary and fiscal policies tend to be relatively loose in election years. Although these effects are not large and systematic, restrictive monetary policies and budget tightening are rare in election years. Overall, this evidence on electoral and opportunistic cycles is generally more consistent with rational expectations models than with the traditional ones.

10.1.4   *Electoral Uncertainty, Polls, and Economic Cycles*

One of the most stringent implications of the rational partisan theory is that the degree of electoral uncertainty should influence the size of macroeconomic fluctuations. Because of rational expectations and wage-price rigidity, the more unexpected is the electoral outcome, the less expected is the policy followed by the winning party (or coalition) and the larger are its real effects. An empirical test of this implication requires a reliable model of ex ante probabilities of electoral outcomes, based upon available information. Because of the difficulty of constructing these models of probabilities, particularly in multiparty systems, we restricted our analysis on this point to the United States. Our results are quite supportive of the theory—the size of postelectoral recessions and expansions is correlated with the degree of electoral surprise. An extension of these tests to other OECD countries is an excellent topic for future research.

10.1.5 Polls, Electoral Uncertainty, and Financial Markets

If different parties follow different policies when in office, expected inflation depends on preelectoral forecasts of the electoral results. To the extent that expected inflation influences the maturity structure of interest rates, the latter should depend on preelectoral polls. Our results for the United States are consistent with this implication. If, indeed, preelectoral polls influence the term structure of interest rates, then financial markets must perceive significant differences in expected macroeconomic policies.

As often is the case for empirical tests on financial markets, however, these results hold under a variety of technical and substantive assumptions, in particular on the behavior of risk premiums, risk aversion, movement in real interest rates, and the like. Although the difficulty inherent in these tests should caution against overinterpreting them, they are sufficiently intriguing to warrant future investigation.

The stock market potentially provides another ground for testing polls' influence on expectations of future policies. However, conceptual difficulties are even greater than for the case of the term structure of nominal interest rates. Should stock holders view favorably or unfavorably say, a Democratic presidential victory? On the one hand, according to the partisan model, a short-term expansion is more likely to occur than with a Republican victory; on the other hand, tax and regulatory legislation may be more favorable to the business community with a Republican administration. Thus, the effects of polls on the stock market are uncertain, even theoretically.

10.1.6 The Structure of Party Systems Matters

In our sample of OECD countries we find very different types of party systems; from two-party systems (the United Kingdom, for instance) to multiparty systems with strict proportionality (Italy until 1993, and Belgium, for instance), to presidential systems (the United States and

France). Party structure matters for the nature of politico-economic cycles and macroeconomic policy. Partisan cycles are larger in two-party (or two-bloc) systems than in multiparty systems with middle-of-the-road coalition governments. Thus proportional representation, which typically delivers coalition governments, avoids policy cycles and achieves policy moderation. The evidence on budget deficits, however, suggests that coalition governments are slower than single-party governments in responding to fiscal shocks; as a result, government debt accumulates more rapidly and to a larger extent in countries with coalition governments .

Thus proportional electoral systems with coalition governments insure policy moderation but create policy deadlocks and delays in fiscal adjustment. On the other hand, single-party governments, typical of majoritarian electoral systems, have the opposite features: They create partisan cycles but insure prompt policy reaction to shocks. Therefore, from a normative perspective, one faces a trade-off, because neither of the two systems dominates the other on all grounds.

10.1.7 The United States Is Not Exceptional

Our findings on the relationship between elections and the economy suggest that the similarities between the United States and other OECD democracies, particularly those closer to a two-party (or two-bloc) system, are much more important than the differences. For instance, results on partisan cycles, on the (lack of) electoral cycles on unemployment and growth, on small electoral cycles in policy instruments are very similar for the United States to those for other OECD democracies. Even on the question of party structure and single-party versus coalition governments, one can detect similarities. "Divided government," where control of the presidency, the house and the senate is not in the hands of the same party, can be considered the American version of "coalition government" in parliamentary democracies. Some of the discussion, both in academia and in the press, about the effects of divided government on achieving not only moderation in policy making but also fiscal deadlocks is strikingly similar to our discussion concerning the trade-off between single-party governments and coalition governments in parliamentary democracies.

10.1.8 Implications for Monetary Institutions

A large body of theoretical and empirical literature suggests that politically independent central banks bring about lower and more stable inflation rates. These benefits concerning inflation should, at least in theory, be achieved at the cost of lesser output stabilization. Empirically, however, the costs of central bank independence in terms of more real volatility appear very small or nonexistent.

We argue that, in fact, the benefits of central bank independence are even larger in a world of partisan policymakers. If monetary policy is insulated from direct political influence, the increased monetary stability reduces the output variability induced by partisan cycles. Thus, inflation-averse and independent central banks may actually reduce real volatility, in addition to reducing average inflation. More generally, we argue that the benefits of central bank independence are even larger than suggested by the purely economic literature, when partisan and electoral incentives of politicians are taken into account. In fact, one of the probable reasons why opportunistic monetary electoral cycles are not very large may be precisely that central banks are, up to a point and to a different degree in different countries, independent from political pressures.

10.1.9 Implications for Fiscal Policy and Fiscal Institutions

The emergence and persistence of large public-sector budget deficits in many industrial countries in the last two decades has generated a widespread concern that policymakers may often engage in excessive deficit financing. This preoccupation is grounded in many recent examples of large fiscal deficits that occurred in the absence of transitory cyclical downturns or transitory spending shocks.

There is an ongoing debate about what is the optimal amount of rule versus discretion in fiscal policy and on whether procedural reforms are better than strict numerical rules. For the reasons discussed at the end of chapter 9, we believe that very rigid numerical targets such as balanced budget amendments are unnecessarily strict and might have greater costs than benefits. On the other hand, appropriate reforms of the budgetary process may be a more effective way to contain politically induced deficit and spending biases. These reforms should enhance budget transparency and enforce a top-to-bottom approach in the budget formation process.

10.2   Are Political Cycles Going to Disappear?

Answers in the affirmative to the question posed in the title of this section often rely on one of three arguments:

1. The process of economic integration in general and in particular the European Monetary Union will make domestic macroeconomic policies much less independent and more constrained by international factors; thus, all parties will have to follow similar macroeconomic policies.

2. Political parties are converging more and more toward similar views on macroeconomic policies because they have learned from previous experiences of excessive and costly partisan fluctuations.

3. In many countries, both left- and right-wing parties will face in the next decade the same problems of fiscal retrenchment and in particular of containment of an overexpanded welfare state.

There is some truth in all three arguments; nonetheless, they do not necessarily imply that politico-economic cycles will completely vanish,

nor do they imply that politics will no longer matter for macroeconomic policies. For a start, we do not find that political cycles have
been less pronounced in the last decade than in the previous two, even
though this result does not necessarily imply that this pattern will
continue for the next decade. Although this is a difficult issue to
resolve empirically, because a complete monetary union is still to
come, our evidence does not support a structural break on the dimension of partisan effects. Nevertheless, the three arguments above are
compelling. Let us consider them in turn.

10.2.1   International Economic Integration

Although countries with flexible exchange rate regimes maintain
monetary and fiscal autonomy, the process of international integration
provides some indirect constraints to autonomous policy making. In
particular, if a country is more integrated with the world economy in
its trade and financial links, asset prices and exchange rate movements
will more quickly reflect macroeconomic policy mismanagement.
Therefore, the effects of surprise inflation on output will be dampened.
For instance, the slope of the expectations-augmented Phillips curve
becomes steeper (in an inflation-unemployment space) in a more open
economy; this reduces the temptation to have surprise inflation and
leads to lower equilibrium inflation. In general, the more open an
economy to trade and financial flows, the stronger might be the effects
of monetary policy on prices rather than on real quantities. Thus, left-
leaning governments may feel particularly constrained in their pursuit
of higher inflation and lower unemployment policies.

However, the idea that international economic integration (often
referred to as "globalization") completely eliminates governments' ability to influence the domestic economy is somewhat exaggerated. Even
in the context of a monetary union, member countries retain flexibility
on the fiscal side; besides it is not yet clear whether the European

Monetary Union will materialize beyond a restricted number of countries. OECD countries that are not members of the European Monetary Union will of course maintain monetary flexibility.

Furthermore, some aspects of the globalization may actually worsen some political distortion. For instance, the easy access that governments have to international financial markets may reduce the effects of large deficits on interest rates, and more generally, may make it easier for fiscally irresponsible governments to borrow. In other words, global financial markets make political distortions less costly for the government budget. Note that the large government deficits that appeared in the late 1970s and continued in the 1980s coincided with a period of financial liberalization and globalization of markets.

10.2.2   Parties Are Converging

The idea that political parties are becoming more alike when it comes to macroeconomic management is also somewhat exaggerated. It is probably true that left-wing parties have learned some lessons from failed attempts at reducing unemployment at the cost of excessive inflation. The first two years of the first term of President Mitterand in France, 1981–82, is the quintessential example. The Carter administration in the United States had a somewhat similar experience when an overexpansion in 1977–78, coupled with the second oil shock, pushed American inflation to double-digit levels. More generally, the policy-induced fluctuations in the late 1970s, and early 1980s may have taught all parties involved a lesson. In the late 1970s, the United States, Germany, and the United Kingdom, among others, under the direction of left-leaning governments, pushed inflation rates to levels unprecedented in the postwar period. In the early 1980s, a right-wing shift in these countries created one of the sharpest recessions in the postwar period. While these experiences have probably made politicians on both sides of the political spectrum more cautious in terms of macroeconomic management, they have not completely eliminated ideological differences.

For the countries adhering to the European Monetary Union, the traditional left/right political conflict on the relative costs of inflation and unemployment may assume a different tone. Right-wing and left-wing governments perceive the *relative* costs of unemployment to other economic problems in substantially different ways. Also, the discussion about demand- versus supply-side policies to reduce unemployment is often grounded in strong partisan ideologies.

10.2.3 Fiscal Adjustments

While it is certainly true that both left-wing and right-wing governments in the next decade will have to face issues of fiscal retrenchment, partisan conflicts are very likely to explode on how to achieve this goal. Decisions on whether to increase taxes or cut spending in high-debt countries—and about which programs to cut or which taxes to raise—are going to increase rather than reduce partisan cleavages. In fact, sharp partisan conflicts on how to reform the welfare state are in the making. The U.S. Congress elected in 1994, and its conflict with the Democratic administration, is a good leading indicator of similar future conflicts in other OECD countries. These conflicts are likely to emerge particularly in high-debt countries that will have to go through several years of fiscal austerity.

Recent experiences suggest that how a fiscal adjustment is conducted —whether on the spending side or the revenue side, whether with cuts in transfers or in capital expenditure, whether with or without reforms of social security systems—may seriously affect the likelihood of success. This is probably the turf for significant partisan conflicts in the next decade.

If we were so bold as to make predictions, we would argue that in the next decade partisan conflicts on the inflation/unemployment trade-off will not disappear, even though they may be attenuated by increased central bank independence and international monetary and financial integration. On the other hand, partisan and distributional conflicts over fiscal decisions, in the context of fiscal consolidation, are likely to become even sharper. Politics is going to be even more important for economic policy in the next decade than it has been in the previous one.

Notes

Chapter 1

1. For a survey of this literature see Persson and Tabellini 1990.

2. This view has a long tradition that goes back to Fischer 1977 and Taylor 1979. Mankiw and Romer (1991) have recently collected many of the major contributions in this area of research.

3. In particular, see Downs 1957, and for a more recent technical treatment, Ordeshook 1986.

4. A related point concerns the issue of "divided government" in the United States and its effects on macroeconomic management. We briefly touch upon this issue in relation to political cycles in the United States. For a more extensive treatment, the reader is referred to Alesina and Rosenthal 1995.

5. See Cukierman 1992 and the references cited therein. For a recent debate, see Walsh 1995b, Fischer 1995, Posen 1995, and Alesina 1995.

6. There is in fact a field in political science called "American politics," whose members in general hardly communicate with those "comparativists" who study other democracies.

7. Only in the last chapter do these two authors briefly discuss how their model of the U.S. economy can be applied to parliamentary democracies.

Chapter 2

1. A classic reference is Downs 1957.

2. An alternative interpretation that is, however, less appropriate for our analysis is the "Lucas supply function," in which misperceptions of the relationship between the aggregate price level and that facing individual agents lead to a similar relationship between unexpected inflation and real variables. Note that this interpretation would imply that the parameters γ and γ' would not be constant but a function of the level

and variability of inflation. In other words these two parameters would not be policy independent, an issue which we do not pursue here. The interested reader is referred to Lucas 1973.

3. Analogous considerations hold for unemployment, which is typically found to be very persistent. For instance, see Blanchard and Summers 1986.

4. Equation (2.7) embodies the assumption that voters do not look back beyond the current government's term of office; in particular, they do not look for comparison at the policies of previous governments. For more discussion on the point, see Fiorina 1981.

5. The speed of convergence to C depends on the value of λ.

6. Lindbeck (1976) suggests that because of time lags between the effects of aggregate demand on output and prices, skillful timing may lead to an increase in inflation only after the election.

7. Note that any information about a challenger's party's competence the last time it was in office is irrelevant if the term of office lasts at least two periods, as we assume.

8. For more discussion of this point, see Alesina and Rosenthal 1995.

9. Obviously, the two-type assumption is an analytical simplification. Even though Persson and Tabellini do not solve for the general case, intuitively one should obtain that the more competent types create a preelectoral boom, the less competent types a recession.

10. Rogoff and Sibert add to (2.18) a preference shock in favor of or against the incumbent thereby adding a stochastic element to the election results. However, it is not necessary to develop this aspect of the model for our intuitive treatment.

11. Note, however, an important difference between the two models. In the Phillips curve example the nature of the preelectoral distortion (i.e., expansion or recession) depends upon the interplay between policy (π_t) and expectations of it (π_t^e). Here, whether seigniorage is expected or not does not change the distortion's economic effect. This is why in this model, unlike in the Phillips curve version of it, the pre-electoral economic distortion has always the same direction, when it is not zero.

12. See Rogoff and Sibert 1988 for a technical discussion of this point.

13. In this formulation, the optimal amount of seigniorage is normalized at zero, but nothing would change if the optimal amount of seigniorage were positive.

14. Rogoff (1990) briefly discusses these issues.

15. For more discussion, see chapter 8 in Alesina and Rosenthal 1995.

16. See, for instance, Lewis-Beck 1988 on OECD countries and Alesina and Rosenthal 1995 and the references cited therein for the United States.

17. An interesting extension would be to consider the incumbency advantage, so that the incumbent has a probability of reelection greater than $\frac{1}{2}$.

Chapter 3

1. One may allow for an opportunistic incentive together with the partisan one. As long as the opportunistic motivation does not become predominant, this hybrid model's implications are qualitatively similar to those of the pure partisan model. See, in particular, Alesina 1988a. For a discussion of voting models with partisan politicians, see chapter 2 of Alesina and Rosenthal 1995 and the references cited therein.

2. In a 1992 review article, Hibbs is more explicit about the role of expectations. More on this point follows.

3. The effect of very high levels of inflation or even hyperinflation on income distribution may be quite different and, in particular, regressive; see, for instance, Cardoso and Helvege 1993. In this book, however, we are concerned with countries and time periods with low or moderate inflation rates.

4. Ellis and Thoma (1991) present an interesting extension of this model to the case of variable electoral terms. In Ellis and Thoma 1995, the same authors extend this model to an open economy.

5. See also the appendix to chapter 2.

6. Remember that we assume no productivity growth.

7. More specifically, we can think of a "monopoly union" that sets the wage unilaterally, while the employers choose, unilaterally, employment. For a review of macroeconomic models with unions, see chapter 9 in Blanchard and Fischer 1989.

8. Phelps (1973) presents the argument on the optimal inflation tax. Mankiw (1990) considers 200 years of U.S. data and concludes that inflation was indeed used as a form of optimal taxation.

9. See Barro and Gordon 1983a,b.

10. This uncertainty can arise from shocks to individual preferences or to random turnout. For a fully developed model with uncertainty about voter preferences, see Alesina and Rosenthal 1995.

11. Since in this model a period coincides with the length of a labor contract, for the U.S. case we are implicitly stating that a labor contract lasts two years, an assumption that is quite reasonable.

12. For an in-depth discussion of time consistency, see Kydland and Prescott 1977, Barro and Gordon 1983a, and the survey in Persson and Tabellini 1990.

13. In practice, polls can generate reasonably good predictions of electoral results. In chapter 5 we use polls as an approximation for the voters' perception of P.

14. That is, we need no assumption except that it is not degenerate.

15. Presumably, the same consideration applies to Hibbs's partisan cycle. Because he does not derive his model from an explicit maximization of welfare function, however, it is not clear how to draw welfare implications from it.

16. Note that expected growth y^e is $\bar{y}$ in either case. In fact, $y_t^e = P[\bar{y} + \hat{\pi}^R - \hat{\pi}^e] + (1 - P)[\bar{y} + \hat{\pi}^L - \pi^e] = \bar{y} + P\hat{\pi}^R + (1 - P)\hat{\pi}^L - \pi^e = \bar{y}$. If growth entered quadratically in the utility function, then the variance of output caused by different inflation policies would be an additional cost of the partisan cycles.

17. Actually, this intuition is more general than the specifics of the Nash bargaining solution (see Alesina 1987). Also, note that because with π^* both parties follow the same policy, the probability of electing R or L should be $1/2$, unless other noneconomic factors influence it.

18. For overviews, see Cukierman 1992 and Persson and Tabellini 1990. See also chapter 8 of this book.

19. A pathbreaking contribution on this point is Kramer 1971. See also Fair 1978 and 1996, Fiorina 1981 and Alesina and Rosenthal 1995 for the United States and Lewis-Beck 1988 for other OECD countries.

20. See Mankiw and Romer (1991) for a collection of papers that well summarize this field.

21. Cohen (1993) provides more discussion of this point.

22. This effect is much stronger in presidential election years relative to mid-term electoral years.

23. Garfinkel and Glazer choose to give a somewhat different interpretation to their results

Chapter 4

1. Tufte (1978) provides several anecdotal examples of the importance of macro-economic performance for voting in U.S. elections. For more formal analysis of the macroeconomy's importance for election results in the United States, see Kramer 1971, Alesina and Rosenthal 1995, Fair 1978, and Lewis-Beck 1988, among others.

2. Nixon's comments are as cited in Tufte 1978.

3. Recent exceptions are the studies by Klein (1996) and Siklos (1994) who consider more than a century of data for the United States.

4. Haynes and Stone (1989) claim to have found some support for the Nordhaus hypothesis on GNP in the United States. In our view, however, a careful analysis of their results suggests that they have found evidence of partisan effects rather than opportunistic cycles. The same point applies to results presented by Nordhaus (1989); on this specific point, see Alesina's (1989) comment on Nordhaus.

5. For a recent survey, see Alesina and Perotti 1995b.

6. Studies by Havrilesky (1993) and Froyen, Havrilesky and Waud (1993) have shown that the executive branch has a stronger influence on the conduct of monetary policy in the United States than the legislative branch.

7. The interested reader can see Alesina and Rosenthal 1995 for a detailed analysis of the U.S. political cycles considering both presidential and Congressional midterm elections.

8. See for instance Blanchard and Summers 1986 on evidence of hysteresis in unemployment rates.

9. Note that incumbent Democratic administrations (only two in the sample, Truman II and Johnson) also inherit low inflation. An explanation is that Democratic administrations are more likely to be reelected if they succeed in keeping inflation low; as discussed in chapter 3, partisan biases on inflation may be tempered before elections by opportunistic concerns about the effects of inflation on reelection chances.

10. The Carter administration is the classic example of such a policy pattern, in which the policies induced by the political business cycle run counter to the conventional political business cycle hypothesis, as pointed out also by Hibbs (1987a).

11. See Alesina and Rosenthal 1995 on this point.

12. These tests are based on the assumption that output growth, unemployment and inflation (the policy goals that we consider in this chapter) are generated by a covariance-stationary stochastic process that can be expressed in auto-regressive form as in (4.1). The results in the tables confirm the stationarity of the variables considered in the empirical tests. Specifically, we use the Aikake and Schwartz tests to find the optimal lag in regression.

13. This is also why we do not test for political effects in a structural VAR model of the economy. Such an approach would require taking a strong stance on an issue open to wide debate, that is, which is the correct structural model and identification scheme of the economy.

14. Note that the variable DRPTXN assumes values different from zero after every election even if the same administration is reappointed, that is, not only following actual changes of U.S. administrations. In several U.S. elections, however, the same party won reelection with little political uncertainty. Rather than trying to estimate the degree of political uncertainty in every period, a task addressed in chapter 5, in this section we first estimate a somewhat weaker form of rational partisan theory by testing for temporary effects on real variables after the beginning of each administration. Later, we also show the results obtained when we define the DPRTN variable to include only actual changes of U.S. administrations.

15. In terms of coefficient values and their significance, the coefficient estimate is largest (in absolute value) for DRPTX4 (-0.74), followed by DRPTX6 (-0.64) and smallest for DRPTX8 (-0.58). In terms of statistical significance, DRPTX6 has a slightly higher t-statistic (4.2) than DRPTX4 (4.1) or DRPTX8 (4.0).

16. Note that, because the DRPT dummy is zero after six quarters, the partisan gap reaches its peak in the sixth quarter. Note also that if the partisan effect were permanent rather than transitory, the estimates in (4.2) would imply that by the end of a Republican administration such a gap from steady-state growth would rise to 2.37 percent.

17. The "steady state" for growth (y^*) is computed as follows: $y^* = 0.91 + 1.1y^* - 0.21y^* - 0.16y^* - 0.64\text{DRPTX6} = 3.37 - 2.37\text{DRPTX}$. This calculation implies a much larger difference between the two administrations than the one reported in the text. However, one has to remember that the partisan dummy is not permanent and goes to zero after six quarters. The value of 2.4 percent reported in the text, takes that into account. Analogous considerations hold for equation (4.3).

18. In the United States, the unemployment rate, although highly persistent, appears to be mean-reverting on the basis of the regression in (4.3) below.

19. Analogous results (available upon request) are obtained if this variable is lagged only one quarter.

20. Note that the dependent variable shows a high level of persistence while being mean-reverting. Thus even a temporary policy shock has rather persistent effects over time.

21. These results are available upon request.

22. We tested alternative ways to control for the world cycle. First, we added as a regressor in the growth equation a proxy for a world average of the same variable. Specifically, we created a variable that is the average growth in the six largest non-U.S. OECD economies, weighted by each country's share of GNP over the total. We also used two variants of this method. One was to redefine each country's variable as the difference between the actual variable and the OECD proxy of the same variable. The other was to add time dummies in the regression that would capture the years of the world business cycle with higher or lower than average growth. In all cases, the proxies for the world business cycle were of the expected sign and significant, and the political dummy remained significant as well.

23. These results are available upon request. When, analogously to the procedure above, we added a world unemployment variable to the basic unemployment equation as an alternative way to control for world effects, this variable turned out not to be significant whereas the partisan effects remained significant as in table 4.5. How can we explain this result? Although the U.S. growth cycle follows closely the world growth cycle, the behavior of the U.S. unemployment rate is quite different from that of other OECD countries. Specifically, though there is some evidence that the U.S. unemployment rate is stationary and mean-reverting, the persistency and non-stationariness of the high unemployment rates in the European countries leads to a desynchronization of the U.S. and European unemployment rates.

24. For the post–1972 period, the higher inflation rate of Democratic administrations is mostly driven by the inflation during the Carter administration.

25. These qualitative results remain the same when we consider separately the pre– and post–1973 sample periods. Results are available upon request.

26. Similar results are obtained using $N = 6, 8$.

27. All the results of these F-tests are available from the authors.

28. See Grier 1987, McCallum 1978, Beck 1987, and Alesina and Sachs 1988.

29. Similar regressions have been performed on U.S. data by Hibbs (1987a), Alesina and Sachs (1988), and Alesina (1988b).

30. The RADM variable is lagged two periods to control for delay in policy change following changes in administration; robustness tests using no lags or different lags of the RADM dummy give the same results. Similar results are also obtained when the quarterly rate of money growth is used instead of the yearly.

31. Other results, not reported here, show that the significance of the partisan dummy holds until 1985.

32. The data on interest rates are available starting at different dates (1955 for the federal funds rate, 1947 for the discount rate and the three-month T-bill rate, and 1953 for the rate on ten-year Treasury notes). The starting period for the regressions in table 4.8 therefore depends on the interest rate measure being used.

33. As in the case of the monetary growth reaction functions, we have included in the interest rate equations a measure of business cycle conditions (either the lagged unemployment rate or the lagged growth rate) to control for possible effects of the economy on the monetary policy stance. Quite surprisingly, such measures turned out not to be significant, so the results presented in table 4.8 exclude this cyclical variable.

34. Again the RADM variable is lagged two periods to control for delays in policy change following changes in administration; robustness tests using different lags of the partisan dummy give similar results.

35. These results are available upon request.

36. Grier (1987) found some evidence of a political cycle (consistent with the political business cycle model) on a sample ending in 1980. His results disappear, however, when we extend the sample to include data after 1980.

37. These results are available upon request.

38. As discussed in chapter 2, Rogoff (1990) emphasizes compositional effects in his theory of political budget cycles.

39. See the appendix to Chapter 9 for a formal derivation of the tax-smoothing model.

40. In fact, both theories imply that fiscal deficits are countercyclical: that is, fiscal deficits emerge during periods of recession and growth slowdown. In fact, in addition to the tax-smoothing considerations stressed by Barro (1979), the tendency toward deficits after a slowdown in growth is exacerbated for two additional reasons. First, many major areas of public spending (*e.g.*, unemployment compensation, social welfare expenditure, early retirement benefits, job retraining, and subsidies for ailing firms) are inherently countercyclical, so that portions of government spending actually tend to rise automatically when growth slows down and unemployment increases. Second, some countries intentionally implement Keynesian aggregate demand policies in the face of a growth slowdown: Right or wrong, many governments reduce taxes or increase government spending during recessions.

41. See Anderson 1987 for a politico-economic explanation of this trend and Alesina and Perotti 1995a for a multicountry discussion of the same phenomenon.

42. Note that because the November elections occur in the middle of the fourth quarter of the year, it is not clear whether this quarter should be considered pre- or post-electoral. Tufte (1978) shows, however, that in several elections the increase in transfer payments occurred in October or even in early November, thus in the fourth quarter of the year but before the elections. In addition, one may argue that transfers actually paid in, say, December may have been announced and approved before elections.

Chapter 5

1. This chapter is based largely upon Cohen 1993.

2. Chappell and Keech 1988 calculate electoral probabilities using presidential popularity data either one or two years ahead and therefore have at most only two observations per election cycle. In addition, because the statistical properties of the probability estimates, which are generated by a regression, are not accounted for in the second-stage money growth estimation, the results are biased. Moreover, the authors fail to account for the fact that the money growth estimates are generated regressors in their third-stage unemployment estimations, further biasing their results.

   Cohen (1993) implemented a model analogous to Chappell and Keech's. The results of this model were less consistent with public sentiment than the option pricing model developed in this chapter. In addition, tests using these probabilities, generated regressor issues notwithstanding, led to less-promising results than those discussed later in this section.

3. In this model, winning the election implies receiving a majority of the two-party vote, not a majority of the electoral college. Although there are many cases of candidates winning an election without a majority of the total vote, in modern electoral history no candidate has ever received a majority of the two-party vote and lost the election.

4. We follow Cohen's (1993) methodology in choosing our trial heat candidates. After the convention, we use each party's nominee. Prior to the convention we follow the results of Gallup's party member preference polls to find each party's front-runner. For an in-depth discussion of the choice of preconvention trial heat candidates, see Cohen 1993.

5. As we incorporate new information, the sample mean and variance may deviate over time. It should be stressed that deviations in μ and σ do not invalidate the model's assumption of identically distributed changes in polls. That is, our assumption states, and empirical analysis supports, the hypothesis that neither μ nor σ move predictably over the course of an election.

6. We feel this is most realistic. In addition to these two techniques, however, we calculate the probabilities using the full sample mean and variance (from 1936, when

Gallup published its first poll through 1994, $\mu = -0.312$ and $\sigma = 4.057$), as well as a model that sets $\mu = 0$ (a realistic assumption given that we cannot reject the hypothesis that $\mu = 0$). A comparison of the results from the different techniques finds that as the election approaches, estimates of the electoral probabilities from all these methodologies converge. Long before the election, however, when τ is large, small differences are evident. This outcome concurs with the discussion in section 5.2.2, which stressed that depending on the value of μ, for large τ, the probabilities converge to either one-half, zero or one.

7. It must be stressed that not only is μ small, but changes in μ over time are minimal. In addition, there is very little movement in σ over time.

8. For the output estimations, the analysis in chapter 4 assumes a one-quarter lag between the start of an administration and its policy impact. The unemployment estimations assume a two-quarter lag to capture the slower response of unemployment to policy changes. For consistency, we assume the same lag structure; the results, however, are not sensitive to these assumptions.

Although the SURPRISE# variable enters equations (5.5) and (5.7) contemporaneously, this lag structure is embedded in our calculation of the SURPRISE# variable.

9. For the present analysis of quarterly output growth, the monthly probabilities are converted into quarterly data by averaging. In addition, a one-period lag is assumed between when contracts are written and when they take effect.

In this analysis, long before an election, when polling data is not available, we assume that P_t^D takes on a value of 0 for a Republican incumbent and 1 for a Democratic incumbent. Since polling usually begins more than two years before an election, however, and given the contract length and lag structure, this assumption is rarely invoked.

10. The results for the unweighted cumulative moving average probabilities are almost identical; they are therefore not presented but are available upon request.

11. The SURPRISE# variable is not a generated regressor; it is calculated using a distributional filter and not from a regression. Therefore the standard errors from the estimation of equation (5.5) are unbiased.

12. From 1948 through 1992, the probability estimate in October of the election year missed by an average of 20 percentage points.

13. The results also indicate that unemployment has significant unit root properties suggesting biased estimations. Following Sims, Stock, and Watson (1990), however, because the SURPRISE# variable is integrated of order zero, $I(0)$, it is asymptotically independent of variables such as unemployment that are integrated of order 1, $I(1)$. Therefore the coefficient on the SURPRISE# variable can be tested using normal inference criteria.

14. In addition to pre- and postelectoral dummy variables, Blomberg and Hess (1996) find that lagged approval ratings, which may capture electoral expectations, affect exchange rates.

15. The post-1948 election S&P500 movement is the only post–presidential election movement in Cutler et al. 1989 Table 4 "Fifty Largest Post-War Movements in the S&P Index," ranking number 15.

16. The implications of this framework fit the significant decline caused by the unanticipated Truman victory in the 1948 election as well as the 5.6 percent gain in the London Financial Times Stock Index caused by the surprise Conservative victory in the April 1992 British general election.

17. For example, the 1980 Reagan victory and surprise gain of Republican control of the Senate may have been very beneficial to defense stocks. The loss of committee seniority due to the defeat of ranking senators may have been harmful, however, to defense corporations that resided in those districts.

18. It is also possible that electoral information affects real interest rate expectations. That is, different administrations' growth rates and fiscal policies may lead to divergent expectations of real interest rates.

19. Although this model characterizes changes in electoral probabilities as influencing inflationary expectations, the results of the estimations cannot specify whether the true mechanism is through some combination of shifts in real interest rate or inflationary expectations or movements in the term premium.

20. This data was obtained from McCulloch and Kwon 1993. To calculate the forward rate revisions, we need yields for off-year maturities such as 23-, 35-, and 59-month bonds. These are calculated by linearly interpolating between the given maturities. At the points between which we interpolate, the slope is very smooth, thus a linear interpolation provides a good approximation of the true yield.

21. The assumption of lack of information about current money growth is questionable. Therefore, an estimation of equation (5.10) was performed using time t money growth, yielding no change in the results.

22. The impact of the political variable is robust to various specifications that include or exclude economic variables.

23. Discussions with the primary dealer community confirmed that this hypothesis is consistent with the views held by Treasury market participants.

The data contain occasional gaps for the twelve months prior to the election when no poll was taken in back-to-back months. Given the properties of the polling data discussed in section 5.2.2 and Appendix A, interpolating polling data does not seem proper. Therefore, we do not calculate electoral probabilities for those dates and exclude them from our estimations.

With the exception of eighteen-month impact, which is very similar to the twelve-month results, the effect of ΔP_t^D lessens as we lengthen the time period over which we assume changes in probabilities matter. That is, if we assume changing probabilities affect financial markets for twenty-four rather than twelve months before the election, the coefficient of ΔP_t^D declines.

24. This analysis is unable to specify the exact consequences on the term structure. That is, it is possible to have a large enough upward shift in the yield curve of the that slope may in fact narrow.

To capture the possibility that the market may heavily discount early electoral information, we used nonlinear least squares to measure the magnitude of the discounting. These estimations, which are available upon request, could not reject the hypothesis of no discounting, further confirming the robustness of the results presented in table 5.3.

25. At present, other measures of electoral probabilities, such as the Iowa political stock market and the British betting market, are unavailable on a historical basis. Therefore, it is currently not possible to compare the calculated electoral probabilities to those produced by the markets. In time, however, these data banks will allow an assessment of the accuracy of the calculated probabilities.

26. The concept of using the two-party vote share is supported by McKelvey and Ordeshook (1984, 1985), who find that uninformed voters use previous polls as an information source, yielding a voter equilibrium that may approach that of decided voters.

27. It is interesting to note that some asset pricing models hypothesize "feedback trading" behavior, similar to that of polling data, that leads to serial correlation in high frequency return data but little correlation over long horizons. See, for example, Cutler, Poterba, and Summers (1990, 1991).

28. A nonconstant variance is also a common problem in the implementation of option pricing of assets. It should be noted that this nonconstant variance issue is very different from the empirical question of incorporating new information gained by the publication of each new poll, which is discussed in section 5.2.3.

29. Not accounting for possible variability in the term premium may bias our estimates. However, the inclusion of lags of the forward rate revision in the estimations, to correct for serially correlated errors, may account for some of the movement of the term premium.

Chapter 6

1. See Lewis-Beck 1988 for a cross-country analysis of the effects of the economy on voting in a large sample of industrial countries.

2. See Hibbs 1987b for a study of such partisan differences in industrial democracies.

3. Fourteen out the eighteen countries in our sample have endogenous elections: Australia, Austria, Belgium, Canada, Denmark, Finland, France, Germany, Ireland, Italy, Japan, Netherlands, New Zealand, and the United Kingdom. Sweden switched in the mid-1970s from endogenous dates to exogenous ones.

4. For a discussion of this point see Alesina 1989.

5. See the appendix to this chapter for detailed information on the sample period for each country and variable.

6. The seven largest countries are (in 1987 order) the United States, Japan, Germany, France, the United Kingdom, Italy, and Canada. An analogous definition is used to construct proxies for OECD unemployment and inflation. In the regressions for the seven countries included in the creation of the proxy for the OECD averages, we have used different proxies that exclude the country in the left-hand side of the regression.

7. It is known that in dynamic fixed-effects panel models the correlation between the error term and the lagged dependent variables might lead to inconsistent estimates of the parameters (Hsiao 1986). The problem is serious in panel sets where the number of agents (N) considered is large but the number of time-series observations (T) is small. In that case, the maximum likelihood estimator of the dynamic model is inconsistent even if the number of agents becomes very large (Anderson and Hsiao 1982 and Nickell 1981). The solution to this problem is to use instrumental-variable methods such as those suggested by Bhargava and Sargan (1983) and Pakes and Griliches (1984). Our panel data set, however, does not suffer from the above problem because of the use of long time series (usually 136 data points). In the case where T is large, the parameter estimates of the standard fixed-effects dynamic model are consistent (Hsiao 1986).

8. A priori, the correct dynamic specification of the model could differ across countries. In country-by-country regressions, we found that the same auto-regressive specification is best for almost all the countries in the sample. Even if the same auto-regressive specification applies to each country, however, the estimates of the coefficients could differ across countries, therefore making the use of a variable-slopes and variable-intercepts model more appropriate. Given the loss of degrees of freedom involved, this procedure was not adopted. We discuss below some country specific results.

9. For instance, in countries where the election timing is endogenous, the probability of a government change is, theoretically, never zero. Also, systematic data on preelectoral polls are available for only a very few countries in the sample, mostly Germany and the United Kingdom (see Blomberg and Hess 1997) in addition to the United States. We leave to future work tests (for countries other than the United States) similar to those performed in chapter 5 for the United States on the relationship between electoral surprise and partisan effects.

10. A second or third lag in the dependent variable does not appear to be significant when added to the panel.

11. These results are available upon request. We obtain analogous results on the political dummy variable when we control for the world cycle with the second and third methods outlined in the text (i.e., using as a dependent variable the difference between domestic and world growth or using time dummies) rather than using the world average variable as a regressor.

12. See for instance Blanchard and Summers (1986) for some evidence of hysteresis in European unemployment rates. Also, comparing the unemployment regression in this chapter with those for the United States in chapter 4, one observes the much higher persistence of the unemployment rate in the full OECD sample relative to the United States one.

13. The estimate is consistent with the hypothesis that the unemployment rate is borderline stationary.

14. Note also that, if we assume that the country dummies already capture country differences in inflation rates, and we do not control for the world inflation rate, we obtain results that are statistically more significant. These results are available upon request.

15. Note that the sample period is much shorter when we consider only the years 1960–1980; this might marginally affect the t-statistics in the comparison of table 6.5 with tables 6.1 and 6.2, because a shorter sample presents fewer political changes and therefore less variance in the political dummies.

16. While we include country fixed effects in these regressions, in the rest of the chapter we do not report the values of these coefficients because they are very similar to those in tables 6.1 through 6.3.

17. It should, however, be observed that capital controls were widespread in the Bretton Woods regime so that national monetary authorities maintained a certain degree of monetary autonomy in spite of the fixed exchange rate parities.

18. Conversely, if we run the regressions on the post-1973 sample, we find results in favor of the rational partisan theory hypothesis even stronger than those obtained for the complete 1960–1993 sample.

19. We also tested whether the dynamic process of inflation has changed moving from the fixed to the flexible rate system. The regressions of tables 6.3 and 6.6 were computed allowing the coefficients on the lagged dependent variable to be different before and after 1972. The results confirm that inflation is significantly more persistent in the post-1972 period with flexible rates. Our results concerning the statistical significance of the variables RADM and ADM remain unchanged, however, even when we allow for a structural break in 1972. These results are available upon request.

20. In these tables, the fixed-effects coefficients are not reported because they are very similar to those of tables 6.1 and 6.2.

21. These results are available upon request.

22. See Gartner 1994 and Hibbs 1994, for example.

23. These results are available upon request. An even more extreme version of this model of voters' myopia would imply that they ignore the world economy's influence on their countries' performance, and thus politicians simply attempt to expand their economies, regardless of the world economy. This hypothesis can be tested running the same regressions as in tables 6.1 and 6.2 without correcting for the effect of the world economy. The results (available upon request) show no support for the political business cycle model.

24. The statistical significance of the coefficient on NPOST is unaffected by allowing for a structural break of the inflation process in 1972. See also footnote 19.

25. The results of these F-tests are available upon request.

26. Several different specifications of the panel were estimated in addition to those presented in equation (6.4); the results, available upon request, were qualitatively identical.

Chapter 7

1. The main difference relative to the monetary reaction function of chapter 4 is the absence in equation (7.1) of a cyclical variable (the growth rate or the unemployment rate). We did actually introduce such a cyclical variable in our regressions but failed to find a significant feedback from business cycle conditions to the rate of growth of money in the large sample considered here. One difficulty here is that reaction functions may be different in different countries, making it difficult to fit a single specification for the entire panel. We therefore dropped such a variable from the regressions presented in this chapter.

We also introduced into the equation a variable representing the average growth rate of the money supply in the OECD bloc, a world average variable similar to that used in chapter 6 for output, unemployment and inflation. We found, however, that this variable was usually statistically insignificant, and we therefore dropped it from the equation. The statistical insignificance of this variable is not surprising. Although world output growth may affect the output growth of a particular country, there is no a priori reason why the growth rate of a particular country's money supply should depend on that in the rest of the world.

2. See chapter 6, footnote 8.

3. As in the previous chapter, we used both definitions of the partisan dummy, RADM and ADM. ADM is a finer classification of governments that distinguishes center-left and center-right governments from those that are more clearly right- and left-wing. The results for RADM were quite similar to those for ADM and are available upon request.

4. The sample period is 1960:1 to 1993:3. Some countries had missing data in the sample; see table 7.A.1 in the appendix for details.

5. These results are available upon request.

6. The results, however, are not dependent on the model's lag specification. For brevity, the coefficients on the lags are not displayed; the coefficient estimates on the lagged dependent variable always add up to a value significantly less than unity, suggesting that interest rates are mean-reverting. Therefore, we need not deal with possible non-stationarities in the interest rate process.

7. These results are available upon request. Alogoskoufis, Lockwood and Philippopolous 1991 find some evidence that the exchange rate regime matters for electoral cycles in the case of the United Kingdom.

8. In this table and the remaining ones in this chapter, we do not report the values of the country fixed-effects coefficients because they are very similar to those obtained in tables 7.1 through 7.3.

9. These results are available upon request.

10. This was found to be the correct specification of the model after estimating the equations on the left- and right-wing governments separately. In particular, the coefficients on the lagged money growth variables were found to be virtually identical.

11. The size of the sample in this section is limited by the availability of consistent OECD data on net public debt (see Roubini and Sachs 1989a). We have data on thirteen countries, and the sample periods are as follows: Austria (1970–1993), Belgium (1960–1993), Denmark (1971–1993), France (1960–1993), Finland (1970–1993), Germany (1960–1993), Japan (1964–1993), Italy (1964–1993), the Netherlands (1970–1993), Norway (1970–1993), Sweden (1970–1993), the United Kingdom (1960–1993), and the United States (1960–1993).

12. This variable is included to capture the effects of real interest rate shocks. For example, after 1979 the increase in world real interest rates significantly and unexpectedly raised most governments' costs of servicing debt. One useful measure of the budgetary costs of higher interest rates is given by the debt-to-GDP ratio multiplied by the change in the differential between real interest rates and growth rates.

13. The main difference between this structural model of the determination of fiscal deficits and the one presented for the United States in chapter 4 is that here we do not control explicitly for transitory components of government spending. We do so only implicitly by assuming that shocks to the cyclical variables (the unemployment and growth rate) might lead to short-run deviation of spending from trend (see Roubini and Sachs 1989a for a more detailed formulation of this model). In fact, a growth slowdown will not only reduce revenues; given legislated spending programs and countercyclical spending programs such as unemployment insurance, it will also tend to increase the spending-to-GDP ratio above its trend and therefore contribute to the fiscal deficit. We do not explicitly try to derive a measure of transitory government spending because, given the strong upward trend in the share of government spending to GDP in many OECD countries and given the lack of large episodes of war in the sample period when spending was temporarily high, it is very hard to distinguish empirically between the transitory and permanent components of spending. We thus let the cyclical variables capture the fact that spending in temporarily high during recessions.

14. Its magnitude suggests that each 1 percentage point slowdown in GDP growth initially raises the budget deficit relative to GDP by 0.50 percentage points. Because the average slowdown in growth was on the order of 3 percentage points, the impact o this effect was a growth of the budget deficit relative to GDP by more than 1.5 percent of GDP.

15. The results in Table 7.7 provide some evidence that during an election year fiscal policy is loose. It would be interesting to investigate which countries exhibit more

pronounced electoral budget cycles. Such a test, however, is difficult for two reasons: First, because the OECD data on public debt (from which we derived the real deficits measures) are available only on a yearly basis, the sample period for each country is quite small (ranging from twenty-two to thirty data points); second, elections are infrequent events, and the data set for each country does not include more than four electoral observations. The problems these small samples present severely constrain the possibility of running meaningful country regressions. Keeping in mind the above caveats, we ran the basic deficit equation for each country separately; we found the coefficient on the electoral dummy to be of the expected sign in eight countries (Germany, Belgium, Japan, Austria, the Netherlands, Norway, Finland, and Denmark) but statistically significant (at the 10 percent confidence level) in only one, the Netherlands (results are available upon request). Although the above caveats might account for these weak results, the inability to find strong electoral effects at the country level would suggest caution in arguing for a strong electoral budget cycle effect in this OECD sample.

16. See Alesina, Cohen and Roubini 1992, 1993.

17. Examples of this fiscal conservatism in left-of-center administrations are the Socialist administrations in France in the 1980s and the Clinton administration in the United States.

18. See also chapter 9 of this book.

19. Our sample on government spending and revenues is restricted to the 1960–1985 period.

20. In the case of taxes, we used the ratio of direct taxes over GDP rather than total revenues, because the chosen variable might be more easily manipulated before elections.

Chapter 8

1. For the United States, for instance, Chappell. Havrilesky, and McGregor (1993) suggest that the most important channel of influence is the power of appointment. Alt (1992) argues that the Federal Reserve cannot displease the President and Congress too much for fear of repercussions. As a matter of fact, proposals to reduce the independence of the Federal Reserve are often on the table in Congress.

2. In the simple specification that we use, ε is, literally speaking, a supply shock. In a more extensively spelled-out model of the demand side, one could also consider demand shocks, such as perturbations of the demand for money. The critical features of the model can, however, be more clearly illustrated in this simple setup. For a more extensive treatment of this point, see Rogoff 1985.

3. In fact, if growth entered linearly as in the models examined (for simplicity) in chapter 3, the central bank would not care about output fluctuations around a target.

4. Substituting (8.1) in (8.2) and dropping time subscripts, one obtains: $U = -1/2\pi^2 - b/2(\pi - \pi^e + \varepsilon - k)^2$. Maximizing with respect to π, holding π^e constant, one obtains the following first-order condition: $\pi = b/(1+b)(\pi^e + k - \varepsilon)$; since $\pi^e = E(\pi) = b/(1+b)(\pi^e + k)$, one obtains (8.3), (8.4), and (8.5) in the text.

5. This discussion in conceptually identical to our treatment of the time inconsistency problem in the appendix to chapter 3. The analytical treatment of this case is more complicated, however, because of the quadratic specification of the objective function on the growth target and because of the shock. The reader is invited to derive the results of the appendix to chapter 3 for this more general model. Canzoneri 1985 may help in this task.

6. For a formal discussion of this problem, see Canzoneri 1985 and Cukierman 1992.

7. It is worth reiterating that there is nothing special about zero, as opposed to a positive constant level. This target is just a normalization.

8. This idea of delegation as a solution to time inconsistency problems is more general than the monetary policy example, for which it was originally formulated. For a discussion of this point, see Persson and Tabellini 1990.

9. Lohmann (1992) discusses an extension of Rogoff's model in which it is in the policy-maker's interest to retain the option of dismissing ex post the central banker. This option forces the central banker, who does not want to be dismissed, to accommodate very large negative shocks when a tough anti-inflationary stance would instead create a very low level of utility for the policymaker.

10. The literature on the relationship between central bank independence and macro-economic outcomes (particularly inflation) is very large, and we cannot review it here. For recent assessments of the literature see Cukierman 1992 and Eijffinger and de Haan 1996. Worthy of special mention in this literature are Bade and Parkin (1982), who, in a paper never published, first pointed out a correlation between inflation and central bank independence in a small sample of OECD countries. Grilli, Masciandaro and Tabellini (1991) provided one of the earliest careful indexes of independence for a broad sample of OECD countries. Cukierman, Webb and Neyapti (1992) extended this analysis to developing countries, uncovering a variety of new interesting issues. For a recent discussion of these issues, see Walsh 1995b, Posen 1995, Fischer 1995, and Alesina 1995.

11. The probability of electoral results could be made endogenous as a function of individual preferences, as in chapter 3. Because this is not our focus, we do not develop this point here.

12. An interesting step forward, which we do not pursue here, is to find the $\hat{b}$ within this range that the two parties would choose. One possibility would be to apply a Nash bargaining solution to find this value. By analogy with results by Alesina (1987) one can conjecture that in the choice of b, the Nash bargaining solution favors the party with the highest probability of victory, because the "threat point" is the non-cooperative outcome, and the higher its probability of victory, the better off a party is in the noncooperative regime.

13. For a related discussion see Alt 1992.

14. See also Persson and Tabellini 1994.

15. For a thorough discussion of this model in the context of other approaches, see Svensson 1995.

16. See Walsh 1995a and Svensson 1995.

Chapter 9

1. We briefly referred to this model in previous chapters; in the appendix to this chapter we provide a brief sketch of it.

2. See, in particular, Buchanan and Wagner 1977.

3. On this approach, see Alesina and Tabellini 1990, Persson and Svensson 1989, Alesina and Tabellini 1990 and, for a survey, Milesi-Ferretti and Spolaore 1994.

4. See Cukierman and Meltzer 1983 and Tabellini 1991 for models of this type.

5. For simplicity and clarity of exposition, this model implies that the optimal tax-smoothing policy implies a balanced budget. This would be the case if the original shock that perturbed the balanced budget were permanent.

6. With some complications, the model can be extended to more than two groups; see Alesina and Drazen 1991.

7. See Shepsle and Weingast 1981; Weingast, Shepsle, and Johansen 1981; and Fiorina and Noll 1978.

8. In addition, a critical issue is the implementation phase of the budget and the associated problem of the bureaucracy's organization. This very important and immense issue has not yet been addressed in the context of multicountry studies on the political economy of budget deficits.

9. See in particular, Alt and Lowry 1994; Poterba 1994a,b; Bayoumi and Eichengreen 1995; Bohn and Inman 1996; and Alesina and Bayoumi (1996).

10. Ferejohn and Kreibel develop their model in a simple setting with complete information, but it is not immediately obvious in which direction the introduction of uncertainty about legislators' preferences would change the results.

11. See Roubini and Sachs 1989a,b for more details on the index's composition.

12. This is perfectly consistent with the war-of-attrition model. Interestingly, recent results on states in the United States are quite consistent with these findings on OECD countries. Poterba 1994b and Alt and Lowry (1994) show that states with "divided government" (those in which the party of the state governor is not the same as the majority party in the legislature) have been slower in reacting to fiscal shocks. In some sense, divided governments in the United States are the analog of coalition government in parliamentary democracies.

13. The reader is referred to the original paper by Alesina and Perotti (1995a) for more discussion.

14. The political classification "left," "right," and "center" is drawn from a different source than those we have used in this book. The two classifications, although very similar, do not exactly match.

15. One potential problem with this finding is that they use a somewhat debatable classification of left- and right-wing government. They adopt a classification according to which both American parties are considered on the right and all the Canadian parties are also right, with no distinction among them. Their results appear robust, however, if one drops these two countries.

16. See Buiter, Corsetti, and Roubini 1993 and Corsetti and Roubini 1996 for a critical analysis of these criteria.

17. See Corsetti and Roubini (1997) for a formal analysis.

18. On this point see, for instance, Poterba 1994a, Bayoumi and Eichengreen 1995a, and Alesina and Bayoumi 1996.

19. In particular, as shown by Sachs and Sala-i-Martin (1992), more than a third of a fall in a state income is compensated by income transfer from the federal government.

20. See, in particular, Alesina and Perotti 1995a, 1996.

References

Aghion, P., and P. Bolton. 1990. Government Domestic Debt and the Risk of Default: A Political-Economic Model of the Strategic Role of Debt. In *Public Debt Management: Theory and History*. R. Dornbusch and Mario Draghi, eds. Cambridge; New York and Melbourne: Cambridge University Press 315–45.

Alesina, A. 1995. Central Bank Independence: A Comment. *NBER Macroeconomic Annual*, MIT Press, Cambridge Mass.

Alesina, A. 1989. Inflation, Unemployment and Politics in Industrial Democracies. *Economic Policy* 8:55–98.

Alesina, A. 1988a. Credibility and Policy Convergence in a Two-Party System with Rational Voters. *American Economic Review* 78:796–806.

Alesina, A. 1988b. Macroeconomics and Politics. In *NBER Macroeconomic Annual 1988* 11–55 Cambridge, MA: MIT Press.

Alesina, A. 1987. Macroeconomic Policy in a Two-Party System as a Repeated Game. *Quarterly Journal of Economics* 102:651–78.

Alesina, A., and T. Bayoumi. 1996a. The Cost and Benefits of Fiscal Rules: Evidence from U.S. States. *National Bureau of Economic Research*, Working paper #5614.

Alesina, A., and T. Bayoumi. 1996b. Budget Deficits and Budget Institutions. *National Bureau of Economic Research*, Working Paper #5556.

Alesina, A., G. D. Cohen, and N. Roubini. 1993. Electoral Business Cycles in Industrial Democracies. *European Journal of Political Economy* 23:1–25.

Alesina, A., G. D. Cohen, and N. Roubini. 1992. Macroeconomic Policy and Elections in OECD Economies. *Economics and Politics* 4:1–30.

Alesina, A., and A. Cukierman. 1990. The Politics of Ambiguity. *Quarterly Journal of Economics* 105:829–50.

Alesina, A., and A. Drazen. 1991. Why Are Stabilizations Delayed? *American Economic Review* 82:1170–88.

Alesina, A., and R. Gatti. 1995. Independent Central Banks: Low Inflation at No Cost? *American Economic Review*, Papers and Proceedings 196–200.

Alesina, A., R. Hausmann, R. Hommes, and E. Stein. 1996. Budget Institutions and Fiscal Performances in Latin American. *National Bureau of Economic Research*, Working Paper no. 5556.

Alesina, A., and R. Perotti. 1996a. Fiscal Discipline and the Budget Process. *American Economic Review Papers and Proceedings* 86:401–407.

Alesina, A., and R. Perotti. 1996b. Budget Deficits and Budget Institutions. *National Bureau of Economic Research*, Working Paper no. 5556.

Alesina, A., and R. Perotti. 1995a. Fiscal Expansions and Fiscal Adjustments in OECD Countries. *Economic Policy* 21:207–48.

Alesina, A., and R. Perotti. 1995b. The Political Economy of Budget Deficits. *IMF Staff Papers* 1–37.

Alesina, A., and H. Rosenthal. 1995. *Partisan Politics, Divided Government and the Economy*. Cambridge University Press.

Alesina, A., and N. Roubini. 1992. Political Cycles in OECD Economies. *Review of Economic Studies* 59:663–88.

Alesina, A., and J. Sachs. 1988. Political Parties and Business Cycle in the United States, 1948–84. *Journal of Money, Credit, and Banking* 20:63–82.

Alesina, A., and L. Summers. 1993. Central Bank Independence and Macroeconomic Performance: Some Comparative Evidence. *Journal of Money, Credit and Banking* 25:151–62.

Alesina, A., and G. Tabellini. 1990. A Positive Theory of Fiscal Deficits and Government Debt. *Review of Economic Studies* 57(3):403–14.

Allen, S. D. 1986. The Federal Reserve and the Electoral Cycle. *Journal of Money Credit and Banking* 18:88–94.

Alogoskoufis, G. S., B. Lockwood, and A. Philippopolous. 1991. Birkbeck College discussion papers in economics, 1/92:29.

Alt, J. 1992. Leaning Against the Wind or Ducking Out of the Storm." In *Politics and Economics in the 1980s*, ed. A. Alesina and G. Carliner, University of Chicago Press.

Alt, J. 1985, Political Parties, World Demand, and Unemployment: Domestic and International Sources of Economic Activity. *American Political Science Review* 79: 1016–40.

Alt, J., and R. Lowry. 1994. Divided Government and Budget Deficits: Evidence from the States, *American Political Science Review* 88:811–28.

Alvarez, M., G. Garrett and P. Lange. 1989. Government Partisanship, Labor Organizations and Macroeconomic Performance. *American Political Science Review* 85:539–56.

Anderson, T. W., and C. Hsiao. 1982. Formulation and Estimation of Dynamic Models Using Panel Data. *Journal of Econometrics* 18:47–82.

Bachman, D. 1992. The Effect of Political Risk on the Forward Exchange Bias: The Case of Elections. *Journal of International Money and Finance* 11:208–219.

Bade, R., and M. Parkin. 1982. Central Bank Laws and Monetary Policy. Unpublished.

Banks, J. 1987, 1989, 1994. *Political Handbook of the World*, NY: CSA Publications.

Baron, D. 1991. Majoritarian Incentives, Pork Barrel Programs and Procedural Control, *American Journal of Political Science* February: 55:57–90.

Baron, D. 1989. A Non-Cooperative Theory of Legislative Coalitions. *American Journal of Political Science* 1048–84 33:1048–85.

Baron, D. and J. Ferejohn. 1989. Bargaining in Legislatures. *American Political Science Review* 83:1181–1206.

Barro, R. 1987. Government Spending, Interest Rates, Prices and Budget Deficits in the United Kingdom 1701–1918. *Journal of Monetary Economics*, 20:221–47.

Barro, R. 1986. U.S. Deficits Since World War I . *Scandinavian Journal of Economics* 88:195–222.

Barro, R. 1989. The Neoclassical Approach to Fiscal Policy. In *Modern Business Cycle Theory*, ed. R. Barro, 178–235, Cambridge, MA: Harvard University Press.

Barro, R. 1979. On the Determination of Public Debt. *Journal of Political Economy* 87:940–71.

Barro, R., and D. Gordon. 1983a. Rules, Discretion, and Reputation in a Model of Monetary Policy. *Journal of Monetary Economics* 12:101–22.

Barro, R., and D. Gordon. 1983b. A Positive Theory of Monetary Policy in a Natural Rate Model. *Journal of Political Economy* 31:589–610.

Baxter, M. 1989. Rational Response to Unprecedented Policies: The 1979 Change in Federal Reserve Operating Procedures. *Carnegie-Rochester Conference Series on Public Policy* 31:247–96.

Bayoumi, T. and B. Eichengreen. 1995a. Restraining Yourself: The Implications of Fiscal Rules for Economic Stabilization. *IMF Staff Papers* 32–48.

Bayoumi, T. and B. Eichengreen. 1995b. The Stability of the Gold Standard and the Evolution of the International Monetary System. *International Monetary Fund working paper*, 95/89.

Beck, N. 1987, Elections and the Fed: Is There a Political Monetary Cycle? *American Journal of Political Science* 31:194–216.

Bhargava, A., and J. D. Sargan. 1983. Estimating Dynamic Random Effects Models from Panel Data Covering Short Time Periods. *Econometrica* 51:1635–59.

Bizer, D. S., and S. N. Durlauf. 1990. Testing the Positive Theory of Government Finance. *Journal of Monetary Economics* 26:123–141.

Blanchard, O., and S. Fischer. 1989, *Lectures on Macroeconomics*, Cambridge, MA: MIT Press.

Blanchard, O., and N. Kyotaki. 1987. Monopolistic Competition and the Effects of Aggregate Demand. In New Keynesian Economics: Imperfect Competition and Sticky Prices, eds. N.G. Mankiw, and D. Romer.1:345–75. Cambridge, MA: and London: MIT Press.

Blanchard, O., and L. Summers. 1986. Hysteresis and the European Unemployment Problem. In *NBER Macroeconomic Annual*.15–78. Cambridge, MA: MIT Press.

Blomberg, S., and G. Hess. 1997. Politics and Exchange Rate Forecasts. *Journal of International Economics*, forthcoming.

Bohn, H., and R. Inman. 1996. Balanced Budget Rules and Public Deficits: Evidence from the U.S. States. In *Carnegie-Rochester Conference Series on Public Policy* 45:82–98.

Buchanan, J. M., C. K. Rowley and R. D. Tollison. 1986. *Deficits*. Oxford: Basil Blackwell.

Buchanan, J. M. and R.Wagner. 1977. *Democracy in Deficit*, New York: Academic Press.

Buiter, W., G. Corsetti, and N. Roubini. 1993. Excessive Deficits: Sense and Nonsense in the Treaty of Maastricht. *Economic Policy* 16:57–100.

Brander, J. A. 1991. Election Polls, Free Trade, and the Stock Market: Evidence from the 1988 Canadian General Election. *Canadian Journal of Economics* 24:827–843.

Calvert, R. 1985. Robustness of the Multidimensional Voting Model: Candidates' Motivations, Uncertainty, and Convergence. *American Journal of Political Science* 29:69–95.

Canzoneri M. 1985. Monetary Policy Games and the Role of Private Information. *American Economic Review* 75:1056–70

Cardoso, E., and A. Helvege. 1993. *Latin America's Economy*. Cambridge, MA: MIT Press.

Chapell, H. W., Havrilesky, T., and McGregor, R. 1993. Partisan Monetary Policies: Presidential Influence Through the Power of Appointment. *Quarterly Journal of Economics* 108:185–219.

Chapell, H. W., and W. R. Keech. 1988. The Unemployment Consequences of Partisan Monetary Policy. *Southern Economic Journal* 55:107–22.

Cho, I.-K., and D. Kreps. 1987. Signaling Games and Stable Equilibria. *Quarterly Journal of Economics 102:179–271.*

Cohen, G. D. 1993. Pre- and Post- Electoral Macroeconomic Fluctuations. Ph.D. diss., Harvard University.

Corsetti, G., and N. Roubini. 1996. European versus American Perspectives on Balanced-Budget Rules. *American Economic Review Papers and Proceedings* 86:408–413.

Corsetti, G., and N. Roubini. 1997. Politically Motivated Fiscal Deficits: Policy Issues in Closed and Open Economies. *Economics and Politics* 9:27–54.

Cukierman, A. 1992. *Central Bank Strategy, Credibility and Independence.* Cambridge, MA. MIT Press,

Cukierman, A., and A. Meltzer. 1986. A Positive Theory of Discretionary Policy, the Cost of Democratic Government, and the Benefits of a Constitution. *Economic Inquiry* 24:367–88.

Cukierman, A., and A. Meltzer. 1983. Money and Economic Activity, Inventories and Business Cycles. *Journal of Monetary Economics* 11(3):281–319.

Cukierman, A., S. Webb, and B. Neyapti. 1992, Measuring the Independence of Central Banks and its Effects on Policy Outcomes. *World Bank Economic Review* 6:353–98.

Cutler, D. M., J. M. Poterba, and L. H. Summers. 1991. Speculative Dynamics. *Review of Economic Studies,* 58:529–546.

Cutler, D. M., J. M. Poterba, and L. H. Summers. 1990. Speculative Dynamics and the Role of Feedback Traders. *American Economic Review* 80:63–68.

Cutler, D. M., J. M. Poterba, and L. H. Summers. 1989. What Moves Stock Prices? *The Journal of Portfolio Management* 15:4–12.

Downs, A. S. 1957. *An Economic Theory of Democracy.* New York: Harper and Row.

Eijffinger, S. and J. de Hann. 1996. The Political Economy of Central Bank Independence. Princeton Special Papers in International Economics, no.19.

Ellis, C. and M. Thoma. 1995. The Implications for an Open Economy of Partisan Political Business Cycles. *European Journal of Political Economy.*

Engle, R. F. and M. Rothschild. 1992. A Multi-dynamic factor model for Stock Returns. *Journal of Econometrics* 52:245–66.

Europa Yearbook, an annual survey of European Politics, Art and Literature, New York: Harper and Brothers.

Fair, R. 1978. The Effects of Economic Events on Votes for Presidents. *Review of Economics and Statistics.* 60:159–72.

Fair, R. 1996. Econometrics and Presidential Elections. *Journal of Economic Perspective* 10:83–102.

Fama, E. F. 1984a. The Information in the Term Structure. *Journal of Financial Economics* 13:509–528.

Ferejohn, J., and K. Krehbiel. 1987. The Budget Process and the Size of the Budget. *American Journal of Political Science* 31:296–320.

Fiorina, M. 1981. *Retrospective Voting in American National Elections.* New Haven, CT: Yale University Press.

Fiorina, M., and R. Noll. 1978. Voters, Bureaucrats and Legislators: A Rational Choice Perspective on the Growth of Bureaucracy. *Journal of Public Economics* 9:239–54.

Fisher, S. 1995. The Unending Search for Monetary Salvation. In *NBER Macroeconomic Annual,* B. Bernanke and J. Rotemberg (eds.) 275–86. Cambridge, MA: MIT Press.

Fisher, S. 1977. Long Term Contracts, Rational Expectations, and the Optimal Money Supply Rule. In *Journal of Political Economy* 85:191–206.

Forrest, J. G. 1948. The Financial Week: Financial Markets Break on Outcome of Election-Outlook Cloudy Until Congress Convenes. *The New York Times* November 7, D1.

Frey, B., and F. Schneider. 1989. Politico-Economic Models of Macroeconomic Policy. In *Political Business Cycles.* T. D. Willett (ed), Duke University Press 239–275.

Frey, B., and F. Schneider. 1978. An Empirical Study of Politico-Economic Interaction in the United States. *Review of Economics and Statistics* 60:174–83.

Friedman, B. F. and K. N. Kuttner.1991. Why Does the Paper-Bill Spread Predict Real Economic Activity? *National Bureau of Economic Research* Working Paper 3879.

Froyen, R. T., T. Havrilesky and R. N. Waud. 1993, Political and Special-Interest Pressures on U.S. Monetary Policy, mimeo, University of North Carolina, May.

Fuerbringer, J. 1992, Bonds Drop on Fears of Clinton's Economic Plan, *The New York Times,* October 20, D1.

Garfinkel, M. And A. Glazer. 1994, Does Electoral Uncertainty Cause Economic Fluctuations? *American Economic Review Papers and Proceedings,* 169–73.

Garrett, G. and P. Lange. 1991. Political Responses to Interdependence: What's "Left" for the Left? *International Organization* 45:539–64.

Gartner M. 1994. "The Quest for Political Cycles in OECD Economies" *European Journal of Political Economy*, 10, 427–40.

Golden, D., and J. Poterba. 1980, The Price of Popularity: The Political Business Cycle Re-examined, *American Journal of Political Science* 24:694–714.

Greenhouse, S. 1992, A Clinton Win: Good for Stocks, Bad for Bonds?, *The New York Times*, October 11, Section 3, p.1.

Grier, K. B. 1987, Presidential Elections and Federal Reserve Policy: An Empirical Test. *Southern Economic Journal* 54, 475–486.

Grier, K. B.. 1989, On the Existence of a Political Monetary Cycle. *American Journal of Political Science*, 33, 376–389.

Grilli, V., D. Masciandaro, and G. Tabellini. 1991, Political and Monetary Institutions and Public Finance Policies in the Industrial Democracies, *Economic Policy* 13:342–92.

Havrilesky, T. 1993. *The Pressures on Monetary Policy*, Norwell, MA: Kluwer Academic Publishers.

Haynes. S. and J. Stone. 1989. An Integrated Test for Electoral Cycles in the U.S. Economy. *Review of Economics and Statistics*, 71, 426–434.

Hershey, R. D. 1968, Bond Rally Fails Despite Election, *The New York Times*, November 7. P. 65.

Hibbs, D. 1994. The Partisan Model of Macroeconomic Cycles: More Theory and Evidence for the United States. *Economics and Politics* 6:1–23

Hibbs, D. 1992, Partisan Theory after Fifteen Years, *European Journal of Political Economy* 8:361:74.

Hibbs, D. 1987a. *The American Political Economy: Electoral Policy and Macroeconomics in Contemporary America*, Harvard University Press, Cambridge, MA.

Hibbs, D. 1987b. *The Political Economy of Industrial Democracies*. Cambridge, MA and London: Harvard University Press, viii–327.

Hibbs, D. 1977. Political Parties and Macroeconomic Policy, *American Political Science Review* 71:1467–87.

Hsiao, C. 1986. *Analysis of Panel Data*, Cambridge University Press.

Ito, Takatoshi. 1990a, The Timing of Elections and Political Business Cycles in Japan, *Journal of Asian Economics* 1:135–46.

Keech, W. 1995. *Economic Politics and the Costs of Democracy*. Cambridge UK: Cambridge University Press.

Klein, M. W. 1996. Timing is All: Elections and the Duration of the United States Business Cycle. *Journal of Money, Credit and Banking* 28:84–101.

Kontopoulos, Y., and R. Perotti. 1996. Fragmented Fiscal Policy. Columbia University Unpublished, December.

Kramer, G. 1971. Short-Term Fluctuations in U.S. Voting Behavior, 1896–1964, *American Political Science Review* 65:131–43.

Kydland, F., and E. Prescott. 1977. Rules Rather than Discretion: The Inconsistency of Optimal Plans, *Journal of Political Economy* 85:473–90.

Levingston, S. E. 1992. Impact of Election Campaign on Stocks Will Intensify as the Tempo Steps Up, *The Wall Street Journal*, 24 August, C1.

Lewis-Beck, M. 1988. *Economics and Elections: The Major Western Democracies*, Ann Arbor, MI: University of Michigan Press.

Lindbeck, A. 1976. Stabilization Policies in Open Economies with Endogenous Politicians, *American Economic Review Papers and Proceedings*, 1–19.

Lockwood, R., A. Philoppopolous, and A. Snell. 1994. Fiscal Policy, Public Debt Stabilization and Politics, University of Exeter. Mimeographed.

Lohmann, S. 1992. The Optimal Degree of Commitment: Credibility versus Flexibility, *American Economic Review* 82:273–86.

Lucas, R. 1973. Some International Evidence on Output-Inflation Trade Offs, *American Economic Review* 83:1113–44.

Lucas, R. and N. Stokey. 1983. Optimal Fiscal and Monetary Policy in an Economy without Capital. *Journal of Monetary Economics* 12:55–93.

Mankiw, G. 1987. The Optimal Collection of Seignorage: Theory and Evidence. *Journal of Monetary Economics* 20:327–41.

Mankiw, G. 1985. Small Menu Costs and Large Business Cycles: A Macroeconomic Model of Monopoly. *Quarterly Journal of Economics* 100:529–39.

Mankiw, G., and D. Romer. 1991. *New Keynesian Macroeconomics*, Cambridge, MA: MIT Press.

McCallum, B. 1978. The Political Business Cycle: An Empirical Test, *Southern Economic Journal* 44:504–15.

McCullough, J. H., and H. C. Kwon. 1993. U.S. Term Structure Data, 1947–1991, Working Paper 93–6, Ohio State University.

McDonald, M. 1991. Political Budget Cycles: Evidence from the States. Senior thesis, Harvard University.

McKelvey, R. D., and P. C. Ordeshook. 1985. Elections with Limited Information: A Fulfilled Expectations Model Using Contemporaneous Poll and Endorsement Data as Information Sources. *Journal of Economic Theory* 36:55–85.

McKelvey, R. D., and P. C. Ordeshook. 1984. Rational Expectations in Elections: Some Experimental Results Based on a Multidimensional Model. *Public Choice* 44:61–102.

Milesi-Ferretti, G., and E. Spolaore. 1994. How Cynical Can a Government Be? Strategic Policy in a Model of Government Spending. *Journal of Public Economics* 55:121–40.

Nickell, S. 1981. Biases in Dynamic Models with Fixed Effects. *Econometrica* 49:1399–416.

Niederhoffer, V. 1971. The Analysis of World Events and Stock Prices. *Journal of Business* 44:193–219.

Nordhaus, W. 1989. Alternative Approaches to Political Business Cycles. *Brookings Papers on Economic Activity* 2:1–49.

Nordhaus, W. 1975. The Political Business Cycle. *Review of Economic Studies* 42:169–90.

Ordeshook, P. C. 1986. *Game Theory and Political Theory.* Cambridge, UK: Cambridge University Press.

Pakes, A. And Z. Griliches. 1984. Estimating Distributed Lags in Short Panels with an Application to the Specification of Depreciation Patterns and Capital Stock Constructs. *Review of Economic Studies* 51:243–62.

Paldam, M. 1989a. Politics Matter After All: Testing Alesina's Theory of RE Partisan Cycles. Working Paper, Aarhus University.

Paldam, M. 1989b. Politics Matter After All: Testing Hibbs' Theory of Partisan Cycles. Working Paper, Aarhus University.

Paldam, M. 1979, Is There an Electoral Cycle? A Comparative Study of National Accounts. *Scandinavian Journal of Economics* 81:323–42.

Persson T. and G. Tabellini. 1994. Designing Institutions for Monetary Stability. *Carnegie-Rochester Conference Series on Public Policy* 39:58–94.

Persson, T. and G. Tabellini. 1990. *Macroeconomic Policy, Credibility, and Politics.* Chur, Switzerland: Harwood Academic Publishers.

Persson, T. and L. Svensson. 1989. Why a Stubborn Conservative Would Run a Deficit: Policy with Time-Inconsistent Preferences. *Quarterly Journal of Economics* 104:325–45.

Phelps, E. 1973. Inflation and the Theory of Public Finance. *Swedish Journal of Economics* 74:67–82.

Plosser, C. I. 1987. Fiscal Policy and the Term Structure. *Journal of Monetary Economics* 20:343–67.

Plosser, C. I. 1982. Government Financing Decisions and Asset Prices. *Journal of Monetary Economics* 9:325–52.

Posen, A. 1995. Declarations Are Not Enough: Financial Sector Sources of Central Bank Independence. In *NBER Macroeconomic Annual*, B. Bernanke and J. Rotemberg eds.. Cambridge, MA: MIT Press 349–55.

Poterba, J. 1994a. Balanced Budget Rules and Fiscal Policy: Evidence from the States. *National Tax Journal*, 48:329–37.

Poterba, J. 1994b. State Responses to Fiscal Crises: The Effects of Budgetary Institutions and Politics. *Journal of Political Economy* 102:799–821.

Roberts, B. E. 1990a. A Dead Senator Tells No Lies: Seniority and the Distribution of Federal Benefits. *American Journal of Political Science* 34:31–58.

Roberts, B. E. 1990b. Political Institutions, Policy Expectations, and the 1980 Election: A Financial Market Perspective. *American journal of Political Sciences* 34:289–310.

Roberts, B. E. 1989. Voters, Investors, and the Consumption of Political Information. In *Models of Strategic Choice in Politics*, P. C. Ordeshook, ed., Ann Arbor, MI: University of Michigan Press 31–47.

Robertson, J. D. 1983. Inflation, Unemployment and Government Collapse: A Poisson Application, *Comparative Political Studies* (January):425–44.

Rogoff, K. 1990. Equilibrium Political Budget Cycles. *American Economic Review* 80:21–36.

Rogoff, K. 1985. The Optimal Degree of Commitment to an Intermediate Monetary Target. *Quarterly Journal of Economics* 100:1169–90.

Rogoff, K., and A. Sibert. 1988. Elections and Macroeconomic Policy Cycles. *Review of Economic Studies* 55:1–16.

Roll, R. 1970. *The Behavior of Interest Rates*. New York: Basic Books.

Roubini, N., and J. Sachs. 1989a. Political and Economic Determinants of Budget Deficits in the Industrial Democracies. *European Economic Review* 33:903–33.

Roubini, N., and J. Sachs. 1989b. Government Spending and Budget Deficits in the Industrialized Countries. *Economic Policy* 8:99–132.

Sachs, J., and X. Sala-I-Martin. 1992. Fiscal Federalism and Optimum Currency Areas: Evidence for Europe from the United States. In *Establishing a Central Bank: Issues in Europe and Lessons from the US*, M. Canzoneri, V. Grilli, and P. Masson, eds., 195–219. Cambridge, UK: Cambridge University Press.

Sheffrin, S. 1989. Evaluating Rational Partisan Business Cycle Theory. *Economics and Politics* 1(3):239–59.

Shepsle, K. A., and B. Weingast. Political Preferences for Pork Barrel: A Generalization. *American Journal of Political Science* 25:96–111.

Shiller, R. J., and McCulloch, J. H. 1990. The Term Structure of Interest Rates. In *Handbook of Monetary Economics*, Vol. 1, B. M. Friedman and F. H. Hahn, eds., 629–722. New York: North-Holland.

Siklos P. 1994 "Politics and U.S. Business Cycle: A Century of Evidence" Unpublished, Wolfred Lewier University, November.

Sims, C. A., J. H. Stock, and M. W. Watson. 1990. Inference in Linear Time Series Models with Some Unit Roots. *Econometrica* 58:113–144.

Spolaore, E. 1993. Policy Making Systems and Economic Efficiency: Coalition Governments versus Majority Governments. Unpublished.

Svensson, L. 1995. Optimal Inflation Targets, Conservative Central Banks and Linear Inflation Contracts. *Centre for Economic Policy Research* working paper no. 1249.

Tabellini, G. 1991. The Politics of Intergenerational Redistribution. *Journal of Political Economy* 99:335–57.

Taylor, J. 1979. Staggered Wage Setting in a Macro Model. *American Economic Review* 69:108–13.

Terrones, M. 1989. Macroeconomic Policy Choices under Alternative Electoral Structures: A Signaling Approach. Unpublished.

Tufte, E. B. 1978. *Political Control of the Economy.* Princeton: Princeton University Press.

Velasco, A. 1995. A Model of Endogenous Fiscal Deficits and Delayed Fiscal Reforms. Unpublished.

Von Hagen, J. 1992. Budgeting Procedures and Fiscal Performances in the European Community. Unpublished.

Von Hagen, J., and I. Harden. 1994. National Budget Processes and Fiscal Performance. *European Economy*, Reports and Studies, no. 3:311–418.

Waller, C. J. 1995. Performance Contracts for Central Bankers. *Federal Reserve Bank of St. Louis Review* 77:3–14.

Waller, C. J. 1992. A Bargaining Model of Partisan Appointments to the Central Bank. *Journal of Monetary Economics* 29:411–28.

Waller. C. J. 1989. Monetary Policy Games and Central Bank Politics. *Journal of Money, Credit, and Banking* 21:422–31.

Waller, C. J. and C. Walsh. 1996. Central Bank Independence, Economic Behavior, and Optimal Term Lengths. *American Economic Review* 86:1139–1153.

Walsh, C. 1995a. Optimal Contracts for Independent Central Bankers. *American Economic Review,* 85:150–167.

Walsh, C. 1995b. Recent Central Bank Reforms and the Role of Price Stability as the Sole Objective of Monetary Policy. In *NBER Macroeconomic Annual,* B. Bernanke and J. Rotemberg, (eds.), Cambridge, MA: MIT Press.

Weingast, B., K. Shepsle and C. Johnsen. 1981. The Political Economy of Benefits and Costs: A Neoclassical Approach to Distributive Politics. *Journal of Political Economy,* 89:642–64.

White, H. 1980. A Heteroskedasticity-Consistent Covariance Matrix and a Direct Test for Heteroskedasticity. *Econometrica,* 48:721–746.

Wittman, D. 1983. Candidate Motivation: A Synthesis of Alternatives. *American Political Science Review* 77:142–57.

Wittman, D. 1977. Candidates with Policy Preferences: A Dynamic Model. *Journal of Economic Theory* 14:180–89.

Index

Accountability, 223
Adaptive expectations, 18, 22
Aghion, P., 232
Alesina, A., 2, 6, 7, 9, 12, 45, 49, 49, 51, 58, 59, 62, 63, 70–72, 83, 85, 96, 106, 143, 144, 158, 160, 173, 198, 201, 205, 218, 219, 222, 229, 231, 233, 238, 239, 240, 242, 243, 265–269, 271, 272, 275, 280–283
Allen, S. D., 72
Alogoskoufis, G. S., 278,
Alt, J., 143, 145, 280, 282
Alvarez, M., 143
Anderson, T. W., 272, 276
Asymmetry of information. *See* Informational asymmetry
Australia, 145, 146, 149, 158, 227
Austria, 145, 158

Bachman, D., 128
Backward-looking behavior, 49
Bade, R., 281
Banks, J., 145
Baron, D., 237
Barro, R., 2, 64, 66, 79, 103, 105, 165, 174, 228, 229, 248, 252, 267, 271
Baxter, M., 132, 133, 137, 138
Bayoumi, T., 282, 283
Beck, N., 72, 271
Belgium, 145, 158, 173, 227, 229, 256
Bhargava, A., 276

Bizer, D. S., 72
Blanchard, O., 62, 266, 267, 269, 276
Blomberg, S., 128, 273, 276
Brander, J. A., 128
Bohn, H., 282
Bolton, P., 232
Buchanan, J. M., 71, 239, 282
Budget
    balanced budget rules, 245–246
    deficits, 227–247, 257, 258
    political models of budget deficits, 230
    transparency, 239
Budgetary institutions, 231, 236
Buiter, W. G., 229, 283
Bush, G., 78, 105, 124

Calvert, R., 49
Canada, 145, 146, 149, 158, 224
Canzoneri, M., 281
Cardoso, E., 267
Carter, J., 261, 269, 270
Capital mobility, 11
Central bank independence, 10, 59, 211, 213, 217, 258
    and the contracting approach, 223
    and credibility, 212
    as a solution to the time inconsistency problem, 66
    degree of, 7, 158, 218
Chapell, H. W., 70, 113, 272, 280
Cho, I. K., 42

Clinton, W., 74, 124, 127, 280
Closed rule, 237
Coalition governments, 5, 7, 8, 10, 141,
   241, 244, 247, 257
Cohen, G. D., 70–73, 113, 126, 127, 144,
   268, 272, 280
Collegial institutions, 239
Competence
 model of, 23, 28
 in the rational partisan model, 59, 63
Competent policymakers, 32
Composition of government spending,
   30
Corsetti, G., 229, 283
Credibility, 64
Cukierman, A., 2, 16, 22, 23, 28, 30, 158,
   239, 265, 268, 281, 282
Cutler, D. M., 128, 275

Debt as a strategic variable, 231, 232
de Haan, J., 281
Delegation of monetary policy, 217
Denmark, 145, 158
Dewey, T., 111, 113
Distribution
 income distribution and inflation, 48
 income distribution and unemployment,
   48
Distributional conflicts, 231
Downs, A. S., 265
Drazen, A., 7, 233, 282
Durlauf, S. N., 72

Efficient market hypothesis, 126
Eijffinger, S., 289
Eichengreen, B., 282, 283
Eisenhower, D., 78
Electoral information hypothesis, 126–
   129, 132
Electoral option model, 112–113, 124
 implementation of, 116
Electoral surprise, 120–124
Ellis, C., 267
European integration, 11

European Monetary System (EMS), 142,
   160
European Monetary Union (EMU), 245,
   259, 261, 262

Fair, R., 268
Fama, E., 132, 137
Ferejohn, J., 237, 282
Financial integration, 11
Financial markets, 111, 124, 126, 128,
   129, 132, 256
Finland, 145, 172, 224
Fiorina, M., 266, 268, 282
Fiscal adjustment, 262
Fiscal illusion, 231, 239
Fiscal policy, 186
 electoral and partisan determinants of,
   201
 institutional design in fiscal policy, 10
Fischer, S., 265, 267, 281
Fixed rules vs. flexibility, 59
Forrest, J. G., 127
France, 145, 146, 149, 158, 256, 261
 socialist government, 6
Frey, B., 64, 72, 144
Friedman, M., 216
Froyen, R. T., 71, 268
Fuerbringer, J., 127

Garfinkel, M., 63, 268
Garrett, G., 143, 144
Gartner, M., 277
Gatti, R., 7, 219, 222
Geographically dispersed interests, 231,
   236
Germany, 145, 146, 149, 157, 158
 left-leaning government, 6, 261
Glazer, A., 63, 268
Golden, D., 71
Gordon, D., 2, 64, 66, 165, 174, 267
Government fragmentation, 242
Great Britain, 224. See also United
   Kingdom
Greece, 229

Greenhouse, S., 127
Grier, K. B., 72, 271
Griliches, Z., 276
Grilli, V., 7, 158, 235, 281

Harden, I., 240, 244
Hausmann, R., 240
Havrilesky, T., 71, 268, 280
Haynes, S., 268
Helvege, A., 267
Hershey, R. D., 127
Hess, G., 128, 273, 276
Hibbs, D., 2, 9, 12, 45–50, 61, 63, 67, 70–
    72, 74, 91, 100, 107–108, 113, 143,
    163, 195, 198, 267, 269, 271, 275, 277
Hierarchical institutions, 239
Hommes, R., 240
Hsiao, C., 276

Inflation, 186
  bias, 65, 165
  inflation-unemployment trade-off, 49,
    262, 263. See also Phillips curve
  target, 53, 224
  unexpected inflation in rational partisan
    models, 46
Informational asymmetry
  in the competence model, 16, 23, 31, 39
  concerning the composition of govern-
    ment spending, 31
Inman, R., 282
Intergenerational
  conflict, 233
  redistribution, 231
International economic integration,
    260
Intuitive criterium, 44
Ireland, 145, 157
Italy, 145, 157, 173, 227, 229, 256
Ito, T., 170–172

Japan, 145, 158, 172
Johansen, C., 282
Johnson, L. B., 269

Keech, W., 12, 70, 113, 272
Klein, M. W., 70, 71, 268
Kountopoulos, Y., 240, 244
Kramer, G., 268
Kreibel, K., 237, 282
Kreps, D., 44
Kwon, H. C., 274
Kydland, F., 2, 64, 165, 267
Kyotaki, N., 62

Lange, P., 143, 144
Left-wing
  constituency, 47
  government in Hibbs model, 50
  parties, 45, 47, 253
  preferences, 52
Levingston, S. E., 127
Lewis-Beck, M., 11–12, 266, 268, 275
Lindbeck, A., 1, 15–22, 32, 174, 198,
    266
Lockwood, R., 72, 278
Lohmann, S., 281
Lowry, R., 282
Lucas, R., 15, 228, 248, 252, 266
  Lucas supply function, 265

Maastricht Treaty on Monetary Union,
    245
McCallum, B., 71, 271
McCulloch, J. H., 137, 274
McDonald, M., 72
McGregor, R., 280
McKelvey, R. D., 275
Majoritarian systems, 7
Mankiw, N. G., 62, 267, 268
Masciandaro, D., 7, 158, 235, 265, 281
Meltzer, A., 2, 16, 22, 23, 28, 30, 239,
    282
Menu costs, 62
Milesi-Ferretti, G., 282
Mitterand, F., 261
Monetary policy, 185
  empirical tests for, 186
Multiparty system, 256

Nash bargaining solution, 58, 268
Neo-Keynesian approach to macro-
  economics, 62
Netherlands, 145, 158, 173
New Zealand, 145, 146, 149, 157, 158,
  224
Neyapti, B., 281
Nickell, S., 276
Niederhoffer, V., 128
Nixon, R., 67, 78, 127, 268
Nordhaus, W., 1, 8, 15–22, 32, 45, 64, 71,
  93, 94, 108, 144, 167, 173, 208, 268
  Nordhaus-Lindbeck model, 16, 17, 22,
  23, 47. *See also* Political business cycle
  model
Norway, 145, 158

Open rule, 238
Opportunistic
  behavior, 9
  voting, 9
Opportunistic cycles, 254
  with rational expectations, 31
  rational opportunistic cycles, 38
  theory of, 16
Opportunistic model, 2, 3, 15
  predictions of the rational opportunistic
  model, 36–37
  predictions of the traditional opportunistic model, 36–37
  rational opportunistic model, 8, 22, 31,
  32, 38, 173
  traditional approaches, 8, 17
Option pricing, 114
Ordeshook, P. C., 265, 275

Pakes, A., 276
Paldam, M., 143, 144
Parkin, M., 281
Partisan cycle, 3–5, 7
  evidence on, 207
Partisan effects on monetary policy, 188
Partisan model, 2, 3, 9, 16, 97, 100
  rational version, 9, 97

traditional approach, 9, 46, 91, 93, 97,
  163, 166
Partisan policymakers, 45
Perotti, R., 7, 201, 205, 229, 231, 238,
  240, 242–244, 268, 272, 283
Persson, T., 2, 12, 16, 23–28, 33, 34, 42,
  44, 64, 66, 94, 208, 224, 233, 265–268,
  281, 282
Persson-Tabellini model, 38
Phelps, E., 267
Philippopoulos, A., 72, 278
Phillips curve, 15, 23, 46, 52, 266
  expectations augmented, 17, 260
  long-run vertical, 21
  short-run, 21, 50
  time-varying, 107
Plosser, C. I., 132, 133, 137, 138
Policymaker's competence, 16
Policy rule, 58
Political budget cycles, 28
Political business cycle
  effects on monetary policy, 196
  evidence, 82, 144, 167, 207
  hypothesis, 80, 102, 269
  model, 15, 17, 45, 93–94, 143, 199
  opportunistic, 70, 71, 74, 108
Political cycles, 1, 3, 5, 259–260
  and central bank independence, 211,
  218
  evidence on, 8
  in industrial economies, 141
  in the rational opportunistic model, 16
  theories of, 8, 10, 11
  in the U.S., 67, 265
Political polarization, 141
Polls, 11, 113, 256
Pooling equilibrium in the competence
  model, 26, 42
Posen, A., 265, 281
Poterba, J., 71, 275, 282, 283
Prescott, E., 2, 64, 165, 267
Presidential systems, 256
Proportional electoral systems, 5, 7, 141
Public choice school, 71, 231

Rational expectations, 9, 255
  in partisan models, 51
  rational expectation models, 3
Rationality of behavior, 15
Rational partisan theory, 45, 46, 51, 74,
    76, 83, 85, 91, 93, 100, 107, 108, 112–
    114, 122, 124, 126, 139, 144, 166, 173,
    195, 196, 255
  criticisms, 62
  evidence, 70, 83, 143–145, 148
  with the rational expectations model of
    financial markets, 135, 139
Rational theory of economic policy, 253
Reagan, R., 78, 105, 232, 274
Repeated game
  in Alesina's model, 58
  and time inconsistency, 64
Retrospective voting behavior, 9, 16,
    254
  in the rational partisan model, 59
  rational retrospective voting in the
    competence model, 27–28, 31–36
Right-wing
  constituency, 47
  parties, 45, 47, 50, 253
  preferences, 52
Roberts, B. E., 113, 128
Robertson, J. D., 172
Rogoff, K., 2, 16, 22, 23, 28, 30, 31, 64,
    94, 170, 173, 207, 208, 213, 216, 222,
    224, 239, 240, 266, 271, 280
Roll, R., 137
Romer, D., 265, 268
Rosenthal, H., 6, 12, 49, 59, 62, 63, 70,
    85, 265–269
Roubini, N., 7, 144, 160, 202, 229, 235,
    241, 242, 279, 280, 282, 283
Rowley, C. K., 71

Sachs, J., 7, 70, 72, 202, 235, 241, 242,
    271, 279, 282, 283
Sala-i-Martin, X., 283
Sargan, J. D., 276
Schneider, F., 64, 72, 144
Seigniorage, 29

Separating equilibrium
  in the competence model, 26, 40
  in the political budget cycle model, 29
Sheffrin, S., 128, 144
Shepsle, K., 282
Shiller, R. J., 137
Sibert, A., 2, 16, 22, 23, 28, 64, 94, 170,
    173, 208, 239, 266
Signal extraction in the competence
    model, 34
Siklos, P., 268
Single-party governments, 7, 241, 247,
    257
Snell, A., 72
Social planner, 65, 224, 233
Spolaore, E., 7, 234, 235, 282
Stein, E., 240
Sticky wages and prices, 5, 45, 62, 255
Stokey, N., 228, 248, 252
Stone, J., 268
Summers, L., 158, 218, 266, 269, 275, 276
Svensson, L., 224, 233, 282
Sweden, 145, 146, 149, 158, 224
Switzerland, 145, 158

Tabellini, G., 2, 7, 12, 16, 23–28, 33, 34,
    42, 44, 64, 66, 94, 158, 208, 224, 235,
    265–267, 281, 282
Tax-smoothing model, 103, 227, 229–
    231, 248, 252
Taylor, J., 63, 265, 268
Term-structure of interest rates, 137
Terrones, M., 170
Thoma, M., 267
Time consistency in Alesina's model, 54
Time inconsistency
  in monetary policy, 64, 66
  time inconsistent rules, 215
Timing of elections, 20, 63, 170
Tollison, R. D., 71
"Tragedy of the commons" game, 235
Truman, H., 74, 78, 11, 116, 127, 128,
    269
Tufte, E. B., 12, 71, 72, 268, 272
Two-party systems, 5, 7, 8, 10, 141, 256

United States, 3, 7–9, 70, 72, 87, 88,
    145–147, 149, 158, 202, 229, 245, 256,
    257
  evidence on opportunistic and partisan
    cycles, 68
  inflation rates, 89
  left-leaning governments, 6, 261
  political cycles, 67
  postwar experience, 69
United Kingdom, 145, 146, 149, 157,
    172, 256
  left-leaning government, 6, 261
Uncertainty
  about electoral outcomes, 19, 49, 55,
    111, 255, 256
  policy uncertainty, 46, 135

Velasco, A., 235
Von Hagen, J., 240, 244
Voters
  naive voter, 15, 35
  non-rational voter, 22
  rational voter, 35
  voters with different preferences, 48, 52,
    53

Wagner, R., 239, 268, 282
Waller, C. J., 7, 218, 223
Walsh, C., 223, 224, 265, 281, 282
Wand, R. N., 71
"War of attrition" model, 233
Webb, S., 281
Weingast, B., 282
Welfare properties of partisan cycles, 57
Wittman, D., 49